*For my wife, Adele Rose,
and our two boys,
Patrice and Pascal*

For thou lovest all things that exist,
and has loathing for none of the things
which thou hast made,
for thou wouldst not have made anything
if thou hadst hated it.

– The Book of Wisdom 11:24

Published in Australia by
Garratt Publishing
32 Glenvale Crescent
Mulgrave, VIC 3170
www.garrattpublishing.com.au

Copyright in this work remains the property of the contributing authors.

Copyright © Chris Geraghty 2020

All rights reserved. Except as provided by the Australian copyright law, no part of this book may be reproduced in any way without permission in writing from the publisher.

Cover Design by Lynne Muir
Text Design by Lynne Muir
Cover image 'Losing Paradise', He Qi © 2004 all rights reserved,
www.heqiart.com
Author Photograph © Adele Geraghty 2018

Scripture taken from the *Revised Standard Version*, Grand Rapids: Zondervan, 1971. Scriptures marked JB are taken from the *The Jerusalem Bible* © 1966 by Darton Longman & Todd Ltd and Doubleday and Company Ltd.

All rights reserved.

ISBN 9781921946059

Cataloguing in Publication information for this title is available from the National Library of Australia.

www.nla.gov.au

The authors and publisher gratefully acknowledge the permission granted to reproduce the copyright material in this book. Every effort has been made to trace copyright holders and to obtain their permission for the use of copyright material.

The publisher apologises for any errors or omissions in the above list and would be grateful if notified of any corrections that should be incorporated in future reprints or editions of this book.

Praise for
VIRGINS AND JEZEBELS

Clearly written, meticulously researched and applying the latest insights of historical critical analysis, Geraghty's work is at once depressing and liberating.

Depressing, because it documents the antecedent basis for the misogyny that saw Pope John Paul II declare, in reference to Catholic belief and tradition that, according to some divine plan, women are inferior beings and incapable of ordained Christian leadership.

Liberating, because it clearly shows the disjunction between the teaching of Jesus and that of the first to fourth century 'weltanscheung' or worldviews of those who came after, particularly Paul of Tarsus, which were fundamentally un-Christian. The pagan patriarchy and primitive biological science of Aristotle and Plato survived because it suited — and still suits — the men who rule the Roman Catholic Church.

— **Paul Bongiorno AM**
Contributing Editor, Network Ten

Virgins and Jezebels is a compelling work which exposes the calculated debasement and marginalisation of women in the early centuries of the Catholic Church. Chris Geraghty explores the enthusiastic transporting of cultural misogyny into the early Christian communities — a pathway antithetical to the attitudes and behaviour of Jesus. This book fleshes out what generations of Catholic women have known, and in the present day still know, in their bones, and in their experiences within the Church.

— **Megan Brock RSJ PhD MAPS**
Psychologist

Jesus shocked his own disciples by his counter-cultural contacts with women. Yet this all went quickly and horribly wrong. How did this happen? Chris Geraghty ably follows the complex trail that leads to the abysmal misogyny of the following centuries. He is not afraid to face the hard questions — questions that are still with us today — about the role of women in the Church. Chris shows us the mistakes and explores the blind alleys which have lead us to our present dilemma. As the author makes abundantly clear, we either learn from past mistakes or we allow them to continue to blind us to the radical vision of God's Kingdom Jesus bequeathed to us.

— **Neil Brown, theologian**

Virgins and Jezebels represents an important and comprehensive addition to Christian self-understanding. Showing himself completely on top of the biblical and patristic literature, Chris Geraghty has written in an easy, engaging — but ultimately angry — manner about the cancerous development of early Christian misogyny that still infects the thinking of the Christian Church. He poignantly shows how it contrasted with the Gospel Jesus' open, relaxed and inclusive way with women.

Dr Geraghty traces the tradition of misogyny back partly to the misuse of the myth of Eve as the evil temptress and femme fatale and partly to the badly mistaken biology of Aristotle and Plato. But most crucial were the early Fathers of the Church such as Irenaeus, Clement of Alexandria, Tertullian, John Chrysostom and others who deliberately sidelined women and brought to birth the Church's virile and destructive misogyny. As a leading scholar, he has done the Church a significant service by bringing together all the research evidence to document the development of an overall patriarchal ideology that still reigns over Mother Church and continues to stunt its growth.

— **Des Cahill, Emeritus Professor, RMIT University;
Senior consultant to the
Australian Royal Commission into Child Sexual Abuse;
Chair, Religions for Peace Australia;
Deputy Moderator, Religions for Peace Asia**

Chris Geraghty has genuinely dug deep into his scholarly soul to reconsider and re-imagine women's crucial contribution to the early Church and all subsequent experience. My initial caution completely shifted to admiration for not just his detailed curiosity but for the conclusions he dared to draw about future Church.

— **Geraldine Doogue AO
Author, Australian journalist, radio and television host**

VIRGINS AND JEZEBELS

The Origins of
Christian Misogyny

CHRIS GERAGHTY

garratt
PUBLISHING

A Table of Contents

A PROLOGUE..1
THE WORLD BEYOND JESUS...7
A SLANTED VIEW OF WOMEN FROM THE
PAGAN WORLD..19
    The Greco-Roman World of Literature 21
    The Pagan World of the Human Sciences and Philosophy....31
A LIBRARY OF UNCOMFORTABLE FACTS...............................46
    Paul's Literary Bequest..48
    A Post-Apostolic and Pre-Nicaean Library......................54
WOMEN IN THE LIFE OF THE EARLY CHURCH
IN AND AROUND PALESTINE..64
THE THIRTEENTH APOSTLE..71
THE WOMEN IN PAUL'S LIFE..81
PAUL ON THE SUBJECT OF WOMEN......................................97
    Women as Witnesses to the Resurrection......................98
    A Man of Traditional, Conservative Values..................103
    Further Pauline Ruminations about Women...............115
    Paul's Reputation as a Misogynist.................................130
    The Adam-and-Eve Myth..138
PAUL'S ALTER EGOS...159
SUPERCHARGING THE MYTH OF ADAM-AND-EVE.............170
THE TRANSGENDERISATION OF FEMALE BELIEVERS........186
A TOXIC VIEW OF WOMEN...205
FEMALE FASHIONS AND ACCOUTREMENTS.......................215

WOMEN'S SODALITIES IN THE POST-APOSTOLIC PERIOD 226
A Sisterhood of Widows 227
Powerful and Troublesome Female Prophets 238
Cliques of Angelic Virgins 262

COHABITING WITH VIRGINS 277

A STRUGGLE FOR A PLACE AT THE TABLE 302

FEMALE PARTICIPATION IN THE MYSTERIES 326

SOME FACTORS BEHIND THE FEMALE HATE SPEECH AT THE HEART OF CHRISTIANITY 334

AN EPILOGUE 342

A BIBLIOGRAPHY 359

A Prologue

This book is about men and misogyny in the early Christian churches – not specifically about women and their contribution to the life of the primitive church – though, of course, the two cannot be separated.

Women became the targets of women-fearers and Christian women-haters of the second and third centuries. While they were part of the daily life of every community (local Christian gatherings in Palestine or North Africa, for example), and while they were making their indispensable contribution (mostly, but certainly not exclusively, as mothers and housekeepers), women were also the targets of the most pervasive prejudices. These were prejudices deeply rooted in the fabric of the daily lives of believers.

In truth, this book is about power, and who should exercise it, about men's clubs and the rules and regulations devised by members to exclude their womenfolk. It is about theological nonsense dreamed up and preached to keep women in their place, to undermine the fundamental and foundational values of Jesus' kingdom – to keep the keys of that kingdom safely in clerical hands. The place of women in the life of the early church is a vast area of historical and theological study, but my principal focus will be confined to the startling prevalence of misogynistic attitudes and practices in the various regions in which Jesus' gospel had spread.

Misogyny is the ugly face of patriarchal societies in which men, often stupid old men, have all the power and make all the decisions. Cicero would have us believe that this misogyny can be traced to a man's visceral fear of women and to the power they exert when they are let loose to roam (Cicero, *Tusculanae Quaestiones*, Bk IV, Ch. 11).

Prostitution might enjoy the reputation of being the world's oldest profession, but misogyny is the world's oldest prejudice. It lay buried in the ground of ancient cultures where women were largely invisible and given limited or no access to power and decision making. Mothers and grandmothers, wives and daughters were in the same category as domestic slaves and children. They had no rights or privileges, no voice and no vote. Men were simply and naturally presumed to be superior and ordained to be in charge. These ancient attitudes have been part of many societal belief systems and reflected in the institutions of a community and in its legal systems. And these very attitudes were contaminating the hearts and minds of men and women, young and old.

A society's hatred or mistrust of women and its entrenched prejudices against them can take many forms. It can manifest in bullying by husbands and brothers; physical, even sexual violence; a conscious and unconscious hostility; paying no heed to one's partner, sisters and daughters. It can show itself in patronising; stereotyping; treating women and girls merely as sexual objects or personal possessions; excluding them from positions of power and influence and from gatherings and clubs. These hostilities against women also led to theological and philosophical arguments to 'support' the belief in women's inferiority; detailing sexual triumphs and repeating tasteless jokes that belittle and denigrate women.

This essay is an attempt to trace the early stages of a patriarchal trend and a misogynistic tradition within the Christian churches. Unfortunately, except perhaps for the author of the *Gospel of Mary*, none of the authors we will meet in the course of our study were women. The female voices in the early Christian communities remain surprisingly absent, and at least for the most part, the male authors who have survived the torment of the centuries saw themselves as speaking to a male audience – their brothers in the Lord.

From the earliest years the local Christian communities were being established along patriarchal lines. It was simply assumed that men were in charge, and that their women were required to remain submissive. The character of power and authority was masculine, whether initially based on the Jewish model of elders and presbyters, or later based on the Roman model of a single leader or supervisor. While a power base founded on a patriarchal model is not necessarily misogynistic, in truth we can't easily avoid the conclusion that such a model provided fertile ground for women-hating, women-fearing values and prejudices to germinate and flourish. Patriarchy robbed women of their dignity, of their status in the community, of their power and of an independent voice. As we will see, patriarchy and misogyny rapidly became bedfellows.

I have extended the period of my present study into the early years of the fourth century (and at times, a little beyond). This is to the time when the Roman emperor became involved in baptizing the world, before the Fathers of the Council of Nicaea had begun to dogmatize their faith in established formulae, before some of the principal Christian leaders had begun to peddle their prejudices. This is before Jerome, Augustine, Gregory of Nyssa and John Chrysostom, for example, had begun to make misogyny the Church's default position. Popes, bishops, monks, poets, theologians and lawyers of the Middle Ages and beyond would learn to recite the same ugly doctrine as their forebears – teachings destined to debase women, except the Virgin Mary, of course, and a handful of other precious virgins. I have chosen to conclude my study in the early fourth century because, by that time, misogyny's dirty paw marks were already all over the literature that was being preserved by the Church in its libraries, schools, secretarial offices and chancelleries.

Various historians and theologians have conducted a search for the origins of misogyny in the Church. As we will see, there are many signposts to follow in any search for the roots of misogynistic practices and attitudes among the Christian churches. These studies that trace the origins of a fear and hatred of women among Christian men are interesting and complex. Whatever the explanation, the fact of prevailing, deep-rooted, women-hating attitudes in different places around the perimeter of the Mediterranean is incontestable. Given the penetration of these attitudes into the flesh of the Church for centuries to come, the bald historical fact of the existence of misogynistic values and prejudices in the early stages of the Jesus movement is, in my estimation, of far greater importance than any causal explanation that history might offer.

How the various ancient Christian authors could read about Jesus in the Gospels, and let their pens scribble bile about one of God's most beautiful works of art, is difficult for a modern man to understand and for a modern woman to accept. It's a cautionary tale to show that prejudice and bigotry will frequently trump faith and common sense, and that there is a natural tendency in any institution to drift away, sometimes far away, from its simple origins, from its pure ideals and policies. Fidelity to a cause, integrity, consistency and the power of pure reason have proved rare commodities in all human societies.

I began this journey trying to understand why, in the face of such obvious and overwhelming considerations, the leaders of the Catholic Church have been so reluctant and so pig-headed about involving women in the sacramental ministry and administrative governance of our institution. Wandering around in the area, I came across the most ferocious, sometimes disgusting attitudes and prejudices written by men whom I had over the years come to respect and admire, men whose writings had been preserved for our edification and formation – Augustine of Hippo, Jerome the exegete, John Chrysostom, Bonaventure, Thomas Aquinas, popes and bishops, monks and theologians. As I journeyed on, the path of inclusion and freedom which had opened up in the life and preaching of the Jesus of the Gospels, suddenly began to close over. I had found side-tracks, potholes, confusing guideposts, theological claptrap, 'straw men' without brains, tinmen without a heart, empty-men repeating the rumours they'd heard, pretend-men peddling blind prejudices of the past. I had to describe the territory I was passing through so that Jesus would not be blamed for leading his followers into this arid place, so that those in authority could abandon the territory without offending their basic principles.

I looked long and hard in an earlier book at the stories the early Church writers and composers were telling about Jesus – the way he related to women and how they reacted to him. The authors of the Gospels obviously wanted their readers and believers to know that women had been involved in Jesus' life and work. Women had been important figures among his followers. He had loved them – and they had loved him. Something revolutionary had been occurring.

Now I want to turn attention to the life of the early communities of believers to see how women were participating in the missionary activities and in the worship gatherings of those groups, how they were included and spoken about. What was said about them? What contribution were they making to the life of the community?

How visible were female members in the groups of early believers? Why were they so silent? So often invisible? What roles did they play? What responsibilities were they able to exercise? How were Jesus' refreshing attitudes and values being translated into practical action, or was his understated policy on the role and importance of women simply ignored? Was the memory of a Jesus who was a supporter of women suppressed, and if so, why? What can be said about the presence of women and their roles in the primitive communities, in the liturgical gatherings, in the governance of the institution, in the daily life of the believers?

What happened after Jesus had left his followers to fend for themselves? Do we have any idea how these people survived and prospered? Can we say anything meaningful about life as it was lived inside the primitive church, about how the apostles and their successors began to engage with the world around them. Can we say anything about how women fitted into the life and mission of the Jesus movement as it drifted away from Jerusalem, from Palestine and its Jewish origins, out into the world?

This lengthy essay is an invitation into a wondrous world of strange practices and beliefs – colourful rivers of mysterious ideas, high rugged mountains of prejudices, vast landscapes populated by angels and archangels, devils and demiurges, giants and aeons, mythical female figures such as Eve, and Lilith as her previous embodiment.

But before I begin to hack a path through the undergrowth, I want to whisper a word of gratitude to my pagan wife for her quiet and patient acceptance of the fact that her life-partner was away for some years on a frolic of his own, doing something of very little significance – not solving the problems of the world (burning poverty, climate change, cruelty to children and to animals), or even the problems of our local community (traffic chaos, parking, greed-driven high-rise dwellings or garbage collection). Now the book is finished, I can turn my attention to these more urgent matters. I also need to acknowledge that my lifelong friend Neil Brown has been a generous companion on this journey of discovery – and all the other trips I have made up and down the highways and byways of my life during the last sixty years. Thank you, Neil. Love and blessings to you, Adele.

The World Beyond Jesus

It's difficult to imagine what it was like living inside a sub-group of believers on the border of the Mediterranean in the first few centuries of our era – in 80 AD, or 180, or 280, for example – in Jerusalem, Ephesus, Carthage, Alexandria, or Damascus. The historical sources available tell us that these early Christians had come into contact with an array of ideas which we now find baffling, maybe amusing, perhaps even offensive. They lived in a messy world of interacting worldviews and mindsets in a muddle of different social, political and religious groupings. They were in contact with beliefs in a pantheon of pagan gods, exotic Eastern deities and festivities, secret ceremonies, popular schools promoting strange cosmologies and theologies. They lived among hordes of people of different ethnic origins coming and going across lands and seas. The people they shared their lives with included Roman officials, preachers, magicians, prostitutes, philosophers, poets and soldiers, businessmen and con artists. In this complex social and religious milieu there were communities of Jesus-followers trying to survive, fighting for a place in the sun. These followers of Jesus were endeavouring to carry on a dialogue with others outside the circle, attracting new followers while keeping their old followers in line.

When Jesus had been cut down in the prime of his life and abruptly disappeared, he had left his little band of followers in a mess. They had been waiting expectantly. He had promised to send them a comforter to fill the terrifying emptiness in their lives. The leaders hadn't even begun to understand the kernel of the Teacher's message. Even at that late stage, they had been expecting Jesus to establish a kingdom on earth in which they could occupy middle management positions. At the point when they were feeling like giving up, they were being challenged to begin again, this time without their leader.

They had a message to preach. A tiny community to nourish, to make secure, to expand and to make its way in the world. Memories to preserve. Decisions to be made regarding his message, his values, his attitudes and sentiments, his way of living in this world and, at the same time, his way of relating to the transcendent world of the Spirit of God. All the work was ahead of them.

We must dive into murky waters to examine how women were treated when Jesus was no longer with them in the flesh, and how they were spoken of by Christian writers (exclusively men). But first it might be helpful to have a cursory look at what was happening in the communities of believers and out in the world. Not where Jesus had lived his life, almost exclusively among Jews, and in Palestine, but out in the Greco-Roman world.

The latter part of the first through to the early fourth centuries constituted a period of rapid expansion for the new religious movement. Those preaching in Jesus' name were attracting believers and camp followers from various urban centres around the Mediterranean and fanning out into the more remote rural areas.

From the beginning, the apostolic and the post-apostolic period was a time of tension and occasional outbursts of conflict. This conflict arose between those who had come over as heretics from Judaism, those who had been former synagogue sympathizers like Cornelius the centurion, Lydia of Thyatira or the Ethiopian eunuch, and the increasing crowd of nondescript converts from the prevailing Greco-Roman culture and various mystery cults – worshippers of Mithra, Osiris, Isis, Dionysius, Cybele, of Attis and others.

Gradually, in fits and starts, the local Christian communities were prising themselves away from their roots in the Jewish culture and from its religious practices, but not without problems. At the same time, however, these communities were claiming Jewish heroes and pivotal historical events to construct a wider theological context around Jesus and his message. Christian preachers and writers were exploiting, for example, the myth of Adam and Eve, the figure of Moses as a divine lawgiver, the symbolism compressed by Jewish authors into the Exodus-Passover event, the institution of priesthood, the notion of Messiah, synagogue liturgical practices, and even the purity laws that Jesus had rubbished. A movement which had grown out of Palestinian soil and which was closely associated with the heroes, the writings and the practices of the Jewish people, was rapidly adjusting itself to attract and accommodate a whole range of people from a wider world. A deep inter-cultural tension between Jewish Jesus-followers and the Gentile converts continued well into the second, and even to the beginning of the third centuries.

For a brief period there appears to have been a level of tension within the communities between those males who had installed themselves in positions of power and who had assumed a controlling authority, claiming to be successors of the apostles, and some female believers who were persuaded Jesus had included them in his work of revealing God's hidden secrets to the world. According to sources such as the Gnostic-Christian gospels, these women were seeking places at the table of the board of directors, but others thought they were troublemakers who had to be brought to heel.

It was an age of religious confusion. The Greco-Roman world, especially in the cities of Asia Minor, was a melting-pot of different religious beliefs and practices. These included the official, institutional religion of Rome with its many deities and temples; secret mystery and initiation cults; Jewish beliefs and practices; mythological characters and stories; a variety of schools of Gnosticism, each with its own complicated system of divine emanations and a bevy of semi-divine figures; and finally, rural superstitions and practices. The intellectual and religious life of the Roman Empire which was infiltrating the fabric of the local churches was itself in a state of flux.

The message of Jesus was almost immediately lifted from its isolated Semitic origins and translated into a new language with its own particular thought-patterns. Then, almost as rapidly, the message was clothed in another set of garments when it took on a life among the people of North Africa. Its Greek language and philosophical points of reference (Plato, Aristotle, Pythagoras and the Stoics) were peeled away and the message began to appear in the world of the Latin language with its legal references. The layman/lawyer Tertullian is the first author available to us who crafted a theological worldview in the Latin language. He came from Carthage and was writing his reactionary treatises and discourses in the second half of the second century. Cyprian, another Latin author from Carthage, was of Berber descent, born into a rich pagan family, educated as a lawyer and trained as a court advocate before he was converted and moved rapidly through the ranks from baptism to the episcopacy.

The post-apostolic period was also a time of intense dialogue between an emerging group of educated, literary Christians and contemporary pagan authors. Origen, for example, was an Alexandrian biblical scholar and theologian from the first half of the third century who produced an important apologetic treatise as a response to the criticisms of a second century pagan philosopher. Celsus wrote the earliest literary attack on Christianity still available, *The True Discourse*, and Origen had replied in a work appropriately entitled *Contra Celsum*. Among many other objections, Celsus had criticised Christians for treason by refusing to conform to the beliefs and practices of the empire, thereby undermining its cohesion and strength, weakening its ability to resist those who would want to bring the whole structure down. The barbarians from outside the boundaries of the empire were flooding in and becoming the refugees and asylum seekers of the age. Celsus regarded Christians as religiously and politically intolerant – uncompromising and unreasonable, and therefore dangerous.

Origen had been well-placed to deal with the criticism of Celsus. He was familiar with the works of the Middle Platonists as well as the pagan philosophers in general and the classical literature of the times. He had been a student of Ammonius Saccas who was, by reputation, the founder of Neo-Platonism.

Clement of Alexandria was another important early Christian writer from the late second century and the beginning of the third. Like Origen before him, he too had been educated in secular Greek philosophy and literature, and had introduced contemporary pagan ideas into his version of the Jesus message. He attempted to explain and enrich the true Christian 'gnosis' by using foreign ideas from the Greek philosophers. According to him, these pagan thinkers had created a rich intellectual world which was also, he believed, God's gift to humanity. A glimpse of the depth of his pagan knowledge can be seen in book VI, Chapter 2 of his *Stromateis* where he quoted and compared the words and ideas of various pagan authors – for example, Euripides, Homer, Thucydides, Sophocles, Menander, as well as Theognis and Hesiod, both of whom (as we will see) had composed imaginative, poetic passages about the mythical origin of the female member of the species. Origen and Clement are witnesses to the attraction of scholars to the Jesus message and the consequential penetration of Greco-Roman thought patterns and ideas into the Christian world. Christian scholars and intellectuals were appearing on the scene.

The post-apostolic period was also a time of brash decadence, of political and social turmoil and intrigue within the Roman Empire, and of border incursions from barbarian tribes. The Roman emperors and their sycophantic entourage were working day-to-day on their reputation for long lunches, spa baths and singing sessions in the local brothels. Some of the emperors were wicked men and a few were truly evil. Other emperors, however, were honourable men who were committed to restoring the glory of Rome and recapturing the lost culture of her golden years. They sought to re-institute those ancient religious practices which had proved so successful in the past – sacrifices offered to the Roman gods, for example, and worship of the divine emperors. By refusing to engage in the traditional religious practices, Christians were judged to be undermining the stability of the nation. Young Christian men were refusing to take the oath of allegiance, to swear the *sacramentum* which was demanded of every Roman soldier on entering the service. Christians were becoming more visible in society than they wanted to be.

This Roman policy of a return to traditional values was causing a great deal of angst for Christian leaders and the faithful. They were being wedged into an intolerable position. As much as Paul had tried to solve the problem of cultural integration for the Corinthians, it became clear that people of faith couldn't remain faithful to Jesus and his message and at the same time publicly demonstrate their loyalty to the divine emperor. Those who believed couldn't bring themselves to offer pagan sacrifices or treat the emperor as a god. They had to accept that their faith was making them hyper-visible rebels. They were seen to be unpatriotic, un-Roman, unwilling to submit to the dictates of Roman law and order. They were seen as bad citizens, atheists and fifth columnists.

But not all the Roman elite were corrupted by a social and moral decadence. They weren't all crazy like Nero or Caligula. Apart from those who were joining the Christian movement, or listening to the teachings of one or other of the many Gnostic-Christian sects, or worshipping an exotic Eastern god of goddess, many citizens throughout the vast empire were choosing to embrace the uncomfortable dictates of the Stoics. These Stoics were living a virtuous and restrained lifestyle, seeking personal peace and integrity through moral restraint and ascetical practices. The spirit of asceticism had become popular inside the

Christian churches and among a significant number of pagan citizens.

The post-apostolic period was also a time of bullying and cruel persecution of the Jesus-followers. From the beginning, according to the author of the Acts, the membership of the community of believers in Jerusalem had come under pressure from the Jewish establishment. As this membership expanded into other regions, there also came pressure from the Roman authorities. The experience of being persecuted by those in power became part of the Christian's experience of his or her new way of life. They were not yet part of the establishment and their meetings were shrouded in secrecy. Surviving on the edge of society, they were tormented by prejudice, suspicion, stereotyping, antipathy, rumours, defamation and imprisonment, and accused of immorality and black magic. Torture and martyrdom were part of the deal. From the beginning, Christians were on guard, looking over their shoulders, waiting for the next move against them.

The sporadic outbursts of local persecutions over the first few centuries resulted in some important consequences. The average Christian man or woman had to contend with the existential experience of being rejected and being subject to violence. However much they sought to adapt and be considered part of the mainstream, they found themselves unable to integrate completely into society. Gradually a cult of martyrs surfaced. Some believers strove to emulate the sacrifices of those who had rejected the world and given their life for the cause – Jesus first, followed by James, the deacon Stephen, Paul and Peter and other believers. Desert fathers, hermits, monks and nuns embraced ascetical practices including tortuous fasting, lengthy vigils and punishing flagellations.

The Roman historian Seutonius, writing about events in Rome in 52 AD, at the time of the Emperor Claudius, reported that under the influence of a 'Chrestus', the Jews were making trouble and Claudius had expelled them from the city.

In about 115 AD Tacitus wrote an account of Nero's arson attack on Rome, and that to exculpate himself, the emperor had blamed the Christians. Tacitus described these Christians as a 'class which was hated for their abominations'. They were guilty of 'hatred of the human race'. According to him, since they refused to honour the gods of Rome (including the emperor himself), they were atheists, involved in 'deadly superstition'.

In the course of the second and third century, local anti-Christian riots broke out in the province of Asia in the Western region of Asia Minor. So began an irregular series of persecutions. Many were involved. There was the savage imperial madman Nero, who is supposed to have martyred Peter and Paul; and Domitian, whom Pliny called 'the beast of hell'. At the turn of the century, Trajan weighed in; the philosopher Marcus Aurelius' encouragement of anti-Christian informers resulted in fierce local persecutions. Perpetua and Felicitas, two Christian virgins, were put to death during the reign of Septimus Serverus. But all these incidents were more or less local skirmishes.

In the middle of the third century the Emperor Decius launched the first empire-wide persecution. Apparently Christians had become too well organized and self-contained and far too visible. They were undermining the empire's traditional polytheism and refusing to bend the knee before the deified Roman rulers of the past. Then the Emperor Valerian intensified the Decius persecution, ordering the clergy to sacrifice to Roman gods. In 258 AD Pope Sixtus II was caught celebrating the liturgy in a Roman cemetery and was beheaded together with four of his deacons. Another of his seven deacons, Lawrence, was barbequed a few days later. A month or so later in the same year, the bishop of Carthage, a former lawyer named Cyprian, was also put to death. Church property was confiscated. Christians were condemned to slavery in the salt mines and the church had become an easy target.

The emperor was scapegoating believers, blaming them for the outbreak of plague and other natural disasters. As the empire was declining, Christians were held responsible for its economic and social problems, for invasions from beyond the borders and the breakdown of morale.

There were reasons why Christians were being persecuted, and the reasons varied from region to region, from one emperor to another. Then, around the beginning of the fourth century the Emperor Diocletian initiated what became known as the Great Persecution.

The sporadic persecutions of members of Christ's fellowship eventually gave rise to a glorification of martyrdom among believers. Christians were being forced to face death for the sake of the gospel. These persecutions involved excruciating torment and heroic courage. The martyrs saw themselves as imitating Jesus' crucified.

Women were numbered among the ranks and became the focus of worship and devotion. A cult of martyrs went hand-in-hand with a spirituality of sacrificial courage and otherworldliness. It was for some of the believers a period of withdrawal from society and the world. The more fervent Christians were being 'called' to live outside society, in the desert, on the top of mountains, in caves. Their intense faith led them to reject the world and its distractions, to turn away from the decadence which was visible inside and outside their communities, to prepare themselves for Heaven and their future angelic existence.

Dramatic changes in the status of Christians and their organisation occurred in the Roman Empire in the early years of the fourth century. In 306 AD, in Britain, the Roman army had acclaimed Flavius Valerius Aurelius Constantinus Augustus (known as the Great and Saintly Emperor Constantine) as emperor. Eighteen years later he acquired absolute power, becoming the sole ruler of the western and eastern regions of the Empire. He exercised this power until his death in 337 AD.

During his thirty-year reign, Constantine would be responsible for many far-reaching administrative, financial, military and social reforms. He would wage successful military campaigns against the various barbarian tribes that were creating chaos on the borders of the Empire – the Franks and the Goths, for example. He would find ways to bring Christians in from the cold and make them (and other foreign religious sects) part of Roman society.

In February 313 AD, Constantine ordered the persecution of Christians to cease. It has been suggested that he enacted an edict (the Edict of Milan) granting religious freedom to all religions and cults throughout the Empire, including the Christian religion. Whether there ever was a formal decree is a disputed question among the historians. In any event, he inaugurated a policy of religious tolerance throughout his empire, in the East as well as in the West, and restored to the various Christian communities the properties which his predecessors had confiscated. He supported the Church financially, built and endowed basilicas and granted special privileges (such as tax concessions) to the clergy. Christianity had arrived. It had taken two and a half centuries, but with the special patronage the emperor was offering, the movement (now an organisation) had come into its own. It was accepted as a visible and powerful part of the ruling establishment.

To unify his empire, Constantine was anxious to promote a policy of peace and stability throughout his territories, and to protect his borders from invasion and crush any internal division or conflict. In pursuit of this goal, he involved himself in the day-to-day affairs of the church. Between 313 and 316 AD, for example, he concentrated his efforts on solving the problems the Donatist schismatics had created in North Africa.

Constantine became involved in the life of the church again when the unity of the Christian communities was seriously threatened by the teachings of Arius, a Libyan from North Africa. Arius had been preaching a troubling doctrine (or 'heresy') about the nature of Christ. Was he both divine and human? Or only human? Was he eternal, or created by the Father? What was his relationship with God the Father (as if anyone could know)? The deacon Athanasius in Alexandria was up in arms, seeking to crush the dangerous doctrine which Arius and his followers were spreading. By alleging that Christ was not divine, Christianity was divided and the imperial policy of peace and unity was threatened.

In 325 AD the Emperor summoned a council of bishops who convened at Nicaea in Bithynia (in modern Turkey). Constantine (almost certainly unbaptized at the time) presided in person over the assembly of bishops and their retinue. He had invited about 1800 bishops to attend and resolve, once and for all, the Christological problem which was undermining the faith of believers and pitting local churches and bishops against one another. The Patriarchs of Alexandria and Antioch both attended. Bishops came from everywhere: from North Africa, Spain, Britain, Gaul and Italy, from Jerusalem, Persia, Armenia, Georgia and India, from many places in Turkey and the near East – Caesarea, Myra, Nicomedia. The number of those who actually attended is in dispute, but a general estimate by scholars hovers between 220 and 318, though the popular estimate of 318 would seem to be a symbolic number, being the number of Abraham's servants recorded in Genesis 14:14.

By dint of its missionary activities and under the patronage of the emperor, the church had emerged as an international organisation. It was flourishing, with a solid male hierarchical structure and an established bureaucracy. It was socially and politically powerful, male dominated, and had rules, regulations and processes to guarantee dogmatic orthodoxy.

Constantine and the Council of Nicaea mark the end of the period of the early Church – the apostolic and post-apostolic times. The movement which had begun in Palestine had become part of the fabric of society, now arm-in-arm with the secular powers, though not without some further stumbles and challenges. The early years had been a period of rapid expansion, confusion and uncertainty, of trial and error, but by the beginning of the fourth century the direction in which the church was heading had been determined. Men were definitely in control and women had been reduced to the status of second-class citizens.

At the council of Nicaea, the bishops passed rules to govern the behaviour of bishops, priests and deacons – rules which demonstrated plainly their attitude towards women and how dangerous they thought they were. In their final declarations, the Fathers of the Council spoke of women as if they were mere dehumanized objects, reduced to articles to be moved around and avoided, and at the beck and call of important men:

> We decree that bishops shall not live with women; nor shall a presbyter who is a widower; neither shall they escort them; nor be familiar with them, nor gaze upon them persistently. And the same decree is made with regard to every celibate priest, and the same concerning such deacons as have no wives. And this is to be the case whether the woman be beautiful or ugly, whether a young girl or beyond the age of puberty, whether great in birth, or an orphan taken out of charity under pretext of bringing her up. For the devil with such weapons slays religious, bishops, presbyters and deacons, and incites them to the fires of desire. However, if she is an old woman, and of advanced age, or a sister, or mother, or aunt, or grandmother, it is permitted to live with these because such persons are free from all suspicion of scandal (Canon IV).

The post-apostolic period ended with dire warnings to clerics – whether beautiful or ugly, women were dangerous and were used by the devil to 'slay' bishops, priests and deacons – so beware.

A Slanted View of Women from the Pagan World

It's often impossible for historians to remove themselves from the official sources, from the formal, established documents produced by emperors and kings, by victors and their followers, and to find material which can give some idea of what the person in the street was thinking. Often there is little of substance to balance the record for the oppressed and vanquished, almost nothing from the common man and woman to colour the narrative. We have nothing from the many women in Jesus' life, from his mother or his best friend, Mary Magdalene (unless she was the source of the *Gospel of Mary*). There is nothing from the beggars and lepers he met in the streets, or from those women who were mentioned by the male notaries, or from those who sat in the pews listening to the sermons of Bishop Irenaeus or in the desks in Alexandria attending the lectures of Origen or Clement. History is necessarily slanted in the direction of power and position.

But by chance we do have some inkling from the first century of what the frontline soldiers were thinking as they were besieging the town of Perugia or resisting the daily attacks from the other side. Some were fighting on the side of Octavian (who was later to become Augustus), others were defending the town, fighting for Lucius Antonius and his wife, Fulvia.

The warring parties were hurling small lead projectiles from slings and catapults back and forth over the high walls. Fossickers have unearthed dozens of these bullets. Some of them were produced from moulds which printed into the lead a variety of slogans of abuse that were often obscene messages about women.

In addition to being an example of the ribaldry among soldiers in the frontline of battle, there is a clear misogynist dimension embedded in those lethal projectiles.

Misogyny was not invented by Christianity. It certainly didn't emerge from the message Jesus preached or from the way he lived his life. Anti-feminine attitudes and prejudices were already there, well-established in the ether, spread throughout the towns and villages, deep within the soil of the cultures around the border of the Mediterranean. Misogyny was waiting to be embraced by preachers and theologians, exegetes and polemicists of an expanding religious movement and ready to be baptized into the service of orthodoxy.

Without entering into great detail, there's no doubt that throughout the Greco-Roman world there were women who exercised some degree of influence, sometimes supreme power, in the public arena. And there were those who enjoyed a visible role in various religious sects, in local or regional ceremonies – priestesses (in Delphi and Dodona, for example), prophetesses and soothsayers. They participated, for example, in the festival of the Thesmophoria which was celebrated in many parts of the Greek world to honour Demeter, the goddess of crops. Women known as Maenads or 'mad women' were also prominent in the ecstatic rites surrounding the worship of Dionysus.

Diogenes Laertius reported that the female philosopher Hipparchia travelled around with her friend Crates, giving lectures and living a life similar to his. There was also a group of women who claimed to be followers of the philosopher Pythagoras. There were female poets in addition to Sappho. Their numbers included Erinna of Telos, Nossis of Epizephyrian Locris, Corinna of Tanagra, and Aristodama from Smyrna.

Although women were largely confined within their domestic world, they were not entirely invisible in the public space. Taken overall, however, and allowing for variations from place to place, their contribution to the public domain was exceptional and sporadic.

The Greco-Roman World of Literature
Homer and Hesiod
Homer and Hesiod were more or less contemporaries, facing one another across the Aegean Sea – two Greek poets who were to become notorious throughout the classical world with each presumed to have been the author of two lengthy poems.

Homer is reputed to have written the epic story of the siege of Troy (the *Iliad*) and the tale of Ulysses' wanderings on his journey home (the *Odyssey*). Hesiod's name appears at the head of *Works and Days* and *Theogony*, the first written in praise of honest farm labour and to denounce corrupt judges, and the second providing advice on lucky and unlucky days for farming. The question of the authorship of these four works need not delay us. All four poems were highly significant in their own right.

In the *Iliad*, Homer depicts the relationship of Hector and his wife Andromache as one of genuine mutual affection. When Andromache, for example, begged her husband not to leave her to go into battle, telling him that 'you are my husband, young and warm and strong!' Hector's reply was replete with tenderness and understanding:

> All this weighs on my mind, too, dear woman...
> It's less the pain of the Trojans still to come
> That weights me down.
> That is nothing, nothing beside your agony
> When some brazen Argive drags you off in tears,
> Wrenching away your day of light and freedom. (*Iliad*, Book 6)

Theirs was a loving relationship of two human beings. It must be remembered, however, that in the literature, the whole Trojan conflict was a blood-thirsty contest involving men fighting over a woman so that one of them could re-possess her.

Penelope and Odysseus were also portrayed by Homer as real people – happily married and faithful lovers.

> And weep he did, with his dear and loyal wife in his arms.
> Such was the gladness she felt to welcome
> Her husband again, as she feasted her eyes upon him
> And could not for a moment take her white arms from his
> neck (*Odyssey*, Book 23).

Yet Penelope and Andromache were essentially housewives restricted to their domestic worlds like the other heroic women in Homer's epic stories. Having addressed his own worries and her anxieties, for example, Hector's last words to his wife before going into battle were:

> So please go home and tend to your own tasks,
> The distaff and the loom, and keep the women
> Working hard as well. As for the fighting,
> Men will see to all that ... (*Iliad*, Book 6).

All Homer's women were status-bound as either wives or possessions, confined to the house and its management, or exchanged, given as prizes, stolen and sold. When Agamemnon wanted to reconcile with Achilles, for example, he promised to give him seven flawless women from Lesbos who 'outclassed the tribes of women in their beauty'.

According to Hesiod, in the beginning the human race had consisted entirely of men who had lived in an idyllic world, free of sorrow, disease and discord.

> Before the time men lived upon the earth
> Apart from sorrow and from painful work,
> Free from diseases, which brings the Death-gods in.

Here are echoes of the Genesis story of creation and of God manufacturing the first man.

In *Theogony* Hesiod traced a history of the world from its primeval chaos to the enthronement of the divine Zeus as supreme king of all the gods. He described a world of primitive gods and chaotic forces – a world which was surprisingly different to the graceful but promiscuous Homeric world of gods far away on Mount Olympus.

According to the story, after much to-ing and fro-ing among the gods, the Titan Iapatos created Prometheus. In turn Prometheus became a friend to mankind and angered the almighty Zeus by stealing the divine gift of fire from the heavens. Zeus devised a way to punish him.

Hephaistos (the god who used to walk with a limp) was chosen to implement Zeus's devious plan. From the earth he fashioned an image of a modest virgin. Zeus's daughter, Athene, dressed this girl in robes of silver, veiled her beautiful face and placed on her head a wreath of blossoms and a miraculous crown of gold. Hephaistos then completed his work and brought his creation to a gathering of men and gods.

> Amazement seized the mortal men and gods,
> To see the hopeless trap, deadly to men.

These attractive creatures were Zeus's curse on mankind. They proved to be lazy and narcissistic. The institution of marriage with 'all the troubles women bring' was the price to be paid for Prometheus' crime.

> From her comes all the race of womankind the deadly female
> race and tribe of wives who live with mortal men and bring
> them harm (*Theogony*, 590-592).

Hesiod wrote that even if a man was lucky enough to find a 'good wife', someone suited to his tastes, he would still be entangled in a mixture of good and evil. On the other hand, if such a man won 'one of a deadly sort' from the lucky dip, he would have to live his whole life with never-ending pain in his heart and torment in his mind. The wound would never heal.

The second poem ascribed to Hesiod is quite different. *Works and Days* is a collation of mythological stories, maxims, wise and superstitious sayings, and advice to farmers about how their lives were to be governed by the seasons. The author pretended to be a grouchy old farmer, hostile to the elite and the city-dwellers, and to women. He was a firm believer in self-denial, self-reliance, piety and the value of work. Conservative, pessimistic, excessively didactic – and a women-hating bad-tempered old man.

The author returned to the burning anger of 'the Gatherer of Clouds', Zeus, who had been hoodwinked by Prometheus and who was determined to punish the fire thief by visiting a plague on him and all mankind.

> They'll pay for fire: I'll give another gift
> To men, an evil thing for their delight,
> And all will live this ruin in their hearts.
> So spake the father of men and gods, and laughed.

Under instructions from Zeus, Hephaistos manufactured an object of fascination and desire, like a piece of pottery. Under instructions from on high, he mixed earth and water together, planted a voice in the mixture and bestowed on it the power to move. He fashioned a face as stunning as an immortal goddess and gave it the shapely contours of a young virgin. Athene taught the girl to weave, Aphrodite taught her to arm herself with charms and strong desires, and Zeus ordered Hermes to plant in her the morals of a bitch. Athene made robes for her and a belt. Divine Seduction and the Graces gave her strings of golden necklaces. Hermes filled her breast with lies, persuasive words and cunning ways. Finally, the gods named this glorious creature Pandora. She was destined to be the ruin of mankind.

The elegant and beautiful Pandora straddled the void between the worlds of the gods and the world of beasts. Like Eve, the myth of Pandora presented women as a necessary evil – necessary for the continuance of the human race, necessary as a means of controlling men and entrenching men's inferior status, necessary as a bridge between the world of gods and the world of animals, necessary as an explanation of chaos, tension and evil in the world.

Pandora was the pagan version of the biblical Eve or of Adam's mythical first wife, Lilith – beautiful but dangerous. According to the myth, when Pandora was delivered as a gift to the brother of Prometheus, she opened her treasure chest and scattered her evil in the world of men. She was the source of chaos in the world. For the first time, all sorts of diseases appeared and began to wreak havoc on mankind.

In *Works and Days* Hesiod recounted the story of the emergence on earth of a series of races, ending in 'the race of iron', mankind. By day, these men would work and grieve unceasingly, and by night they would waste away and die. He collected a catalogue of maxims by which to live, a series of aphorisms capturing the wisdom of a simple farmer. Among his list of admonitions, the poet included the following:

> Don't let a woman, wriggling her behind,
> And flattering and coaxing, take you in;
> She wants your barn: woman is just a cheat.

Semonides of Amorgos

Hesiod's malevolent description of Pandora and her daughters was taken up by the poet Semonides (from Amorgos). Little is known of him apart from the fact that he died in his late eighties (around 465 BC) and that he had a reputation for being both a sage and a miserable miser. Like his friend Pindar, he worked as a travelling poet, earning his living by imposing himself on the wealthy, narcissistic, self-important aristocrats. These prominent men used to put him up in their villas and pay him good money to write poems and songs in their honour.

Semonides began his poetic diatribe against women by stating the obvious fact that the gods had made women different. Then he proceeded to tell his readers just how different they were. Some had been created from a pig. These women were 'hairy sows' whose house was like a rolling heap of shit. They were fat and dirty, dressed in filthy clothes, lounging about on 'the shit-pile'. The gods had made another group from a fox – these were 'pure evil', their moods changing from one moment to the next. And like a fox, they were aware of everything going on around them, always on the alert. Some husbands were driven to acts of domestic violence – their wives having made their lives intolerable.

> One type is from a dog – a no-good bitch,
> A mother through and through; she wants to hear
> Everything, know everything, go everywhere,
> And stick her nose in everything, and bark
> Whether she sees anyone or not.
> A man can't stop her barking; and with threats,
> Not (when he's had enough) by knocking out
> Her teeth with a stone and not with sweet talk either.
> Even among guests, she'll sit and yap.

Semonides believed some women were two-faced like the sea – calm one day, wild and unapproachable the next, unbearable to look at, filled with snapping hatred, ferocious like a bitch with pups. Like the ocean, they had their own perplexing ways.

And there were some female types who were 'from a drab, grey ass', used to being smacked and when it came to sex, they welcomed any man who happened to be passing by. Another loathsome, miserable type was 'from the weasel'. She was ugly and repulsive, and sex-crazed to boot. 'Any man who climbs aboard her will get seasick' – presumably from the constant, violent lurchings. Other women always wore their hair combed-out like a horse with a flowing mane and dressed with overhanging flowers. These wives were beautiful for others to look at, but for their 'keepers', unless they were heads of state who could afford extravagant delights, they were simply a pain.

Then there were the women who were 'from the ape'. These were Zeus' gift to men, but no Pandoras. Hideous faces, no necks, no bums and all legs. The poet said he pitied the poor man who held this type of woman in his arms. Like apes, they were well-versed in every kind of trick. They never thought of doing some kind act for anyone, but plotted to see how they could do the greatest harm.

The poet didn't condemn all women. Some men were uncommonly lucky and found wives who were 'from a bee'. Their households thrived, their children prospered and their husbands were content, surrounded with love. Grace enveloped them. These wives shone brightly among their horrid sisters. And they didn't like to sit around with other women discussing sex. But …

A man who's with a woman can't get through
A single day without a troubled mind.
Just when a man seems most content at home
And ready for enjoyment, by the grace
Of god or man, that's when she'll pick a fight,
Her battle-helmet flashing, full of blame.

As the poet viewed the world through his blurred spectacles, all men, without exception, shared in the same level of misfortune. Zeus had locked them in a shackle hard as iron, never to be broken, and that prison was called 'marriage'.

Juvenal

In the early years of the second century AD, The Latin poet Decimus Iunius Iuvenalis (Juvenal) was composing savage satires about life in pagan Rome. His longest poem, described variously as bitter, hysterical, exaggerated, brilliant and amusing, was probably published in 116 AD, during the reign of the Emperor Trajan. However, it depicts life in the upper echelons of Roman society during the chaotic times of emperors such as the sadistic Caligula, the brutal clown Nero, the gentle invalid Claudius and the paranoid hypocrite Domitian. This poem of Juvenal's attracts our particular attention because, while his other satires touch here and there on the subject of women, his sixth satire is exclusively dedicated to a prolonged diatribe against marriage and the 'lecherous' female.

Juvenal presented himself in his satires as a man of old-fashioned, conservative Roman values – a waspish commentator on the mores, the proclivities and stupidities of Roman society. He was the pagan version of a Tertullian from Carthage or a Jerome – educated in the Greek and Latin languages and mythology, a gifted but intemperate author, ultra-conservative in temperament, a man with a venomous pen in his hand. Although he was obviously observing his society through mischievous, prejudicial eyes, he was providing a detailed, if slanted, picture of the city in which the early Christians, including Paul of Tarsus and his companions (male and female) had been living and working.

His poetry naturally proved unpopular at the time. The ancients also disliked seeing themselves portrayed in edgy cartoons. His sixteen satires dropped out of view until the early third century when they were rediscovered by Tertullian of Carthage (c 160–220) and later, in the early fourth century, by Lactantius, both early Christian writers.

At the opening of the sixth satire, the Juvenal pretends that he had learnt that one of his male acquaintances, Postumus, was contemplating marriage. In an attempt to persuade him that marrying was even more stupid than attempting to commit suicide and more disastrous than engaging in sexual concourse with young boys, Juvenal wrote,

> Why stand such bitch-tyranny when there's rope available,
> When those dizzying top-floor windows are all wide open,
> When there's bridge nearby from which you can make your jump?
> Supposing none of these exits catches your fancy,
> Don't you think it better to sleep with a pretty boy?
> Boys don't quarrel all night, or nag you for little presents
> While they're on the job, or complain that you don't come
> Up to their expectations, or demand more gasping passion
> (lines 30–37).

With these lines, the author launched on his extended denunciation of women, rich and poor, young and old. According to him, women were hyper-sexed, promiscuous and predatory creatures.

> All women now, high or low, share the same lusts: the peasant
> Trudging barefoot over black cobbles is no better
> Than the lady who rides on the necks of tall Syrian porters
> (Lines 349–50).

On every street, according to the author, the reader could find a replica of the notorious wife of the Emperor Claudius, Clytemnestra, a whore-empress who crept out of her husband's soft bed as soon as she heard him snoring and, under cover of a hooded night-cloak with her black hair hidden beneath a tart's blond wig, she would hurry down to the local brothel where she traded herself to the patrons as 'the Wolf Girl'. 'Naked, with gilded nipples' she absorbed her many clients' heavy battering and reluctantly headed home in the early hours of the morning. An insatiable nymphomaniac. She made her way through the back streets to her palace, weary and exhausted but never satisfied. This was the woman-wife who had ultimately poisoned her imperial husband a year before the author was born.

They were all the same, according to Juvenal. That was what women were like.

> If they draw a blank there, they try slaves.
> If enough slaves cannot be found
> The water-carrier's hired. If they can't track him down either,
> And men are in short supply, they're ready and willing
> To go down on all fours and cock their dish for a donkey
> (lines 331–34).

For some reason, although he had been nurtured by a mother, slept and ate with a wife, Juvenal wrote nearly seven hundred lines of female invective – amusing to his male readers, exaggerated, and verging on the psychotic.

Women were cruel, superstitious, self-indulgent, arrogant, avaricious, gluttonous and sex-crazed, Juvenal continues. Some were boring know-alls and intolerably perfect. 'Who can stomach such wifely perfection? I'd far sooner marry a penniless tart than that haughty prig, Cornelia', he wrote.

> Worse still is the well-read menace, who's hardly started
> dinner Before she's praising Virgil, forgiving the doomed
> Dido, Comparing rival poets, Virgil and Homer suspended
> In opposite scales, weighed up one against the other.
> Critics surrender, academics are routed, everyone there
> Falls silent, not a word from lawyer or auctioneer.
> So avoid any woman's company at a dinner-party
> Who affects a rhetorical style, who hurls well-rounded
> Syllogisms like slingshots, who has all history pat:
> Far better one who doesn't grasp all she reads.
> I detest
> The sort who are always thumbing, and citing – some standard
>   grammar,
> Whose every utterance follows the laws of syntax,
> Who with antiquarian zeal quotes poets I've never heard of:
> Such matters are men's concern
>
> (lines 434–455).

According to Juvenal, intelligent, outspoken women existed in Roman circles, but they were to be avoided. One of his contemporaries, as we will see, an anonymous author who inserted a short passage into one of Paul's letters to the Corinthians, insisted, in Paul's name, that women had to remain silent in church and wait till they were at home to ask questions of their husbands.

The Pagan World of the Human Sciences and Philosophy

As each grew to become a giant of the western world, it is important to examine Plato the mystic philosopher, Aristotle the Philosopher-

Scientist and Claudius Galen, Marcus Aurelius's surgeon. Each of these has had a powerful influence on the development of Christian thought.

Over time Plato was to become a disembodied philosophical figure who haunted the pagan and the Christian worlds for centuries. History has enticed him out of its shadows to appear on stage as the Universal and Eternal Idea of a philosopher *par excellence*. In his day and through his Academy outside Athens, he laid down a thinking grid for the Greco-Roman world. His reality was made up of two fundamental realms – a world of ideas and spirits which was immutable, and a world of shadows, our world, which was comprised of the senses and physical matter. He developed a mindset which classified everything neatly into a binary system – matter and spirit, universal ideas and shadowy images of them in some material form, good and evil, male and female, intellect, reason and order on the one hand versus desires and chaos.

At approximately the same time, Aristotle emerged as a giant scientific brain which set out the rules for thinking and research, the logic for disciplined reasoning, categories for reality, a system of metaphysics and ethical behaviour, and a program for governing families and states. He devised an intellectual system which would eventually rival Plato's influence and which would come to dominate the schools of learning throughout Europe. Aristotle's ideas were taken up by the Arab world, then returned to Europe around the eleventh century. They were simply accepted as scientifically established and repeated by scholars and thinkers in the Middle Ages throughout the Renaissance and Reformation periods. Late in the nineteenth century, Pope Leo XIII canonised Aristotle as the pagan patron saint of philosophy. He was destined to inspire the systematic theology of the Roman Catholic Church, from Thomas Aquinas in the thirteenth century to almost the end of the twentieth century.

The questions we confront here, however, are: what did these two giants of Western thought think about women? How did women come to exist down here on the earth? What was their status and role in society? How did women relate to men? What was their biological makeup? And, of course, how did Plato and Aristotle come to exercise such a powerful influence over the minds and systems of those who came after them?

Plato

In his *Divine Institutions* (III. 19), Lactantius told his readers that the noble Plato had given thanks that he had not come into the world as a foreigner, or a woman. This same chauvinist sentiment is reflected in the traditional morning prayer Jewish men (men, of course) have been accustomed to reciting for many centuries:

> Blessed are you, Yahweh, King of the Universe, for not having made me a Gentile. Blessed are you, Yahweh, King of the Universe, for not having made me a slave. Blessed are you, Yahweh, King of the Universe, for not having made me a woman.

Almost four hundred years before Jesus was preaching his message in Palestine, Plato had been telling his pupils how women had originally become part of creation. At about 360 BC, he produced his *Timaeus*, written in the style of a philosophical discussion involving four erudite participants. The work took the form of a long monologue spoken by one of the characters, Timaeus of Locri.

Plato's *Timaeus* is an elaborate and imaginative account of the formation of the universe. It describes a time when the divine master-craftsman, the demiurge, the father and maker of the universe, had instructed the gods to manufacture a world of lesser creatures, and so they set about making human souls. Through his character Timaeus, Plato observed that since human nature was two-fold, the superior sex was the one which was designated as 'man'. This was standard thinking of the time. Aristotle would agree, as would his successor Theophrastus, and St Paul of Tarsus, Tertullian, Clement of Alexandria, Jerome and his pen-friend Augustine, the three Cappadocian theologians, the archbishop of Constantinople, John Chrysostom and the endless line of bishops, monks, church lawyers and theologians dancing to the same beat down through the Middle Ages. This thinking was accepted by everyone of importance – everyone except Jesus.

In *Timaeus*, the human souls which had been created by the gods, 'by virtue of necessity', were implanted in bodies which were subject to a range of sensations, desires and emotional responses. According to Plato, the first-born creature (a type of pagan Adam) was meant to 'grow into the most god-fearing of living creatures', and that if he was able to gain mastery over the sensations, desires and emotions swirling about inside him, he would be living 'justly' – and if not, 'unjustly'.

> He that has lived his appointed time well shall return again to his abode in his native star and shall gain a life that is blessed and congenial. But whosoever has failed therein shall be changed into woman's nature at the second birth (*Timaeus*, 41–42).

Plato's imaginative view of the world continued to inspire his students. He wrote that even though reduced into a lowly, female form by his failure to live well, if 'she' still persisted in her wickedness, 'he' would be changed again and again, 'into some bestial form which would reflect his true evil character' until eventually 'he' acquires some sense and 'returns to the semblance of his first and best state'. According to Plato, in the ideal world we were all created as males but those who proved unable to govern their urges would turn to wickedness and become females. Some of the men who had been created by the demiurge would go on a journey of descent through the hierarchy of lesser creatures until they eventually would return to where they had begun – to their masculine existence, and living in their native star in the heavens.

Plato, Aristotle and the pre-scientific 'scientists' were limited in their research, and their observations led to interesting theories of gender flexibility and transgender myths to explain human existence. Perhaps we can read Plato's imaginary creation story as a peculiar mixture of a version of the Adam and Eve story (man superior, woman inferior, woman unstable and emotional and prone to wickedness) coupled with the pervasive belief that all the members of the human race were created to return to their original state of perfection, thereby achieving their ultimate destiny as male dwellers in the stars.

Aristotle

Aristotle was seventeen when he walked from Macedonia to study philosophy under Plato at his Academy in Athens. After his initial training, Aristotle became a colleague of his master teacher and stayed at the Academy for twenty years, until Plato's death in 347 BC.

Plato's gifted student also had his say on the subject of women and their role in society – and what he said had influence for at least two millennia. His 'scientific' views and pre-scientific prejudices were to contribute to the way Western society learnt to see women and their relationship with men.

Aristotle claimed that on the observable evidence, women differed psychologically and physiologically from their partners. They differed fundamentally in the psychological characteristics and social skills which were peculiar to them, but they were also physiologically inferior. In brief, according to him a woman was a misbegotten and constitutionally retarded male.

While the marriage partnership was one in which a husband and his wife each made their own contribution (to produce children and create a family unit), according to Aristotle it was not a partnership of equals. The relationship was more like a form of aristocracy in which the husband ruled by right and by virtue of his natural merit. The female was by her nature the passive member of the partnership – intellectually and biologically passive and inferior.

As a scientist, Aristotle recorded one of the observable and obvious differences between the male and the female members of a species. The 'male' animal reproduced itself outside its own body, and the 'female' procreated its offspring through a process which occurred inside the body. While both the man and the woman (the male and female animals) made their own particular contribution to this process of procreation, Aristotle concluded that the male semen was the active, ensouling element which produced life, while the discharge or secretion associated with females was the passive element in the process.

The Greek playwright Aeschylus (and others) shared Aristotle's view of the mystery of how babies were made.

> The woman you call the mother of the child is not the parent,
> just a nurse to the seed,
> the new-sown seed that grows and swells inside her.
> The man is the source of life – the one who mounts.
> She, like a stranger for a stranger,
> keeps the shoot alive unless god hurts the roots (*Eumenides*, 658–61).

The Philosopher-Scientist Aristotle also observed that blood vessels were less prominent in the female body than they were in males. As a consequence, women were paler than their counterparts, also finer in their physique, softer and smoother. The reason Aristotle gave for this 'phenomenon' was that the secretions or semen which produced such male characteristics as muscle mass and hair, were discharged as a waste product in a woman's menstrual fluids. As a scientist in a pre-scientific age, he concluded that women had an observable deficiency in their physical makeup. On the evidence, they were weaker, smaller and slower than men.

Aristotle also concluded 'on the evidence' that a woman was really the equivalent of an infertile male. As he said, she was something like a 'deformed male' (*The Generation of Animals*, 737a, 27). Because of the observable coldness which characterised her condition, she lacked the power 'to concoct' or thicken her own semen. The significant heat variations within the male and female bodies (as well as in the sexual act) explained why it was that some couples gave birth to male offspring, while others became the parents of daughters. The more heat generated by the breathless coupling agents, the more likely it was that after a period of nine months, a male would emerge.

Temperature controlled the sex of a child. Warmer semen was the liquid secretion which had been compacted, or concocted, or cooked properly. The more compacted the male semen, the more fertile it was, and the stronger. Strong semen ensured the delivery of a hot member of the species rather than a cold one, a son rather than a daughter. Furthermore, if the secretion or semen, for example, came from the right side of the body (a side which was observably hotter than the left), a male would be produced, and conversely, if from the left side, a female would emerge from the oven.

Aristotle was the pre-eminent scientist of his day and his reputation as a scientist and philosopher was restored to the West in the late Middle Ages and went on to flourish in the Renaissance period. He considered that theories were proved by observable facts, and he had observed that when copulating couples danced together when a north wind was blowing, they produced males. But if they did their arduous work during a southerly, they produced females. This was because during the season when southerlies blew, animals secreted a greater quantity of liquid which was harder to concoct or compact. The weather affected both male semen and female menstrual discharge. When the moon was on the wane, when the temperature was colder and the weather more humid, less perfect humans were generated. But when everything was working perfectly and the vital heat was at its full strength, the end-product would invariably be a boy.

> The shepherds maintain that it not only makes a difference in the production of males and females if copulation takes place during northern or southerly winds, but even if the animals, while copulating, look towards the south or north (*On the Generation of Animals*, book IV, Chapter 2).

Aristotle had other contributions to make on the topic of women. For example, he thought that females had a predisposition to depression. They tended to be more brazen, more untruthful and devious. They also had a sharper memory, especially for detail, and were softer than men, more compassionate, more emotional, more easily moved to tears, more prone to jealousy, more argumentative and rather passive. They lacked initiative and energy. Aristotle was simply passing on the details of a convenient stereotype which was reflected in the literature of his people and which would endure down the centuries.

He even contributed to a stereotypical theory about blondes. According to him, only fair-skinned women enjoyed a sexual discharge when they copulated, and only they could experience an orgasm. This white woman's discharge was similar to an infertile or emasculated male's secretions when he was aroused. Gentlemen have always preferred blondes. In ancient Greece, where most women had dark hair, blondes were prized as sexual partners.

The end result of Aristotle's research was that the male was the perfect member of the species; the female, lower on the scale of perfection, was approximately on a par with slaves and children. As we will see, this view of society is reflected in several of those epistles which appeared under the name of Paul the Apostle (Col 3:18–22 and Eph 5:22–6:9).

In his *Politics* (1.2.12), Aristotle stated in simple, direct words, the obvious 'scientific' truth about men and women: 'The male is by nature superior and the female inferior; the male is the ruler and the female the subject'.

The philosopher's ideas about the importance of heat, about female coldness, about a hierarchy of perfection within the human species, with a male at the head of the pyramid (again, echoes of Paul of Tarsus), and about procreation – these ideas appear a little crazy to any modern, scientific person. However, they were to dominate the medical and biological sciences, philosophy and theology for almost 2000 years.

Crazy ideas are not necessarily harmful, provided they can be buried with their thinker and their damage can be contained. But sometimes, when the genius is dead, however crazy his ideas were they take off and assume a life of their own. It is not what Aristotle or any of his successors taught that is historically significant. What is important is how far their ideas travelled and what influence they exerted on successive generations.

Theophrastus

A particularly crass anti-feminist passage from the philosopher Theophrastus' lost work *On Marriage* was preserved verbatim by Jerome in his treatise *Against Jovinian* (Book I, Chapter 47). This single passage was regularly lifted from Jerome's essay and repeated with approval in various texts throughout the Middle Ages – quoted again, several times, for example, in Chaucer's *The Wife of Bath's Tale*.

Theophrastus had been a close friend and colleague of Aristotle. They had met as young men when Aristotle moved to the island of Lesbos. They worked there together as philosophers; Aristotle as an animal biologist, Theophrastus as a botanist. On Aristotle's death, his colleague became the guardian of his son and took over the management of the Lyceum school Aristotle had founded. The students and their teachers became known as the Peripatetics.

Theophrastus features in the historian Diogenes Laertius' *The Lives of the Philosophers* and is reputed to have written more than 227 books, though most have either been lost (including his work *On Marriage*) or survive only in small fragments.

The extract which Jerome reproduced opened with the perennial chauvinist question of whether a wise man should ever marry. After exploring the issue inside and out, the social commentator from Lesbos came to a firm conclusion: of course not. In any ideal marriage, a wife had to be beautiful, of good character and born of honest parents; and a husband had to be healthy and wealthy. However, according to the author, these preconditions were seldom, if ever, satisfied.

To begin with, as any serious philosopher soon discovered, marriage interfered with the study of philosophy and was an unnecessary distraction. Paul of Tarsus was of the same opinion.

And Theophrastus thought that as a general rule, women were unreasonable and very demanding. They demanded, for example, expensive dresses, gold, precious jewels, servants, fine furnishings and gilded coaches. And they were always complaining. This was powerful, destructive stereotyping.

One of the obvious problems for anyone planning marriage, therefore, was that he couldn't find out what he was getting himself into until he was well and truly stuck with the merchandise. No guarantees. No fit-for-purpose test. No right of return if dissatisfied. Horses, asses, cattle and slaves, and kettles, seats, cups and clothes could all be examined and tested before the purchase was concluded. A woman might be bad-tempered, foolish, disfigured, arrogant or smelly, but the poor, deluded man would never know until it was too late: 'A wife is the only thing that is not displayed for assessment before she is married, for fear she might not come up to scratch.'

'Behind the curtains' a wife was constantly grumbling to her husband. She complained that another man's wife was better dressed, that her husband was ogling 'that creature next door', that she had seen him talking to the maid and that 'I'm an invisible nobody at the ladies' soirées.' Supporting a poor wife might be difficult, but dealing with a rich one could be torture.

As he wrote, Theophrastus warmed to his task of persuading his students and readers that a truly wise man should avoid getting into bed with a woman. Wives were unreasonable. A man had to be constantly praising her beauty. He couldn't afford to let his gaze stray from her face. He had to remember to celebrate her birthday, respect her nursemaid, her handsome hanger-on, the curly-haired darling who managed her affairs and the eunuch who titillated her and satisfied her lusting indulgences.

Theophrastus declared that a man could never win. If he let his wife manage his household, he inevitably became her slave. If he kept some control himself, she inevitably punished him for his disloyalty. Petty household strife, domestic warfare and premature deaths by poisoning – that was what a marriage normally entailed. If he welcomed old women into his household (soothsayers, prophets, carpetbaggers, or traffickers in jewellery and silken ware), he was putting his wife's virtue in peril. But if he excluded these people, she alleged that her husband was harbouring groundless suspicions about her.

I list here a litany of complaints that sound like the mutterings of a long-suffering, unreconstructed male, sharing with his mates in the tavern over a few glasses of wine.

> If a wife is fair, she soon finds lovers; if she is ugly, it's easy for her to be ruttish. It is difficult to protect what many men long to possess and annoying to possess what no-one thinks worth taking.

So why do men marry? Theophrastus couldn't imagine why. A good and agreeable wife was a rare a bird – or as Juvenal said, a 'black swan' – an unimaginable creature for anyone living on the Mediterranean. A faithful slave was a much better household manager, more submissive and more observant. Male friends and slaves were better, more attentive to a man in his sickness and in his old age. In the final analysis, men were far better companions that any woman, as Augustine of Hippo would advise his readers seven hundred years later.

This was the message Theophrastus was sharing with his students and his readers, the same message Jerome was inviting his Christian readers to accept, the same one the monks and scholars who followed him into the Middle Ages and beyond would swallow mindlessly, the same message which would amuse the multi-married and sex-crazed widow in Chaucer's *Canterbury Tales*.

Galen of Pergamon

During the second century of the previous era, Claudius Galenus was working as a surgeon for Emperor Marcus Aurelius, and he would polish his professional skills by treating injured gladiators. Without much humility, he reported that his emperor had described him as 'first among doctors and unique among philosophers' (*De Praecognitione XIV/660* in the series *Corpus Medicorum Graecorum* V 8.1).

Galen (and professionals such as Aretaeus, a physician from Cappadocia) simply accepted Aristotle's 'scientific' view of the world and his ground-breaking ideas about how men and women conducted their intimate relationships, and about how babies were made. Biologically, men were seen as superior to women. Maleness was determined in the womb where the foetus amassed a critical surplus of 'heat' and 'vital spirit'. If it was able to realize its full potential, a foetus naturally developed into a male and, according to Galen, a female was an incomplete or an 'unfinished' male (*De Semine* 2. 5, 60, in the series *Corpus Medicorum Graecorum* V 3.1).

> When the semen is possessed of vitality, it makes us men, hot, well-braced in limbs, heavy, well-voiced, spirited, energized

to think and act (Aretaeus, *De causis et signis diuturnorum morborum*, 2.5).

A further proof of the fact that the male was superior was based on 'scientific' observations made from dissecting other warm-blooded animals. Galen came to the conclusion that men and women essentially had the same body parts. The only difference was that female organs were situated inside the body. Whereas for men the same parts were external, dangling in the area known as the perineum.

> Consider first whichever one you please, turn outward the woman's, turn inward, so to speak and fold double the man's, and you will find them the same in both, in every respect (*De Usu Partium Corporis Humani*, XIV, 6-7).

For many centuries, and based on Galen's 'observations', male and female genitalia were considered to be basically the same in structure, though located in different places on the body. The procreative bits embedded in the female body were a mirror image of the male equipment. The male body was the standard: the female body was simply an imperfect version of the prototype and unable to generate the same degree of heat.

Another reason why the Greek specialist surgeon considered the male more perfect than the female was based on what he 'observed' was occurring in the womb. When a female was born, something had gone wrong in the development of the foetus. The procreative parts, the penis and the testicles of the unborn, had not been receiving sufficient heat to enable them to be projected outside the body as they should have been if the process had gone to plan. As a result the foetus was incomplete.

The creator had designed half the human race to be 'unfinished'. However, as Galen conceded, there were some advantages in creating some members of the species in this way. The creator had planned the whole complicated system to embody a perfect member of the species and an imperfect one.

Like Aristotle, Galen was also fascinated by the significance of left and right orientations. He completed his treatment of male and female by reflecting, as Aristotle had, on the significance of the two sides of the human body. His 'scientific' observations had led him to conclude that the left testes of the male and the left side of the uterus of the female received a flow of blood which was unclean and full of residues, watery and serous. The right testes and the right side of the uterus, on the other hand, received purified blood which was naturally warmer than the blood flowing on the left side. Thus he concluded that, 'It is no longer at all unreasonable to say that the parts on the right produce males and those on the left, females.'

In those ancient times, and throughout the Middle Ages and the Renaissance, men and women were not seen as different because they were made differently. They had been created the same. Both had similar body parts. The difference was in their relative degree of excellence. Men were at the top of the species, and because of the coldness of women they occupied a lower position on the hierarchical scale of excellence. For Galen and his Aristotelian predecessors, as well as for the world of medicine, philosophy and theology up into the eighteenth century, the difference between men and women was thought of in terms of degrees of perfection, of pre-eminence, and men were more pre-eminent than women.

According to Galen, a human being, male or female, was brought into being when a man and his sexual partner rubbed their genitalia vigorously together, thereby generating a degree of heat sufficient to concoct or thicken the liquid semen which oozed from the private parts of the male and the female, compacting the two seeds into one and thereby generating life. The heat associated with orgasm produced the female seed. The medical practitioners at the time believed that frigidity caused infertility and enhancing sexual pleasure in the female was a classical treatment.

These strange notions might have been interesting in themselves, but they are worrisome when considering how a universal genius like Aristotle could stray so far off the mark. But what is much more significant (and the reason why I have spent a little time focusing on these giants of antiquity) is the deep and lasting influence Aristotle and others exerted on leaders and thinkers over the centuries, how they skewed many people's thinking, how they underpinned cultural beliefs and prejudices.

In the second century, we see their ideas rising to the surface in the writings of Clement of Alexandria, for example. Since Adam and his male relatives were covered in body hair, he concluded that they were warmer than Eve and her female relatives. Men were able to generate more body heat than the smooth, hairless, gorgeous version of humanity. Men were life-empowering, tougher, bigger, stronger — and therefore obviously more perfect. That's how God had made them. At least that's what Clement believed and the reason he thought that men should wear their hair with pride.

Perhaps a taste of what the best theologians of the Middle Ages were teaching about women might prove instructive. We can hear echoes of the ancient Greek scholars in the musings of Albert the Great, who was in turn the man who introduced Thomas Aquinas to the world of theology:

> Woman is less qualified [than man] for moral behaviour. For the woman contains more liquid than the man, and it is a property of liquid to take things up easily and to hold onto them poorly. Liquids are easily moved, hence women are inconstant and curious. When a woman has relations with a man, she would like, as much as possible, to be lying with another man at the same time. Woman knows nothing of fidelity. Believe me, if you give her your trust, you will be disappointed. Trust an experienced teacher. For this reason prudent men share their plans and actions least of all with their wives. Woman

is a misbegotten man and has a faulty and defective nature in comparison with his. Therefore she is unsure in herself. What she herself cannot get, she seeks to obtain through lying and diabolical deceptions. And so, to put it briefly, one must be on one's guard with every woman, as if she were a poisonous snake and the horned devil ... In evil and perverse doings woman is cleverer, that is, slyer, than man. Her feelings drive woman toward every evil, just as reason impels man toward all good (Albertus Magnus, *Opera Omnia*, tome 12, *Quaestiones super De Animalibus*, XV, q. 11).

The world of Plato and Aristotle, of Theophrastus and Galen, the world of Homer and Hesiod, of Juvenal and the classical Latin poets, was a world totally alien to Jesus the Palestinian lay preacher. Yet it was a world inhabited (at least in part) by Paul of Tarsus, the Greek-speaking Pharisee and Roman citizen. It was a world in which Christian scholars and essayists such as Tertullian, Clement of Alexandria, Origen and many other converts to the gospel, were increasingly at home.

A Library of Uncomfortable Facts

For the first three centuries AD, before the catalogue of accepted books to be included in 'the New Testament' had been authoritatively restricted to twenty-seven, each region had its own library of sacred Christian literature. During this early period the Christian movement was under stress.

Jesus-followers were being confronted with a variety of philosophical and religious beliefs and practices. In order to preserve some semblance of contact with Jesus and his initial message, each small group of believers needed some basic, authentic and tangible expression of what the original eyewitnesses had heard and seen. Their memories of Jesus and his message had to be preserved in permanent form before they disappeared, or before the original experience had been diluted by the many forces at work within contemporary society.

The message and the stories which supported the beliefs of the early followers could no longer simply be handed down just in oral form. Written records begun to appear and circulate – letters from Paul, to begin with, and recorded sayings of Jesus which later became known as 'Q', followed by the Gospels. And there was a history of the missionary activities of the early church; the interface between the early communities of believers and Jewish officialdom, and later with the Greco-Roman world. Other letters written under the names of various apostles – Paul, Peter, John, James, Jude, Barnabas – were also found to be circulating.

I have elected to confine my attention to the three hundred years following Jesus' death, ending in the period just before the meeting of bishops at Nicaea in 325 AD. The council summoned by the emperor Constantine provides a convenient point to conclude my examination of the early Christian tradition of misogyny. The library of essays and treatises and the like which I have drawn on has come largely from these first three hundred years.

In the initial chapters of this book I look at the role women enjoyed in the very early Christian communities and how some leaders, especially the Apostle Paul and those writing in his name, spoke about them. Some of the early Christian literature written by these leaders was eventually canonised and sacralised. Then for sixteen hundred years Christians received Paul's letters and other literary pieces as the authentic word of God. Believers have revered these texts as divinely inspired documents. They have handled them with reverence, quoting them as irrefutable authorities guaranteeing the truth of various dogmas and establishing the authenticity of different practices and prohibitions. This sacred literature is contained in a canon of writings which were put together over time from a library of primitive material and endowed with the status of revealing what Christians have come to recognize as the acid test for the genuineness of their faith and practice.

What became known as the New Testament canon consists of twenty-seven books ranging from the four Gospels (of Mark, Matthew, Luke and John), the book of Revelation (also known as the Apocalypse), the Acts of the Apostles, the various authentic letters of Paul the Apostle and a number of other letters, some of which have been attributed to him and to other apostles as a mark of respect as well as to ensure they were accepted as having the same status and authority as the equivalent Jewish library of sacred books. This canon of revered books, however, was not concluded until the second half of the fourth century, after Constantine had died, and outside our period of interest.

In the eastern territory of the church, the thirty-ninth Paschal Letter (written by Athanasius of Alexandria in 367 AD) recorded the list of twenty-seven books which now constitute the official canon. He excluded from his list the writings of those men now known as the Apostolic Fathers (people like Clement of Rome, Ignatius of Antioch and Polycarp). But he also made an allowance for some holy books to be read privately – books like the *Didache*, the *Shepherd of Hermas* and the *Wisdom of Solomon*. This list of Athanasius, though created for use only in his hometown, was widely approved and rapidly accepted throughout the East. His list was confirmed by a papal declaration in 405 AD, but was probably first approved earlier in the West at the Synod of Rome in 382 AD. At the Synods of Hippo Regius (393 AD) and Carthage (397 AD) the North African churches followed the lead of Rome and Alexandria, and at a later Synod of Carthage (419 AD), these local churches finally put any doubt to rest about the inclusion in the canon of the Epistle to the Hebrews and the epistles of James and Jude.

So what was the situation before the canon of the New Testament was finally and officially confined to the canon of twenty-seven books? What books were being copied and circulated? What were people reading – or at least hearing from? What books were included in a local church's collection, and how did they get there? Which of these texts were received as sacred, as authoritative and authentic? Was there a fixed catalogue of books that was available for Christians to refer to, and if so, when did this catalogue came into existence? Did it vary from place to place? Were some books excluded? If so, by whom, and on what basis was this determined?

Paul's Literary Bequest

When the early Christian literature was being composed, from about 50 AD to the end of the first century, the figure who set the fashion in the Christian world was Paul. Jesus had disappeared from the earth as a physical force and Paul's presence soon began to overshadow the emerging organisation – not Peter, or James or John, or any of the other apostles, many of whom, as far as we can see, simply disappeared into the shadows. While there was some rivalry between those barracking for Peter, or for James the brother of Jesus, and the fierce supporters of Paul and the fans of other male preachers, and while there was competition for leadership within the different communities, Paul fought with passion to establish his position and seems to have won the contest. Consequently he emerged as the dominant figure in the primitive Church.

Paul's published portfolio of correspondence includes thirteen, perhaps fourteen, letters (which have come to be called epistles, though only one or two could be classified as epistles in the classical sense). Thirteen letters in the New Testament were attributed to Paul. The Epistle to the Hebrews could constitute the fourteenth, if Cyril of Jerusalem is to be believed (*Catech*.4:36 PG. 33/499). Of the thirteen, only seven can be said with any certainty to have been written (or dictated to a secretary) by the man himself.

In an earlier book I examined the original four Gospels of Mark, Matthew, Luke and John to examine how the early Christian authors wrote about women – how they sought to depict Jesus' attitudes to women, how he related to them and how they responded. Women of all sorts – relatives, friends and strangers – had been included in his life and mission. His contact with women had not been restricted by Jewish cultural taboos and prejudices. He had not simply taken on board the prevailing patriarchal paradigm. Jesus had involved women in his daily life, eaten and drunk with them, showed them respect, enjoyed their company and related to them in a new, counter-cultural manner.

Was Jesus' new and radical attitude towards women incorporated into the system of beliefs and values of the life of the early Christian communities? To examine how the message of Jesus was launched outside Palestine and prosecuted, the letters written by Paul the thirteenth apostle are critical.

The thirteen letters appearing under Paul's name can be divided into three categories:

1. *The authentic letters*: This category is comprised of Paul's First Letter to the Thessalonians, his letters to the Galatians and to the Philippians, his Epistle to the Romans, his short note to his friend Philemon, and both his remaining letters to the Corinthians (though one brief critical passage in the first of these letters was more than likely introduced into the text later by an anonymous hand).

   Some scholars (L.L. Welborn, for example) have suggested that Paul's first epistle to the people of Corinth as it appears in the New Testament is an amalgamation of three distinct letters – one warning against associating with citizens who were immoral and who worshipped idols, a second in reply to a letter he had received from the community in Corinth (1 Cor 7–9 and 12–16), and a third giving advice in an attempt to establish peace and communion among his people in Corinth (1 Cor 1:1–6:11). But we don't need to be concerned over this issue. We will treat the letter as it has been published and read over the centuries.

2. *Three doubtful or deutero-Pauline letters*: Paul's Second Letter to the Thessalonians, his letters to the Colossians and to the Ephesians. Scholars generally agree that these pieces of correspondence were written by someone close to Paul, probably by one of his disciples or a member of his school of theology, but not by the man himself.

3. *The Pastoral Epistles*: The pseudonymous Letter to Titus and the two addressed to Timothy were written after Paul's death but attributed to him. They appear even today (falsely) under his name.

From a few references in Paul's letters we can conclude that there were other letters he wrote, and which have been lost.

Furthermore, from his observation in 2 Cor 10:10, we can also conclude that Paul was aware his letters were being collected and circulated, and the author of the Second Epistle of Peter knew that these letters were circulating among the various communities and were being quoted. The members of the early churches considered that, like Jesus and the other apostles, Paul was speaking with authority, and for two thousand years Christians of all persuasions have continued to quote passages from his letters as well as from the pseudonymous letters as though their message came directly from the Spirit of God.

But the author of 2 Peter also thought that there were some things in Paul's letters that were hard to understand (and as you will see, I tend to agree), things which 'the ignorant and unstable' twisted to suit themselves 'as they do the other scriptures'. The author warned his readers to be careful that they were not carried away by 'the error of lawless men' (2 Cor 3:15–17).

Some critical passages of the sacred scriptures have been used and abused down the centuries, and modified and misinterpreted, mostly unconsciously, to bolster spurious argument. As we will see, one of these passages consists of a few chauvinistic verses in 1 Corinthians 14. Paul was himself constantly on his guard to warn against shysters, charlatans, humbugs, loud-mouths and false prophets. Some passages from his various epistles have been quoted by the Fathers, twisted, misinterpreted and exaggerated, taken out of context and planted in the middle of acrimonious disputes to 'prove' some particular proposition. Jerome the exegete fell into this trap towards the end of the fourth century with his expansive treatment of Paul's Delphic statement, 'It is well for a man not to touch a woman', in 1 Corinthians 7:1.

Paul wrote his letters some decades before the earliest Gospel would appear. This was most likely the Gospel of Mark. The first letter we have which Paul wrote was to his people in Thessaloniki. He had visited them during his second missionary journey, in the summer of 50 AD (Acts 17:1–10). He had converted some synagogue Jews, some God-fearing people and some Greeks as well as some 'rich women', but we don't know who these women were. No names, no details. He wrote this first letter during the winter months of 50 to 51 AD and it was addressed to his 'brothers' (1 Thess 1:4; 2:1, 14 & 17; 4:9 & 13; 5:1, 12, 14 & 27) – which probably also included his 'sisters', since the masculine form, by usage, included the feminine. But that's another story and has its own message about where women have sat on the gender spectrum, between superiority and inferiority, or visibility and invisibility. Other letters followed this first epistle to the Thessalonians – several to the Corinthians, to the Galatians, the Romans and the Philippians.

Paul and those writing in his name were far more expansive than Jesus had been when talking about women. But before we look at what Paul and the others had to say on these topics, there are a few general observations to be made.

First, Paul (and some of the others) was writing letters – and only letters. These were not treatises, essays, pamphlets or Gospels. These letters were addressed to a particular person, or more often to a specific group of people – not to the world at large, or to all Christian communities. Not like a pope's encyclical letters or a blog on the internet. When he was writing, Paul had a specific local audience in mind.

These letters were then copied and collected, and much later canonised. They came to be generally available to other believers, century after century. But when they first appeared, they were written by one man to a discrete group of people whom he knew and who knew him (although Romans was an exception as he had not yet arrived there). The author and his readers were united by a common memory of what had passed between them. Consequently, when interpreting what Paul (and others) were saying, and its relevance to other cultures centuries down the track, we must take account of the literary form of the writings and the context of the words.

Second, his letters often addressed particular problems and answered questions his churches had been asking. They had a specific context and therefore a reasonable reader has to interpret them as part of some continuing dialogue – a dialogue, unfortunately, which was interrupted by long gaps and is disturbed by background static when a modern reader attempts to tune into the message.

Third, great care must be taken in our interpretation of what Paul wrote and of what was written in his name. We don't have the other side of the correspondence and only a limited knowledge of the authors and of the people they were addressing. We know little about what they knew, how they went about their daily lives, the pressures they were experiencing and the cultural context in which they lived. Therefore it is easy to misinterpret the words, to push them out of shape, to plant them in a different context, and so exaggerate or distort the message.

Fourth, since the author's advice was being given to one community, since answers were being provided to problems within a particular church, great care must be taken when that advice, those answers, are removed from their context and made to apply generally, to all communities, to every church and without modification. What Paul and the others wrote should not be applied automatically across the board.

We should be mindful that in the New Testament literature we are listening to one side of the story – to men only. We have to read between the lines and under the text. When the author of the Pastoral Epistles, for example, insisted that he would not permit any woman to teach or exercise authority over men, we can be reasonably sure that there were women doing what was being expressly forbidden. Otherwise the author would have had no reason to raise the subject. And the voices of the women involved are now lost. Presumably they were being heard at the time and later suppressed. Any texts reflecting a contrary view, if they ever existed, were never copied and preserved in the institutional libraries.

Finally, it's clear that Paul was not producing a rounded theology or a philosophical treatise on the subject of women, their role in society and their place within the Christian churches. Unlike Jesus, he and those who wrote under his alias did focus some of their thoughts on the general topic of women and the male/female relationship. We should not presume, however, that the few letters and the scattered passages we have to hand exhaust the topic. Paul wrote other letters which are lost to us. We don't know what they said. And Paul was writing on the general topic to various communities, addressing problems, dictating his own insights, and at other times trying to reflect ideas which had been handed down to him. We should not presume that the few letters and scattered passages we have to hand addressed all the issues relating to women. They didn't.

A Post-Apostolic and Pre-Nicaean Library

We are not left to our imagination to create a picture of the world of women and their place in the life of the early Christian churches. Apart from Paul and those who wrote under his name, there are a number of authors from the second, third and early fourth centuries who addressed the topic of women, their fashions, their foibles and behaviours. These authors – Tertullian of Carthage; Clement of Alexandria, the author of the *Didascalia* and the *Didache*; and to a lesser extent, Irenaeus, the bishop of Lyon in Gaul – addressed the place of women in society, their relationship with men, and their role within the Christian communities. The Christian-Gnostic literature (including the various apocryphal gospels and acts which have been rediscovered in recent years), the *Shepherd of Hermas*, the *Testaments of the Patriarchs* and other documents all offer fertile territory where we can fossick for insights into the mentality and practices of the period.

The world in which the early Christian communities were functioning in Asia and around the borders of the Mediterranean was more fluid than we imagine. In a world where there were no standards yet established to separate heresy from orthodoxy or distil wheat from chaff, the ordinary believer would have found it difficult to know where to look for the genuine message of Jesus. With no agreed canon of sacred literature to guide them, even from the beginning there were disputes about who was the leader, who should be followed – Peter, Paul, Apollo or someone else.

What is clear is that the first, second and third centuries constituted a period of flux and uncertainty. Some of the Jewish converts were adapting some of their own literature into a Christian idiom, or at least mimicking their traditional Jewish literary forms when they were composing Christian texts. Members of the Gnostic sects were causing chaos by their claims to have received new revelations independently of Jesus and the apostles, and preserving these revelations in written form. There was a high level of cross-fertilization between the various communities, the different sects and the competing theologies. And the followers of the successful apocalyptic, ascetical and prophetic movement which Montanus and two female friends had established were making damaging inroads into the Christian communities in Asia Minor and North Africa. They had produced a large library of texts to record their revelations.

There were gospels, acts, treatises, poems, testaments from different local churches, some with a distinctive Jewish tone, some with a marked Gnostic orientation – all inviting attention. Claiming to be authentic, they were each asserting contact with the apostles, with Jesus, with the Spirit, and all were being circulated. The churches needed to know with some degree of certainty where they could find the true, authentic message of Jesus. This could only be achieved by establishing a canon or an official list of the truly sacred and authenticated books, another catalogue of books which were approved and could be read in the local community, and finally, a list of dangerous material to be avoided.

At one stage scholars such as Origen and Eusebius were distinguishing three clear categories of books: books generally accepted, books which were on the edge but more or less suitable, and those which had to be definitely excluded from any list.

The texts which eventually found their way into the canon of the New Testament were not the only literary material which was being copied, circulated and made part of a collection of books to nourish the faith of the local followers of Jesus. By the middle of the second century, in addition to the collection of letters of Paul and of the four Gospels which were circulating, there was the *Didache* and the *Shepherd of Hermas* (both of which were considered in some circles as part of the scriptures), the letters of Ignatius of Antioch and those of Polycarp, the *Martyrdom of Polycarp*, the *Odes of Solomon*, a letter of Clement of Rome, the works of Justin the Apologist (two apologies – one addressed to the Emperor Antoninus and the second to the Roman Senate, and his *Dialogue with Trypho*), the *Testaments of the Twelve Patriarchs* and other pieces of Christian literature (Athenagoras on the *Resurrection of the Dead*, the *Epistle to Diognetus* as well as the works of Papias, of Melito and Theophilus). All this material was being circulated in and between the local churches.

A little later, the works of Tertullian, Irenaeus, Origen, Cyprian of Carthage, Hippolytus, and Clement of Alexandria, and the *Didascalia* were being read and preserved for posterity. All this material provides (limited) insights into the life of women and the attitudes and prejudices of those early Christian communities which had spread throughout Asia or which had gathered around the edges of the Mediterranean.

In the general confusion of ideas and spiritualities circulating at the time, apart from the more orthodox and conservative religious trends, there were various rival groups parading their beliefs and attracting followers. These 'heterodox' groups became known as 'Gnostic', and the movement itself as 'Gnosticism'. As the more orthodox conservative forces came to exercise their dominance, they took steps to suppress their rivals, ridiculing their teachings and burying their manuscripts. Until recently, our knowledge of these rival movements of religious ideas and spiritualities was restricted to the writings of conservative 'orthodox' authors like Irenaeus, Hippolytus and Epiphanius.

Fortunately, since the end of the nineteenth century and especially since the middle of the twentieth century, scholars have had an extensive library of original Gnostic literature to examine. They no longer need to rely entirely on the opponents of Gnosticism to fill the void. There is a substantial number of original documents of early origin known to us as the Christian Apocrypha. These texts were so named because they were written in a style or in a format which mimicked those works which became known as the canonical books – the four Gospels, Acts and the Book of Revelation (also known as the Apocalypse).

In December 1945 some local youths were riding their camels along the banks of the Nile near Nag Hammadi and, while digging for fertilizer to nourish their family crops, they came across an old jar buried in the sand. When the seal was broken, they discovered that it contained 13 ancient Coptic codices. The jar had been buried around 400 AD, probably by monks from a local monastery who were 'disposing' of some of the subversive material in their library. The 50 different ancient texts contained in the codices were Coptic translations of material which had been written in Greek sometime between the middle of the second century through to the end of the third. They were largely Christian documents but, as we would say now, 'contaminated' by Gnostic ideas and beliefs, and from different Gnostic traditions – Sethian, Valentinian and Hermetic. Some were only a matter of a few verses (less than a page in length), but others were much more substantial.

The codices from Nag Hammadi, however significant, are not the only original Gnostic material which has become available in recent times. In 1896, for example, the Berlin Gnostic Codex was rediscovered, again after many centuries. The next year some Gnostic documents were found on a rubbish dump in the ancient city of Oxyrhynchus. In 1967 the *Gospel of the Saviour* was put back together from a jumble of ancient parchment fragments. The *Gospel of Judas* and other texts were found in the 1970s.

The Christian Apocrypha include a number of gospels – gospels of Philip, of Truth, of Thomas and the Greek Gospel of Thomas, of Judas Iscariot and of Mary Magdalene. They include also the *Dialogue of the Saviour* and a series of Acts of individual apostles. The acts of John, Peter, Paul, Andrew and Thomas were composed to fill in the history of the early church that was missing from the canonical books, telling stories of the journeys undertaken by some particular apostle to distant lands, stories of the ascetical lives lived by believers, often demanding that they renounce the matrimonial state. A few apocryphal apocalypses were styled on the Book of Revelation and were offshoots of Jewish apocalyptic literature (texts ascribed to Peter, or Paul, or Thomas). And there were other texts such as *The Nature of the Rulers*, *Three Forms of First Thought*, the *Holy Book of the Great Invisible Spirit*, the *Secret Book of James*, the *Prayer of the Apostle Paul*, the *Treatise on the Resurrection*. Historians and theologians have a wealth of early Christian and semi-Christian sources to work on.

The apocryphal gospels, like their relatives (the four canonical Gospels of the New Testament), purport to record eyewitness recollections of Jesus including details of his birth and childhood, his sayings, stories providing additional details about his passion and resurrection, and post-resurrection dialogues in which Jesus continued to reveal spiritual truths to one or other of his favourite disciples or to Mary Magdalene, for example.

The historical accuracy of this apocryphal material is difficult to assess from this distance. Some material seems to be an imaginative gloss on the stories told in the canonical Gospels. Other parts appear to be an attempt to combine canonical material with popular oral traditions. Perhaps some of the material relied on a stream of tradition running in parallel with the tradition on which the composers of the canonical Gospel were relying – a stream which wasn't being adequately controlled by someone in a position of power.

The Gnostic-Christian literature which has recently come to light provides evidence of the spiritual depth of the Gnostic world of the second and third centuries, the diversity of the prevailing traditions, and a different slant on the theological significance of Jesus. This literature deals with secret revelations, with the communication of a hidden knowledge or a deeply personal and spiritual *gnosis* which was believed to lead to a state of perfection. In some of the gospels, Jesus was the revealer of a hidden knowledge which he had not shared with his followers during his lifetime but which he had shared privately with one or two chosen disciples, male and female. They in turn became the repository of his secrets for the community.

The newly found literature records stories of male and female spirits, aeons living up among the stars, a mysterious hierarchy of male and female emanations in the heavens – stories of characters who were engaged in the cosmic process of perfection or striving for redemption. These documents recount manifestations of God as a father and as a mother, and describe all reality – divine, human, spiritual and physical – as based on a radical dualistic paradigm. All reality was comprised of male and female elements. Those who possessed the genuine knowledge or *gnosis* were both male and female.

This dualistic view of reality and of the world which was propagated by the Gnostics and the Gnostic Christians was not reflected in the theology or philosophy of the Catholic Church. Its view of the world was based on a God seen exclusively as a father, and on male authority figures only – popes, bishops, monsignors and abbots. As the Church's orthodox position developed over the centuries, God the Father mysteriously gave birth to a son, God the Son, but without the need to engage the services of a female figure. Then together (at least in the Western church tradition) the Holy Spirit proceeded from the mysterious union of the Father and the Son – a story heavily dominated by heavenly male characters and devoid of any heavenly female figure.

The *Gospel of Thomas* is one of these Christian-Gnostic Apocrypha. It was probably written in Greek, in Syria, perhaps as early as the first century, about the same time as the canonical Gospels. It is a collection of Jesus' secret sayings which were supposed to have been communicated directly to his apostle Thomas Judas. This early collection of sayings was similar to what became known to scholars as the 'Q' document which was used by the composers of Matthew and Luke in conjunction with the Gospel of Mark to put their Gospels together.

If it is true that the *Gospel of Thomas* dates from the first century, it takes the reader to a time much closer to the historical Jesus, and to a Jesus who was a teacher of wisdom. This document does not focus on Jesus' titles or his miracles, and does not concentrate on a heroic figure who faced death by crucifixion to redeem mankind from the powers of evil. The figure at the centre of the *Gospel of Thomas* is that of a man who possessed a special knowledge of secrets, who enjoyed a special gnosis, and who revealed his secrets to an elect group of those who could understand and who were thereby liberated to achieve a state of perfection.

> The Jesus of Thomas is also somewhat different from the Jesus of the New Testament gospels, and it would appear that the Gospel of Thomas is not fundamentally dependent upon the New Testament gospels but is an independent gospel and a primary source of the Jesus tradition. Jesus in the Gospel of

Thomas performs no physical miracles, reveals no fulfillment of prophecy, announces no apocalyptic kingdom about to disrupt the world order, and dies for no-one's sins.

(Marvin Meyer, *The Gnostic Discoveries*, pp. 61–62)

This early literature in all its forms would have been read by the early Christians – at least by those who could read. None of it was thought of in the early days as apocryphal, unorthodox or heretical. These were categories that had no purchase for the early Christians, they would emerge slowly over time. And even after the canon of the New Testament literature had been finally established, the texts of some of these authors continued to be copied and circulated. Others, for some reason, were destroyed, dumped on rubbish heaps or hidden away in jars buried in the desert. Nonetheless, they all witness to beliefs, attitudes, values and prejudices which circulated in the minds of some believers and their communities in a particular part of the world. Fortunately, modern readers now have access to a library of foreign but fascinating ideas and beliefs from these early centuries.

In the course of our study, we will make our way 'round the perimeter of the Mediterranean, from North Africa anticlockwise to the south of France. We will visit Tertullian in Carthage, Clement and Origen in the city of Alexandria, and the deserts of Egypt where the Christian-Gnostic texts had been buried for safekeeping.

We will pause in Syria on the eastern border of the Mediterranean where the *Didache* and the *Didascalia* first saw the light of day, in Asia Minor or modern Turkey to trace the behaviour of the prophet Montanus and his two girlfriends, and in the Greek community of believers in Lyon, the capital of Gaul and the episcopal seat of Irenaeus.

We will encounter ideas and beliefs exceedingly strange to the ear of any modern reader, ideas which found their way into different gospels and acts that were never canonised by those in charge. Strange voices from the past, ideas from a variety of sources – orthodox and heterodox believers, mysterious religious cults and Gnostic sects.

In the course of our study, we will discover a world of ideas and beliefs that was deaf to any notion of a kingdom of heaven on earth as preached by Jesus. These were ideas which would never have entered Jesus' head, ideas which clashed with his world. These early Christian writers who followed after Jesus and his apostles were preoccupied with evil and sin, sex and desire, heaven and angels, Adam and Eve, with women at the primordial source of chaos in the world, and as brain-troubling and genital-tantalising temptresses of God's most gifted creature.

We must, however, be careful how we deal with these documents. We don't know how much we know of the ancient world, or what we don't know about the life, the beliefs and practices of the local churches during their first few centuries of existence. Nor do we know how accurately these documents reflect the life of the early church. A substantial quantity of early texts has perished. One expert has calculated that approximately eighty-five percent of the second century texts he saw referenced in the existing sources has perished.

Furthermore, a thoughtful reader has to ask herself why a particular text survived while others disappeared. Obviously someone (usually a monk) preserved those texts which were of particular interest to him or to his superior, or to the principal librarian or its benefactor. The documents which survived were those which men in control, those with authority (and money) considered acceptable, or orthodox. We can be confident that the surviving texts certainly don't tell us the whole story – and perhaps not even the right slant. It's a possibility that they don't even provide a more or less accurate picture of the day-to-day existence of the average Christian and their local community. At this late stage, we have to be careful not to proceed with over-confidence.

Instead of Jesus' kingdom being established in the ordinary world of men and women, Christianity gradually became an established institution and a process by which a believer could withdraw from the earth. Inside this organisation, the institution of marriage came to be seen as second-rate, somehow tainted and passé. The authors contributing to the libraries of the local churches were trying to convince their readers that the sexual coupling promoted by the creating divinity was to be avoided as much as possible, and to be engaged in reluctantly, without pleasure, as an act of duty. Celibacy, virginity and sexless living would become the gold standard offered to the followers of Jesus. And to achieve this regime, writers were laying down strict regulations about female dress and ways of behaviour, about bathing and social contacts between the two sexes. These were dangerous, marshy areas of human existence, into which, we can say with some confidence, Jesus had not ventured. If the literature which is available to us can be accepted, Jesus' message was travelling far from its origins in Palestine. The message was butting up against many pressures and undergoing profound modifications. And women were suffering the consequences.

Women in the Life of the Early Church in and around Palestine

From the beginning women were part of the life of the early church. They were visible and included, some by name, others as part of a group – of widows, of prophets, as servants or deaconesses, as teachers and hostesses.

The Acts of the Apostles is a complex historical document purporting to tell the story, albeit heavy with theology, of the spread of the Good News of Jesus throughout Palestine, Asia Minor, Greece and as far afield as Rome. It was composed some decades after Paul's letters, probably somewhere between 80 and 90 AD. The story begins in the days immediately after Jesus' disappearance from Galilee and Jerusalem, when Peter had assumed the leadership of a fringe group of what appeared to be Jewish heretics. Among its many other features, Acts records something about women's presence within the movement from the beginning, before Paul arrived on the scene.

The author of Acts paid special attention to Paul's missionary journeys, establishing communities outside Palestine. There he adapted the message to other cultures, attracting pagans to join the ranks of the early Jewish believers.

The author began his story with Jesus' departure from the scene and the dramatic events of Pentecost a few days later. Like Paul's letters, the Jesus message as presented in Acts had undergone a radical change. In Acts the principal topic is not Jesus' post-Resurrection conversations (Acts 1:3). Instead the author was telling a story about the spread of a message which dealt principally with the significance of Jesus as the Christ-Saviour. This message tells of his rejection by his fellow Jews, about his death and return to life, and about the establishment of structured communities of believers around the rim of the Mediterranean.

The story narrated in Acts covers pastoral activities in the broad territory from Jerusalem to Rome. It covers successes and failures during the brief period from approximately 35 to 70 AD. The narrative involves a long list of characters – apostles, deacons, prophets, missionaries, Roman officials and Jewish functionaries, and of course a number of women. Several are identified by name.

While there are a number of examples in Acts of women playing a role within the primitive local communities, there is no recorded incident of women travelling out on the road with Paul or anyone else as they had done with Jesus. Elsewhere in the letters of Paul we read of women engaged as missionaries on the road, of women accompanying their husbands or other male co-workers, giving them support and comfort. But the author of Acts mostly confines his story to the journeys and exploits of Paul and his male companions who were travelling without female company. He does not trace in any detail the journeys of any of the other apostles or make mention that some of them had been travelling with female companions.

After addressing his imaginary reader, Theophilus, and having completed his story of the life and times of Jesus as recounted in his Gospel, the same author continued his colourful account of the foundation of Christianity, beginning with the first days in Jerusalem.

We read how Jesus' followers coped after his disappearance, about the basic message they had begun to teach. We can see how the message had changed from Jesus to Peter, and again from Peter to Paul. We read how the leaders interacted with officialdom and the general population, and how the followers had attracted large crowds to their movement.

The story moves rapidly from scene to scene, from region to region, the focus forever shifting – colours, shapes, brushstrokes merging into one another. We are left with the impression of a miraculous surge of energy, a feeling of a Spirit-filled movement with a bright future – groups of men and women sharing what they possessed and what they believed. The daily grind behind the narrative, however, may have been more humdrum and demanding.

The reader is left wishing that the author had told more. Yet amongst the *dramatis personae* – sometimes sympathetic, sometimes hostile – we meet a number of important women who were playing a part in the unfolding story of Christianity. Although they do not feature as much in his second volume as in his gospel (the Gospel of Luke), the author nonetheless introduces his readers to women members of the Christian community – to Sapphira, the wife of Ananias, to Mary, to the mother of John Mark, to Tabitha, to Lydia, to the four daughters of Philip, and to Priscilla.

After Jesus had finally disappeared from the scene, a group withdrew to the upper room where they were staying and devoted themselves to prayer. This group comprised the eleven apostles (absent Judas the traitor), 'the women', Mary the mother of Jesus and his brethren. Quite a crowd – about one hundred and twenty according to the author – and a mixed bag. This upper room was either very spacious or the attendees were crushed in like sardines. Men and women staying and praying together. Apparently, the customary segregation of the sexes was no longer viewed as obligatory by these 'heretics'. They did not consider themselves part of the establishment. Jesus had encouraged them to think differently, to be different. They were special, and on the fringe. The men and women had become used to being in one another's company. Following Jesus' example, at least some of the taboos and prejudices which were part of the cultural heritage of the Jewish people at the time were being ignored.

It wasn't acceptable in those days for men to associate freely with women, to converse male to female or mingle in public, certainly not to be together in any 'upper room'. Before they had met Jesus, when these people had been at prayer in the local synagogue or Temple, the sexes had been segregated. Women had been tolerated in the synagogue, but only if they were veiled, if they occupied a place apart and if they remained silent. And they were not counted in the quorum which the law required for a proper prayer meeting. There was no active female participation in what was essentially men's business.

But these early Jewish Christians were living by a different standard. Jesus had set the example. Women had been an integral part of his group. No longer fringe-dwellers. A woman was not just some man's wife or daughter, but they were real life-members of the new community. The author of Acts was not announcing this new regime with any shrill trumpet-blast, making a policy statement for all to sit up and listen. He was stating a simple fact, leaving it to others to read between the lines. A seismic shift within the cultural settings of the period was gently taking place.

According to Acts, the message was spreading like wildfire. Numbers had increased dramatically, though 'thousands at a time' was perhaps a romantic exaggeration. Early in the story, the author tells us that the apostles had performed many signs and wonders among the people, and that multitudes, 'both of men and women' (Acts 5:14), had been added to the ranks. Women formed part of the rapid expansion of the movement, just as men had, though they were certainly not as visible as the men, and not able to exercise the same level of authority. However, according to the author at least, when Paul was on the hunt and persecuting the filthy Christians, he couldn't suppress the troublemakers unless he took out the female members as well as the men.

> Saul laid waste the church, and entering house after house, he dragged off men and women and put them in prison (Acts 8:3).

One of the first women we meet in Acts (apart from Jesus' mother) is the scheming, dishonest wife of Ananias.

According to the story, Sapphira and her husband Ananias had been a team. In telling the story of their dishonesty and punishment, the author gives us no sense that 'the wife' was inferior to her husband. In this community they were equal partners and treated equally. Equal owners of the property. Equally free to dispose of the property, equally free to contribute or not to the common purse, and equally guilty and equally punished. In this movement, women were not treated as possessions or slaves. They were not silent or invisible within the ranks of this start-up organisation. And it was hoped that the new movement would continue as it had begun.

The author continued his story, going on to name other female members within the ranks – women who were occupying positions of some significance and playing a visible part in the emerging institution.

Before he begins to write about Paul's missionary activities, the author pauses at several points to speak favourably of several women – Tabita of Joppa, otherwise known by her Greek name, Dorcas, meaning 'Gazelle' – Mary, the mother of John Mark (whoever he was) and her slave Rhoda.

Tabita is described by the author as a disciple 'full of good works and acts of charity'. She was undoubtedly one of those charitable, energetic women who were visible in her community and ministering to an identifiable group known as 'the widows'.

Tabitha had spent her time before her death weaving for the widows of Joppa. After her death they had gathered, as widows used to do, to prepare her body for burial, to mourn her passing with groans and tears and to give her a fitting farewell. More than likely, these widows were also believers and members of the community like Tabitha. Following Jesus' example when he had raised the daughter of Jairus (a story which the author of Luke's

Gospel had also recounted, Luke 8:51), Peter dismissed the weeping widows and restored Tabitha to life, and though we will continue to read about numerous groups of widows in the early church (in the Pastoral Epistles, for example) we never hear of her again. Widows were destined to become an important part of the early Christian communities – not thrown out onto the streets to fend for themselves as they generally were at the time, with no social security or old age pension. Widows would quickly organise into identifiable groups or associations and supporting them would become part of the church's mission. They were treated with more respect than they attracted out in the general community and were destined as a group to become powerful and troublesome.

When he told the story of Peter's arrest, his imprisonment and miraculous escape, the author of Acts modelled his narrative on some of the Gospel details associated with Jesus' appearances after the resurrection, or more probably, on an oral tradition later recorded by the author of John's Gospel. Two women are prominent in the story – Mary, the mother of John Mark, and a slave girl called Rhoda.

In the Gospels women had been central to the resurrection narratives. They had been reliable witnesses of Jesus' appearance and conveyors of a message to the apostles. The evidence of women was generally regarded in Jewish culture as unreliable and not usually accepted in Jewish courts. In the Christian community, however, this prejudice had been buried. Women were participating in the life of the community.

As the story unfolded (and like the Gospel story involving Thomas), the Apostle James and some of the brethren had been absent from the prayer meeting in Mary's home when Peter had appeared out of the mist, so the group of women were entrusted with the task of giving a message to them, telling them what had happened.

In his Gospel, as well as in his Acts, the author showed a special interest in the role of women in Jesus' life and in the new communities. In Acts, as elsewhere in the New Testament, women were associated with hospitality. The author of these Acts tells us that the Christian community used to gather for prayer in a particular person's home and that the host would provide lodgings for itinerant disciples. In some cases the host was a woman. Jesus had instructed his disciples that they could rely on a warm welcome into other people's homes and could expect to share at their tables. Jesus had enjoyed the hospitality of Martha and Mary, for example, and of Peter's mother-in-law. The early missionaries were following their founder's example, and women were responsible for the offer of hospitality which was an essential aspect of the kingdom. And their homes became the place to gather for prayer and preaching.

In due course, we will come back to Lydia, Priscilla and the four daughters of Philip.

The Thirteenth Apostle

After Jesus had drifted out into the clouds and away from his little band of followers (if the New Testament accounts can be accepted as true versions of events), the person who eventually emerged as a dominant figure and muscular missionary from among the believers was a man called Saul, an educated Pharisee from Tarsus. According to him, he had been an ambitious young man who had risen higher in the ranks than any of his contemporaries and had proved himself unusually zealous in protecting the traditions of his ancestors (Gal 1:14). For some time he had worked as an enthusiastic tormenter of those who were pilgrims on the Way of Jesus. An unflattering description of him appeared perhaps two centuries after his death:

> At length they saw a man coming, namely Paul, of small stature with meeting eyebrows, a bald head, bow-legged, strongly built, hollow-eyed, with a large crooked nose. He was full of grace. Sometimes he appeared as a man; sometimes he had the countenance of an angel (*The Acts of Paul and Thecla* 1).

At several stages in Acts we read about the stunning, life-changing *volte-face* Saul the Pharisee experienced just outside Damascus. Like Moses before him (and Jesus), following his powerful experience of the transcendent, he had withdrawn into the wilderness to communicate one-on-one with the divine. At approximately the same age as Jesus had been when he had journeyed into the desert before beginning his public ministry, rather than going straight up to Jerusalem to meet with those who were 'apostles before me', Paul disappeared into Arabia (Gal 1:17) where, as he said, he was caught up into the third heaven – whether in the body or out of the body, he did not know. In the desert he was assumed into Paradise where he heard things that could not be told, that no man would even utter. Private revelations, startling dreams and amazing visions (2 Cor 12:1–4). He was taken up into the mystical world of the prophets of God.

Following these destabilising experiences, Paul went up to Jerusalem to meet the apostles and become a fully-fledged member of a new, heretical Jewish movement. According to Acts, from the leaders in Jerusalem he received a special commission to the Gentiles and went on to become the movement's most notorious missionary.

Paul's career as a travelling preacher lasted much longer than Jesus' fleeting three years. He journeyed to far distant lands, to cities and villages in Asia Minor and Greece. We read in Acts about his preaching and about his companions on the road – and his encounters with women. We glimpse some details as to how the communities in Jerusalem and beyond were functioning, how they came together to pray and celebrate, the problems they experienced, the content of Paul's preaching, his grand visions, his emotional attachment to the figure of Jesus Risen, the regulations he wanted to enact, and a little of who did what. In the course of his missionary work, before he was put to death, Paul alienated many of his Jewish brethren while attracting large numbers of pagan followers.

Tertullian tells us that the apostle Paul was beheaded. Legend would have it he died in Rome, about 67 AD, a few years before the catastrophic destruction of Jerusalem. He was then in his 60s. In his youth, before he went public, the magnetic but divisive hero to whom Paul had pledged his allegiance had probably worked with his father Joseph as a carpenter. Paul had been a tentmaker – both tradesmen, though as far as we know only one of them had earned his living by plying his trade.

As he travelled around the world Paul was writing letters to various communities he had founded. In this as in other matters, he proved to be different from the Jesus he was preaching.

As far as we know, Jesus had written nothing. He had travelled on foot around a confined area, almost entirely within one culture, whereas Paul was travelling in and out of many cultures. Jesus had been a charismatic figure and a force of nature. He had been a blunt man from the north with no formal tertiary education. A preacher and a gifted teller of stories. These stories were breathtakingly beautiful, simple parables such as the Prodigal Son, the Good Samaritan, the Lost Sheep and the Good Shepherd. He had been a testy layman on a spiritual journey, an outsider, an advocate for the poor and the marginalized, moving in and out of people's lives, but apparently not laying down roots in any particular place.

Paul, on the other hand, was an educated Pharisee trained in the school of Gamaliel with the blessings and burden of a university degree. He was a citizen of Rome, an entrepreneur, an organiser and a theologian. Paul was called to interpret the message of Jesus, to adapt and translate it into a foreign language and implant it in a different cultural setting. He was a gifted, high-ranking follower who was charged to carry the message of Jesus outside Palestine, to the world, and to establish a functioning institution.

Paul had a personal investment in the various communities he had founded. For example, he regarded himself as the father of a family of daughters and he had arranged a marriage for each of them with a wealthy, suitable bridegroom – Jesus Christ. He was an emotional (some might say theatrical) man, with all the vulnerabilities which came with being a passionate human being. He was not afraid to express his feelings – sometimes fiery, but often warm and affectionate – 'Therefore, my brethren, whom I love and long for, my joy and crown ...' (Phil 4:1).

But Paul was also someone who found himself under attack from those he saw as his opponents. As he was travelling here and there, he was aware that some people were trying to undermine his work, to tamper with his message and replace him. He felt surrounded by critics and opponents, and that he needed to defend his reputation. Though he was prepared to argue his case strenuously, he was also rather authoritative in his style. Even while he was appealing to the common sense of those in the community, he did not seem inclined to engage anyone in dialogue in order to find common ground with his enemies. No compromise. No middle way. Paul's way or the highway was his pastoral policy: 'To anyone who might still want to argue: it is not the custom with us, nor in the churches of God' (1 Cor 11:16).

Paul appears to have been unusually thin-skinned. Always on the defensive. In his first letter to Corinth, for example, he complained bitterly that some people had been questioning his motives, claiming that he had been feathering his own nest, sponging on the community and leading an easy life. In his mind he had the right to his 'board and lodgings', to his food and drink. He saw himself as a worker, covered in grime, dripping with perspiration. According to him, no worker would plant a vineyard without eating some of the fruits, or tend a flock without drinking some of the milk. In the course of pleading his cause and defending himself from his critics, he reminded his people in Corinth that he was leading a lonely, celibate life, stating: 'Do we not have the right to be accompanied by a woman or a sister as the other apostles and the brethren of the Lord and Cephas?' (1 Cor 9:5).

In context, the words 'woman' and 'sister' are ambiguous. 'Sister' could be a blood relative or, as Paul often used the word, a female companion and co-worker who was also a believer. The Greek word *gunaika*, which is translated here as 'woman' could also have meant 'a wife'. In his Vulgate version, Jerome translated the word as *mulier*, which, again, usually meant 'woman' in general, or by extension it could also have referred to a wife.

The translator of the Jerusalem Bible cut to the chase and rendered the meaning of the text, 'And the right to take a Christian woman round with us ...'. Maybe she would have been a pious woman like those who had accompanied Jesus on his journeys. Perhaps a wife, since many of the apostles, Peter included, would have been married. Their wives would have joined them on their journeys, and looked after their needs, whatever those needs might have been. Later writers could hardly entertain the thought that holy men like the apostles would have acted as any normal man would in the circumstances and have regularly exchanged their bodily fluids with their partners. Paul had complained that he did not enjoy the natural comfort of a female companion and he wanted that sacrifice noted.

Paul's language was different, not just because he was writing in Greek and Jesus had been conversing in Aramaic, but the tone of the message was changing compared to the tone Jesus had used. No stories. No reports of breathtaking wonders amazing the bystanders. No repetition of the abuse and condemnation Jesus had levelled at the religious leaders and Jewish officials of whom Paul had once been a colleague. The primitive energy and translucent simplicity reflected in the Gospel stories of Jesus' ministry were transformed in Paul's writing into practical advice and guidance, into cerebral theology, into complicated, often shallow rabbinical arguments and a search for order and organisational stability.

Jesus' kingdom message, with its emphasis on the poor and vulnerable and its vision of a future reality on earth, disappeared like a stone dropped into a pond. Within a decade or two Paul's teachings about church order and structure rose to the surface. He stressed the notion of the faith community as the body of Christ, of communion among the faithful and the gifts of the Spirit. Paul's mission was to establish communities of believers, to ensure orthodoxy and order within his churches, to encourage his communities to live an ethical life free of scandal. He wanted his communities to be able to attract and welcome pagans. He pushed to consolidate the administration and leadership structure and to suppress damaging, deviant preaching.

Jesus had been keen to preach his grand kingdom vision, and he did this right to the end (Acts 1:3). Paul was about developing a program and interpreting the meaning of Jesus' life for his readers. The main focus of Paul's life was to encourage his followers to live virtuously and to preach about the Christ who was now a heavenly being, to preach about his death and resurrection and about his mystical body, the church. In his letters he practically ignored the kernel of Jesus' message – the kingdom – though not entirely. In promoting aspects of his theology of the church he included some elements of Jesus' primary message – for example, in his analogy of the body and its various parts reflecting the different roles and functions at work within the various communities.

Paul's image of his church in action (which he was sharing with his Corinthian readers) contained echoes and undertones of Jesus principal message about a kingdom which the Gospel writers would explore and expand some decades later. But while the Kingdom was the major theme of the message Jesus had preached, for Paul it was merely a minor variation which was almost inaudible amid the drums and trumpets in the heroic, theological and pastoral symphonies Paul was composing around the theme of the glorified Christ.

What is strange about Paul and the other early Christian writers inside and outside the New Testament (including the authors of the Gospels) is that none of them seem to have had any interest in letting their readers know what the real, historical Jesus was like. Men such as Ignatius of Antioch, Justin Martyr, the author of the *Shepherd of Hermas* and others said nothing about Jesus being short and fat, or tall and slender, bearded or clean-shaven with a head of short curly hair or dreadlocks, tense or relaxed, charming or aloof, calm or explosive. And unlike the four Gospel composers,

Paul seems to have had no interest in the details of Jesus' life such as his parables and sayings, his journeys and crowd minglings, his wonder-working or his now famous Sermon of the Mount. He had no interest in the people who had wandered around with Jesus. Martha, Mary and their brother Lazarus do not receive even a mention. There is no word on the widow of Naim, or the Canaanite woman by the well, or the women on the hill of Calvary, or even of Mary Magdalene or Jesus' mother. He did not quote even one of Jesus' sayings. Jesus' colourful stories must have been recorded and circulating in the churches at the time Paul was writing his letters. The essential message which Paul and the other early leaders were preaching in the local synagogues and marketplaces was confined to Jesus' suffering, death and resurrection, and to the meaning of those pivotal events for his followers.

Paul was more interested in discipline and order in the ranks and in transforming Jesus into the Risen Christ. He wanted to proclaim Jesus as the Messiah, the Saviour of humankind, a second Adam, another Moses, the true son of Abraham, the redeeming scapegoat, a man touched with divinity. It's as if the historical Jesus of Nazareth had disappeared while undergoing radical cosmetic surgery to reappear as the mysterious figure of Christ the Lord and Saviour.

Throughout his missionary years Paul was developing his own ideological interpretations of the person of Jesus and exploring the theological significance of his hero's truncated life. He was translating the historical Jesus into a celestial being, into a cosmic, redemptive figure. He was facilitating an ongoing dialogue between the message Jesus had preached and the Christian movement on the one hand, and the Greco-Roman world on the other, translating, for example, Jesus' ethical behaviour adages into statements reflecting contemporary Stoic values. He was responsible for devising basic structures for his nascent institutions – setting up leadership roles, giving directions, establishing rules, providing advice and giving practical answers to a series of pressing pastoral problems.

Paul told his Corinthian readers in what we now label his second letter that by believing in the risen Jesus and being baptised, they had effectively left this world and placed themselves on the other side of earthly history. They were now heavenly beings, new creatures in a new creation.

> From now on, therefore, we regard no-one from a human point of view (*kata sarka*). Even though we once regarded Christ from a human point of view (*kata sarka*), we regard him thus no longer. Therefore, if anyone is in Christ, he is a new creation. The old has passed away, behold, the new has come (2 Cor. 5:16–17, Revised Standard Version).

This is a very strange passage and difficult to interpret. Many attempts have been made to capture what Paul was trying to say. What did he mean when he wrote that now we don't know anyone 'according to the flesh'? Unlike Jesus who lived on earth among people, Paul seemed to regard himself as living somewhere else. According to him there were two worlds – the world of the flesh and the world of the spirit. There was the old creation commencing with Adam and Eve and involving sin and temptation, and the new creation established after Jesus' death and resurrection. Followers of Jesus, according to Paul, live in this other world by being 'in Christ' by baptism. This is a new way of being, living in a new dimension, in a new reality under a new dispensation.

It seems strange for a follower of Jesus to assert that he regarded no-one from a human point of view and that he no longer thought of Jesus as an historical and human figure. The old way of seeing reality, of viewing Jesus and ourselves, was obsolete. Christ belonged to a new reality. He existed now in a different dimension. Paul's followers were all in a new creation – no longer earthbound or what used to be regarded as human. By baptism a follower of Jesus was 'in Christ' and therefore no longer part of the earth, no longer a human being walking the earth as Jesus had done, but a heavenly being like Christ.

Paul had travelled a long way from the simple Kingdom message of Jesus. Jesus had been preaching about a kingdom here on earth, a heavenly kingdom begun in the here and now, a regime of love and forgiveness, of inclusion and compassion where real human beings live and share with one another. However, according to Paul, a true believer did not look at anyone from a human point of view. They did not assess others on the basis of their wealth or prestige. They did not see others as flesh-beings, as part of human history, as bodily creatures. While once upon a time some believers knew Jesus in the flesh, as an earth creature among us, that's not how Paul came to know him. After his conversion Paul had disappeared into the deserts of Arabia. He had been transported into the third heaven and experienced unimaginable, unspeakable visions. After Jesus death, resurrection and ascension into heaven, believers no longer could know him in the flesh. He was no longer an earthbound being. He had become a new, heavenly, spiritual creature.

Underneath Paul's new teaching about Jesus we can find the dualism that Plato and his followers had taught. Jesus had been a Jew in Palestine: Paul was a man of the world and a Roman citizen who spoke Greek. Jesus had come from a culture which promoted the idea of God's presence in its history of salvation; Paul's mind had been geared to the idea that reality was radically divided on the basis of a system of dualism. While Jesus' message was one of continuity, Paul had adopted a message of discontinuity. According to him there was a fundamental rupture between Jesus' previous earthly existence and his life after his death, paralleling a similar difference between a believer's flesh-bound existence and his life with Christ in baptism.

The primary meaning of the Greek word *sarx* was the substance or matter comprising the body with its senses and passions. It was the opposite of *pneuma* or spirit. It denoted the perishable, corruptible element of all human beings. By extension, the word *sarx* or flesh became a metaphor for the old dispensation as opposed to the spirit-filled dispensation. It was also employed as a shorthand way of talking about passions, sin, corruption and death, and therefore personified the power of Evil as the enemy of God's plan. While Jesus' kingdom message was based on the continuity between God's original plan and an earthbound regime of love and forgiveness blossoming into a future dream sequence of life with God, Paul's vision was based on a contrast between the old and the new, the flesh and the spirit, and on a fundamental dualism involving two realities – earth and heaven.

In the light of what we know of him from the Gospels authors, Jesus would have been surprised to have read what Paul was writing about him in his letters, about what he had achieved in his earthly life and about the life he was living beyond the grave.

The Women in Paul's Life

Saul the Pharisee appears out of nowhere in the Acts. Saul the persecutor of the followers of Jesus was blinded and converted to the Way on the road to Damascus.

Turning our full focus from Jesus to Paul and his journeys reveals that, with a few exceptions, it was downhill for women in the life of the early Christian communities.

Unlike with Jesus, we have no genealogy for Paul. There was no mention of his mother or father, or his sisters or his wife (if he ever had siblings or a partner). But writing towards the end of the second century, Clement of Alexandria seemed to think that Paul did have a 'consort' or a 'partner' just like the other apostles, though we don't know from this distance whether, after the lapse of so many years, Clement knew what he was talking about.

> Even Paul did not hesitate in one letter to address his consort. The only reason why he did not take her about with him was that it would have been an inconvenience for his ministry. Accordingly he says in a letter: 'Have we not a right to take about with us a wife that is a sister like the other apostles?' (*Stromata*, book III, Chapter 6, 53)

Paul told his readers in one of his letters that for a missionary, the best way to travel was in the state of celibacy, though this was only his personal opinion. The other early missionaries obviously didn't agree. In his commentary on this passage from 1 Cor 9:5, Clement made an anachronistic attempt to protect the reputation of the early missionaries and to put an asexual spin on Paul's words. His interpretation is a sad commentary of those times.

They take their wives with them, not as women with whom they had marriage relations, but as sisters, that they might be their fellow ministers (*syndiakonous*) in dealing with housewives. It was through them that the Lord's teaching penetrated also to the women's quarters without any scandal being aroused (*Stomata*, III.6:53, 3f).

No sex on the job. According to Clement, if you can believe it, they were all celibates. By the time Clement came to be teaching in Alexandria, there was no chance Paul and Barnabas could have mingled with Lydia's crowd or stayed in her house. Jesus would not have been speaking with the Samaritan woman, or travelling with his female friends, or sharing a meal with Martha and her sister Mary. Jesus' followers were travelling off in another direction and the women who accompanied them as sisters were meant to be dealing with the housewives. Their ministry was restricted to the women's quarters – to places where men couldn't venture without causing scandal.

When they came to Philippi on their second missionary journey away from Jerusalem, Paul and his male companions, Timothy and maybe the author of the Acts, made contact with a group of women including a rich and famous woman who used to sell luxury purple textiles in the city where she lived. She had become part of the business scene in that area of Macedonia, which had the status of a Roman colony. Lydia had attached herself to the Jewish synagogue in her hometown, in Thyatira, where there was a school in prophetesses and where she had been a 'worshipper of God', though she had never actually converted to Judaism.

As he tells this story, while the author of Acts had been travelling around with Paul in Asia, they had been pestered by a gifted slave girl soothsayer who had been following them 'for many days' and publicly advertising that they were servants of the most high God. Paul was so annoyed that he exorcised the spirit of divination from her. During this same visit, they had met Lydia and some of her female friends and had engaged them in conversation by the river. Just as Jesus had done with the Samaritan woman by the well: 'We sat down and began to talk with the women who had gathered' (Acts 16:13).

In Macedonian society during the Hellenistic age, women seem to have enjoyed an unusual degree of freedom and a comparatively high level of status. Lydia was one of these women – wealthy, liberated and assertive. She welcomed the mysterious message Paul was spreading, sat with other women listening to him and eventually prevailed on him and his companions to stay with her in her house. Like the mother of John Mark back in Palestine and other women, Lydia transformed her home into a meeting place for Christians of the area. For his followers, as Jesus had foretold, hospitality was high on the agenda. Eventually Paul baptised Lydia 'and her household'.

Despite Paul's Jewish background and especially his strict Pharisaic upbringing, he had joined a group of women and had begun to teach them about Jesus. As a rule, and especially in Judaism, women were not considered eligible to be students of philosophy, legal studies or religious teaching.

We don't know whether Lydia was married or a spinster, divorced or widowed, or whether she had a family. In any event, her behaviour in associating with strangers, and a group of men, at least from the point of view of a fervent Jew, was socially and religiously inappropriate. If mixing with men had been okay for Lydia (since she was not strictly speaking a Jewess), for Paul it should have been taboo.

Furthermore, Lydia had offered these foreigners lodgings in her home, and apparently without seeing the need for consulting a male member of the family – her husband, for example, or her father. Furthermore, since Paul and Barnabas had been in prison in Phillipi and had been required to leave town, she was tempting fate.

Lydia had begun as an out-of-town businesswoman on the edge of a Jewish prayer group and ended up becoming the first convert to Christianity in Europe and a prominent figure in the local Christian community. However, despite this, she doesn't rank even a brief mention in any of Paul's letters. She just disappeared.

Apparently, the freedom with which Jesus of the Gospels had preached his message was having some effect. Women like Lydia could associate with strangers, with men, could include them in their prayer group and offer them hospitality. At least for a time, Jesus' kingdom message was at work in Phillipi – and in Corinth.

As the author of Acts told the story, a Jewish man by the name of Aquila and his wife Priscilla (or Prisca) had recently arrived in Corinth from Rome because the emperor had ordered the authorities to banish all Jews from the capital city.

Aquila and Paul were both tentmakers and for a short time before leaving Corinth, they had worked together at their trade. The married couple then travelled with Paul before dropping out of his party in Ephesus and coming in contact with Apollos who had arrived there from Alexandria. People were on the move in those far distant days, travelling round the perimeter and across the waters of the Mediterranean, using the available public transport or trudging along the Roman roads and rocky pathways which crisscrossed the empire.

As Luke reported, this Apollos was already familiar with the scriptures and had been instructed in the way of the Lord. He had been teaching the people of Ephesus about Jesus and was speaking to Jews in the synagogue. We are told, however, (and this is a detail which cries out for some explanation) that he only knew of one baptism, the baptism of John, so on meeting Priscilla and her husband, he was destined to embark on a steep learning curve: 'But when Priscilla and Aquila heard him, they took him and expounded to him the way of God more accurately' (Acts 18:26).

Although Apollos was already well educated, it was part of Priscilla's job to instruct him 'more accurately'. The author depicts her as an important co-worker travelling with Paul, able to be left at certain spots to continue his missionary work and available to instruct male members of the community.

This married couple is mentioned on six occasions throughout the New Testament, and although it was unusual in Jewish and Christian circles for wives to be mentioned first, on four of the six occasions Priscilla's name precedes her husband's. This might give some clue to her status within the community.

In wrapping up his first letter to the community in Corinth and writing from his residence in Ephesus sometime in the mid-50s, Paul sent 'warmest wishes' from 'Aquila and Prisca' (whom they knew) and from those who used to meet in their house: 'The churches of Asia send greetings. Aquila and Prisca, together with the church in their house, send you hearty greetings in the Lord' (1 Cor 16:19).

Apparently this missionary couple returned to Rome after Claudius' expulsion order had been repealed and were offering open-house hospitality to the members of the community.

At the conclusion of his epistle to the believers in Rome, Paul sent greetings to them (using Prisca's proper name rather than its diminutive form), adding that all the churches among the pagans owed them a debt of gratitude.

> Greet Prisca and Aquila, my fellow workers in Christ Jesus, who risked their necks for my life, to whom not only I but also all the churches of the Gentiles give thanks. Greet also the church in their house (Rom 16:3–5).

They were obviously an important couple – a good team – teaching, preaching and providing hospitality to fellow believers. Paul obviously regarded both of them as close friends who had worked together with him over a number of years.

The storyteller of Acts reported that towards the beginning of their third missionary journey, Paul and his travelling party had landed at Philip's place in Caesarea. This was Philip 'the evangelist' (not to be confused with the apostle Philip) who had been commissioned, second in line, as one of the seven servants or ministers to care for the Greek speaking widows who had joined the church. A story is recorded in Acts about this Philip converting an Ethiopian eunuch on a journey from Jerusalem down to Gaza (Acts 8:25–39). He and his family eventually settled in a town on the coast north of Gaza, in the province of Samaria.

Paul's party stayed with Philip and his family of four unmarried daughters who, as the author reported, 'prophesied'.

Hospitality was one of the more pleasant features of the life of the early church. There is no mention in the records, however, of Philip's wife and mother of his girls, or of any brothers. Nor does the author of Acts think to tell us the names of any of these (presumably) young women, though tradition later identified one of them as St Hermione of Ephesus, who would die a martyr under Trajan in 117 AD.

This passing reference to Philip's four daughters records the appearance of identifiable Christian prophetesses in the apostolic church. Among the Jews at the time of Jesus (and before), the ministry of God-given prophecy had not been restricted to men. At the beginning of Luke's Gospel, for example, the author had described the elderly Jewish widow Anna as a prophetess. Female prophets were also well-known to those familiar with the literature of the Old Testament – Miriam, Deborah, Huldah, Noadiah and Isaiah's wife come to mind. Although it was possible for any member of the community to act occasionally as a prophet on a one-off basis, more than likely these young women were exercising a special function – performing an established, recognised service for the community, though we don't know exactly what that entailed.

The author of Acts reserved the title of prophet or the gift of prophesying for members of a specialised group – to leaders like Silas and Judas (also called Barsabbas) who were specially chosen and commissioned as messengers, 'leading men among the brethren' (Acts 15:22), and they as 'prophets, were able to inspire and strengthen the members of the church' (Acts 15:32). While Paul and his crowd were with Philip in Caesarea, a prophet named Agabus arrived from Judea. As prophets sometimes did, he foretold what Paul was later to face when he returned to Jerusalem (Acts 21:10–11).

Philip's four daughters (all unmarried and probably virgins), were part of the local elite. They had the reputation for being endowed with a gift from the Spirit and were able to fulfil an important function among the believers. We will return to these important topics – the place of virgins and prophetesses in the life of the early church. As we will see, prophets and prophetesses were to become for a time a central feature in the church's life and ministry, one which would challenge the institutional structure of the organisation. As the church historian Eusebius reported in the fourth century, these four daughters and the other prophets 'occupied the first place among the successors of the apostles'.

> Among those that were celebrated at that time was Quadratus, who, report says, was renowned along with the daughters of Philip for his prophetical gifts. And there were many others besides these who were known in those days, and who occupied the first place among the successors of the apostles. And they also, being illustrious disciples of such great men, built up the foundations of the churches which had been laid by the apostles in every place, and preached the Gospel more and more widely and scattered the saving seeds of the kingdom of heaven far and near throughout the whole world (Eusebius, *Eccl. Hist.* III. 37.1).

Apart from Lydia, Priscilla and the four daughters of Philip, at least fifteen of his female companions receive a mention in Paul's various authentic letters, and several more in the second Epistle to Timothy. (The two epistles to Timothy have always been ascribed to him, though scholars now consider it was written by some anonymous author, almost certainly after Paul's death.) These fifteen or so women had been living and working with Paul and others with authority inside his little communities.

In the final chapter of his Epistle to the Romans Paul mentions ten women, perhaps eleven or twelve if Olympa and/or Hermas are female followers rather than being the names of male companions. It is sometimes difficult to determine whether the person Paul was naming was male or female.

A woman called Mary had been working hard among the believers in Rome and was part of a team of women who had been serving side by side with him and his male co-workers. Paul also mentioned a Junia whom he described as a fellow Jew, a prisoner with him, more senior in the service than he was himself and a woman who was 'outstanding among the apostles' – using the title 'apostle' in a wider sense, as someone sent to preach the gospel as an itinerant missionary. He sent his greeting to Rufus 'who is eminent in the Lord, and to his mother and mine', and further on, to Nereus and his sister; and to Tryphaena and Tryphosa as 'workers in the Lord'. In writing to the believers in Rome, he said that Persis was someone he regarded as his 'beloved'. And this was the type of affectionate language Paul was not reluctant to use.

The significance of these greetings can be gauged from the simple, casual, off-handed manner in which Paul expressed them. No fanfare. No embellishment or policy statement. The visible presence of women within the local church, women with names, status and authority of their own, women as middle-management leaders, seems to have been normal and taken for granted.

Euodia and Syntyche also accompanied Paul as his co-workers in Macedonia, in a city called Philippi. They were labouring side by side with him (and others) in the work of the Gospel.

> I entreat Euodia and I entreat Syntyche to agree in the Lord. And I ask you also, true yokefellow, help these women, for they have laboured side by side with me in the gospel together with Clement and the rest of my fellow workers, whose names are in the book of life (Phil 4:2–3).

The author's reference to a 'yokefellow' (*syzygus*) may be Paul's affectionate nickname for some leading figure in the local community. He was sure the names of these two women were already 'in the book of life'.

The title of 'co-worker' was one he had used at the conclusion of his first letter to the Corinthians when he exhorted his readers to be obedient to 'every fellow-worker and labourer', and to extend to them some recognition and respect. The same title used to describe these two women would suggest that those who belonged to such a special group enjoyed some role of leadership and a level of prestige. Although a modern reader is desperate for more details, there is no flesh on these historical bones.

In his letter to Rome, Paul provided a character reference for someone called Phoebe:

> I commend to you our sister Phoebe, a *deaconess* [or a minister or servant] of the church at Cenchreae, that you may receive her in the Lord as befits the saints, and help her in whatever she may require from you, for she has been a helper [a *patroness*] of many, and of myself as well (Rom 16:1–2).

The city where Phoebe was ministering used to be one of the two harbours of ancient Corinth. She was introduced to the community in Rome as someone who had been a *deaconess* to the believers in Cenchreae as well as someone who had been a patroness to Paul and to others.

The origin of the office of male deacon or servant was described early in Acts when the apostles commissioned Stephen, Philip and five other Gentile men to minister to those widows who were not of Jewish stock and who were being neglected (Acts 6).

The origin of the female version of this ministry, however, is lost in the shadows of history. When their ministry was officially established (if ever), and where, remains a secret. What is certain, however, is that women (as well as men) were, from the earliest times, carrying out the functions which later became associated with an order of deacons. Women such as Tabitha were serving the community by providing material aid and ministering to the needy (Acts 9:39). That was what Phoebe had been doing in Cenchreae.

When Pliny the Younger was governor of Bithynia early in the second century, he wrote to Emperor Trajan seeking his advice as to how to deal with the Christians who were appearing before him. As he reported to his boss, these people had become numerous in his part of the world, and rather troublesome. Pliny told the emperor some basic details which had come to his notice about the Christian liturgical meetings, commenting that these meetings had been stopped after he had published an edict forbidding political associations.

> I thought it necessary to extract the real truth, with the assistance of torture, from two female slaves, called deaconesses (or *ministrae*), but I could only uncover what was depraved and excessive superstition.

Pliny had adjourned the proceedings and sought advice because the number of those concerned was so impressive: 'Persons of all ranks and ages, *of both sexes*, are and will be involved in the prosecution.'

The superstition called Christianity had been visible in the cities and had spread through the countryside. By the end of the first century, by the time the authors were composing the Gospel of John and other authors were putting their finishing touches on some of the remaining works (the epistles to Timothy and Titus, the letters of Peter and the epistle to the Hebrews, for example), the Christian communities could pride themselves with having attracted large contingents of female members. Some of these women held positions within the institution and exercised identifiable ministries, and some were acting as slaves or servants. 'Deaconesses' or female ministers were known to pagan officials such as Pliny the Younger outside the closed ranks of believers. Phoebe was one of them.

The other Greek word Paul used to describe Phoebe, *prostatis*, can be translated as 'patroness', or president, governor or superintendent. At that early stage the female deacons, or more probably simple community servants, could have been itinerant missionaries, or else women who held some type of leadership role in the local communities. They were also recognised as teachers and preachers. Phoebe would have exercised some or all of these functions, as well as being a person of importance who enjoyed some degree of influence, as the title *prostatis* indicates. In the First Letter to Timothy, for example, the same title pointed to the functions performed by a bishop, a deacon or one of the presbyters. They too were 'patrons'.

Phoebe had been someone special in and around her hometown, one of Paul's sisters in the Lord, a servant or minister to the community and an influential patroness who had lent her support to him and many others. She was a woman of importance and Paul wanted her to be treated properly in the capital city.

In his first letter to his brothers and sisters in Corinth, Paul refers to a female member of the local community. 'Those of Chloe' had informed him that their community was fractured on the basis of leadership. Some vowed their allegiance to Paul, others to Apollo, some to Cephas (or to Peter) and of course, others to Christ (Cor 1:11–12).

Though it appears she was an important member of the crowd in Corinth, this is the only reference to Chloe in the New Testament. She was clearly a woman who exercised a level of authority as a leader, but we don't know whether she was a friend or foe. Was she a supporter of Paul or a member of a rival faction? A wealthy pagan perhaps, whose household slaves were Jesus followers and reporting to Paul? Or a Christian troublemaker? Or someone concerned for the welfare of the community and enlisting Paul's help to restore peace?

While some English translations speak of 'Chloe's household' or 'some of Chloe's household', the phrase Paul used does not refer explicitly to her household. It simply refers to 'those of Chloe', to Chloe's mob, her crowd, her people – 'those who belonged to Chloe' (1 Cor 1:11). The unwarranted addition of the word 'household' could accurately capture who she was, the woman of the house in charge of the family and domestics, but it might equally lead the reader off on a tangent.

Chloe was calling on Paul to exercise his authority and to remedy the situation in Corinth. In dealing with the problems, Paul did not simply dismiss the reports of Chloe's people as rumours, as baseless complaints of whingeing malcontents, or as evidence of a leader who was out to cause trouble. The fact that he treated the reports seriously and tried to address them suggests that Chloe had been on his side – one of his supporters, one of his patrons.

The phrase 'Chloe's mob' also suggests that Chloe was one of the leaders among the Christians in Corinth, or maybe in Ephesus. She was someone of importance.

In the very early days, in addition to those women who worked closely with Paul as his co-workers and who exercised a special ministry as teachers or as dreamers of dreams, as prophetesses, there were other women who were at the forefront of the life of the local churches. Their houses became the focus of Christian activity. This was one of the identifying features of the apostolic church and of Paul's mission – the house-church. We have already seen how the house of Mary, the mother of John Mark, was available for meetings in Jerusalem, as was the home of Lydia in Philippi (Acts16:40), and of Prisca and her husband in Ephesus, and later in Rome (1 Cor 16:19 and Rom 16:3–5). Probably the home of Chloe in Corinth also served as a meeting place for prayer and celebration. But many of these women disappeared without trace.

The travelling preacher would reside with these prominent Christian women and the local community would meet in their homes to pray together. The whole household, including servants and tradesmen, would join the assembly, welcome the preacher, live with him and listen to his message. Though the writer does not say so, the kingdom of heaven was already in the process of being realised, and women were involved.

'The elected lady' of the second letter of John was probably another important figure who conducted prayer meetings and instruction sessions in her own home. In his letter the author was warning her to be on her guard against 'the many deceivers who have gone out into the world': 'If anyone comes to you all and does not bring this doctrine (the doctrine of Christ), do not receive him into the house or give him any greeting.'

It is not clear how these churches were organised or who led the gathering in prayer, but it would be reasonable to assume that there was a large degree of flexibility from one house-assembly to another, from one centre to another. Each community would have been free to lay down their own rules, though there would have been at least loose connections between the various churches. Probably in some communities the lady of the house, being in charge of the household and a patron of the believers meeting there, would have exercised a leadership role and more than likely organised the prayer meetings and even presided at them.

The prominence of women in the early stages of the movement can be seen from many passages spread through the Acts and Paul's letters. Like Jesus, there were many women in Paul's life and in the lives of the other apostles, and like Jesus, they treated them with dignity, valued their contribution and none of them, Paul included, uttered a hostile, abusive word to them, or about them. There were certainly some women among the prominent missionaries, and their work among the believers was not initially limited to an exclusive ministry to women, or to specific gender roles. These limitations appeared later.

As far as we can read underneath the texts of the Acts and his letters, Paul's contact with women was of a different character to the close relationship Jesus enjoyed with women. While the Gospels record in detail a number of encounters between Jesus and women in his life, what he said, what she said (an adulterous women, Martha and Mary, Mary Magdalene, the Samaritan woman drawing water from a well, the Syro-Phoenician woman), there is nothing similar on the record involving Paul or any of the other apostles. Jesus had enjoyed a degree of intimacy with his female friends and followers. The Gospel authors depicted him as comfortable and relaxed in their company. Paul, however, seemed conscious of his decision to remain celibate while being remarkably short on details regarding his female co-workers. The readers of his collected letters are left to fill in the gaps and imagine who these women might have been. They appear and almost immediately disappear without trace, just as most of Jesus' companions had done, including his apostles. But Jesus had not promulgated any rules to regulate female dress or reflected on their status as Paul would do. He hadn't drawn on his Jewish traditions to establish women's inferiority in the scheme of things, as Paul did.

However, Paul enjoyed a productive, professional relationship with a good number of women. It was his theology, his ideas, his background as a visionary and theologian in the Pharisaic mould which finally determined how women would be seen and treated within the expanding Christian communities.

Furthermore, the rich theme of kingdom which Jesus had preached was beginning to disappear, and with it the concentration on the poor and dispossessed, the lame and the blind, the sinner and the outsider – and women. We don't see the relationship which Jesus had enjoyed with his female followers and with other women, or the part they played in his life mirrored in the life and mission of the early communities. None of the apostles seem to have followed Jesus' lead. We don't read of Peter or Paul or of any of the others paying special, personal attention to women in their lives. We never hear of Peter's wife or his mother-in-law, of Paul's mother, or his sisters, or his wife, or any details of his relationship with his female missionary companions. Important Gospel figures like Mary Magdalene had disappeared – and the mother of James and John, and women like Joanna and Salome. We have no record of the details of conversations Paul engaged in with women – friends, co-workers or strangers. The female atmospherics within the Acts and Paul's letters are of a different order to those pulsating throughout the Gospels.

Faced with the profile of women in the early apostolic churches, their involvement in Paul's missionary work and their prominence in the house churches spread around the Mediterranean communities, it is a shock to come across a number of passages in his authentic letters and elsewhere which provide both practical and theological grounds for the subordination of women. The idea of the headship of man over women, the theological use of the Adam-and-Eve myth, and the veiling regulations in Corinth, were all Paul's ideas.

The situation for women deteriorated further in the Pastoral Epistles and the writings of later community leaders. Women were forbidden to teach, or to exercise any authority over men. Jesus' lofty message about the kingdom was being put to rest.

Paul's attitude to women might be thought to have been somewhat nuanced, and perhaps confusing, even contradictory insofar as his pastoral involvement of women was not supported by his ideas. Before the end of the first century, however, the position of women within the movement was clear. While the emerging Christian-Gnostic sects might have been happy to engage the services of women in ministry and in the liturgy, the more orthodox Fathers of the church would preach and practise a regime of patriarchy with distinct features of misogyny.

Paul on the Subject of Women

Jesus didn't speak about women, except in his parables. He did, however, speak about people – about human beings of all sizes. And he did speak to women and engaged with them on a person-to-person level. He lived and worked with them. They travelled about with him. He suffered and died in their presence. They had been the first witnesses of his new presence among his followers. His life as told in the Gospels speaks of his attitudes towards women and the values by which he lived.

Paul, on the other hand, did occasionally address the subject of women in his letters. And from the available evidence his missionary relationship with female co-workers and what he wrote on the subject of women was somewhat at odds. While he conducted his life in their company, and while he welcomed their contribution to the growth of the movement and paid tribute to them, he was anxious to ensure that they complied with at least some of the culturally determined customs of the day. Paul regarded himself as a bachelor. A man of the world who had been brought up and educated at the interface of the Jewish and Greco-Roman worlds.

When Paul raised the subject of women, as he did in a number of places and from a variety of angles, his observations were pastoral rather than theoretical, argumentative rather than reflective. He trotted out his ideas to defend a practical, pastoral position. His remarks seem to have arisen spontaneously and witness to his ingrained belief-system, to unreflected attitudes and prejudices hidden underneath his thought-patterns and which were tempering his pastoral theology and practices.

Paul and the other apostles and community leaders seem to have quickly and unconsciously fallen back into the cultural groove of the day. They appear to have embodied, without any resistance or reflection, the attitudes and prejudices generally accepted in the society where they were ministering and where they had grown up.

Women as Witnesses to the Resurrection

Three of the four canonical Gospels provide evidence of the central role women played in the resurrection events. According to the authors of the Matthew and John Gospels, women were present as the first witnesses to the new reality of a Risen Lord.

> So they (Mary Magdalene and the other Mary) departed quickly from the tomb with fear and great joy, and ran to tell his disciples. And behold Jesus met them and said, 'Hail!' And they came up and took hold of his feet and worshipped him. Then Jesus said to them, 'Do not be afraid; go and tell my brethren to go to Galilee, and there they will see me. (Matt 28:8–10).

With the Gospel of John this same women-first tradition burst into bloom when the author gave Mary Magdalene the principal role in his post-resurrection narrative. The details of the involvement of women as recorded by the author of the Luke Gospel are somewhat different. According to him, the women did not encounter Jesus risen. They received a message from 'two men in dazzling apparel' who told them that Jesus was not to be found among the dead, but that he had risen. They were invited to deliver a message to the eleven apostles and 'to all the rest'. As the author of Luke reported, the women told their story to the apostles, but the men thought they were speaking nonsense. This story of the women's involvement was repeated (with a few variations) by two disciples to the stranger on the road to Emmaus.

> Moreover, some women of our company amazed us. They were at the tomb early in the morning and did not find his body; and they came back saying that they had even seen a vision of angels who said that he was alive. Some of those who were with us went to the tomb, and found it just as the women had said; but him they did not see' (Luke 24:22–24).

The authors of three of the canonical Gospels are witnesses to the fact that women were seen by the early church as true exemplars of the faith, as messengers of the Good News and credible witnesses to extraordinary events.

Even before the Gospels appeared on the scene, however, Paul had dealt with the resurrection event and its significance. He had identified a series of witnesses to Jesus' post-resurrection appearances as proof of the extraordinary claim of the apostles that Jesus had in fact conquered the terrors of death. But in the series of mysterious encounters he listed he made no reference to women, though they may have been included, anonymously, among the five hundred he mentioned.

> For I delivered to you as of first importance what I also received, that Christ ... appeared to Cephas, then to the twelve. Then he appeared to more than five hundred brethren at one time, most of whom are still alive, though some have fallen asleep. Then he appeared to James, then to all the apostles. Last of all, as to one untimely born, he appeared also to me (1 Cor. 15:3-8).

Paul is silent about the presence of women in Jesus' life and on Calvary, and about their special role in recognising his new presence among his followers after the resurrection.

Yet within a decade or two, three of the four Gospels were prioritising women in this wildly significant event. In the face of what was recorded later by the Gospel authors, Paul's omission screams out for some explanation. Where are the women in Paul's summary of the resurrection witnesses? Where is Mary Magdalene, and the others? Did he not know that stories were abroad that women were there on the scene to witness the mystery of their Lord's presence and to receive and transmit a message from two mysterious men on guard at the empty tomb?

As a Pharisee trained in the school of Gamaliel (and like the other apostles in the story), did he also refuse to place any persuasive value on the evidence which a woman could give? Or did he presume his readers in Corinth would not value their evidence, or that they would be put off by their presence?

Paul claimed he was delivering to his readers what he had received. Had the apostles failed to tell him about Mary Magdalene, Joanna, Mary the mother of James and the others, and if so, why?

Or had the whole institution become male dominated? Were men feeling threatened and sensing the need to assert their top-dog status within the institution?

Or did Paul decide not to give the female members of the community any further reason to inflate their status and demand a greater share of the action? Were women on the move in the Jesus movement and ready to assert their importance? Perhaps they were already rowdy and rebellious enough. From this distance Paul's silence on the subject is deafening.

Immediately after his conversion, Paul had spent a few days with the disciples, including Ananias, in Damascus. Later he had travelled to Jerusalem for instruction in the faith and stayed with Peter for fifteen days. He had met with James the son of Alphaeus, perhaps also with Barnabas. It is beyond belief that his apostolic contacts had not filled him in on some of the critical details of what he came to believe was the principal event in Jesus' life. He had been told of Jesus' appearance to Peter, whom he mentioned first, to the twelve (though there were only eleven by that stage), to James, to 'all the apostles' (presumably a larger group than 'the twelve') and surprisingly, to five hundred or more of his followers – and yet he omitted any reference to Jesus' women, to Mary Magdalene and the others.

The leaders in Jerusalem may have been reluctant to accept that women had played such an important role in Jesus' life and mission. They may have wanted the community's attention to be focused on male authority to avoid their power being dissipated or disrespected. Who had the authority and the basis for its exercise had become a point of tension in the primitive communities. Was Peter in charge or one of others? Perhaps James, the brother of Jesus? Did the tension lie between Peter and Paul? There was some bitter rivalry between Paul and other preachers who were interfering in his pastoral bailiwick. Was one man in charge or a committee of apostles and elders? Did the power rest with those members with special gifts (prophets and prophetesses, for example) or with the apostles and their successors? Perhaps there was an audible level of tension between the male leaders and the women. Inject powerful women like Mary Magdalene into the mix and the result would have been chaos.

Maybe we can also look to Paul's audience to partly explain his silence. He was writing to his church in Corinth where female participation in the life and worship of the community had perhaps become a problem. Women misbehaving, causing trouble. He could hardly tell them how important they had been in spreading the news of the resurrection and then tell them that they had to be silent in the liturgical gatherings, that they were second-class members with a status inferior to their menfolk.

Maybe the women in the early church had taken to Jesus in a big way and had frightened the male members. The spontaneous outbursts of raw enthusiasm and excessive devotion had to be tamed by rules and prohibitions. Women had to be put back into their customary places. In the face of disputes and power struggles, the leaders had worked hard to keep the peace, to remain in control, to keep women 'pregnant and in the kitchen'.

New converts from far and near were joining the ranks. We can safely assume that there was a dramatic increase in the numbers of those who were reluctant to accept women into positions of power, people who had grown up in a patriarchal culture, members who had crossed over from Judaism and those who came from the Greco-Roman world. These 'players' were all educated to be suspicious of women leading prayer groups, prophesying, joining in the discussions and challenging their male counterparts. After all, these new converts had not met Jesus, or heard him preach. Involving women in the life of the community and establishing their roles had become a difficult message to sell. Perhaps, to add to the problem, Paul may not have been a supporter of Jesus' radical feminist policy and was reluctant to promote it. The converts from Asia Minor had retained their cultural prejudices about the presence of women in public places. They believed their place was in the home and female misbehaviour in the mystery cults throughout the region only reinforced the stereotypes.

Finally, in his theological mind Paul linked the fact of witnessing Jesus' resurrection appearances with membership of the college of apostles, and with being able to exercise authority within the community. In accordance with the Jewish law that was well-known to any Pharisee, men were the appropriate and credible witnesses, not women. Women were not part of the specially selected band of apostles. Men, and only men, had constituted the seventy members of the Jewish Sanhedrin. In the society at large where Paul was preaching and establishing his communities, men were in charge. The future of the churches could not be assured if women were seen to be dominant and if the role of women in the resurrection of Jesus was made public. The women's involvement was an uncomfortable historical fact. Any reference to them could only cause further trouble – maybe undermine the emerging power-structures within the community and alienate those who otherwise were showing interest in applying for membership.

Whatever the explanation, the omission of Jesus' female friends from the resurrection narrative would not enhance Paul's reputation as a promoter of women within his organisation.

A Man of Traditional, Conservative Values

In 315 BC, Cassander of Macedon established the colony of Thessaloniki and called the city after his wife, the half-sister of Alexander the Great and the daughter of Phillip II.

In about 50 AD citizen Paul and his travelling companions established a Christian presence in this bustling metropolis on the border of the Aegean Sea. In the winter of that year, after he had left them for Corinth and Athens, Paul sat down to write a letter to his 'brothers' there.

During his stay in the city, Paul had confronted a number of problems. He had been told by the community leaders, for example, that some of the male members were continuing to live the lives they had enjoyed before, as pagans. Fornication had been a popular recreational past-time and the social norms of the time tended to turn a blind eye to such activity. In towns like Thessaloniki or Corinth at the time when Paul was walking the land and preaching, premarital sex, adulterous activities and visitations to brothels were considered minor offences for warm-blooded males.

While the elder Cato had expressly justified fornication (Horace, Sat. i. 2), Cicero was only prepared to argue the case for leaving men, especially young men, free to 'sow their oats' as being negligible. In his defence of Marcus Caelius Rufus, Marcus Tullius Cicero proclaimed in a speech delivered on 4 April 56 BC that:

> Anyone who thought young men ought to be forbidden to visit prostitutes would certainly be the virtuous of the virtuous, that I cannot deny. But he would be out of step not only with this

easy-going age but also our ancestors, who customarily made youth that concession. Was there ever a time when this was not habitual practice, when it was censured and not permitted, in short when what is allowable was not allowed? ... Imagine a woman with no husband who turns her house into a house of assignation, openly behaves like a harlot, entertains at her table men who are perfect strangers, and does all this in town, in her suburban places, and in the crowded vacation land around Baiae; in fine, imagine that her walk, her way of dressing, the company she keeps, her burning glances, her free speech, to say nothing of her embraces and kisses or her capers at beach-parties and banquets and yachting-parties, are all so suggestive that she seems not merely a whore but a particularly shameless and forward specimen of the profession. Well, if a young man had some desultory relations with her, would you call him an adulterer, Lucius Herennius, or simply a lover? Would you say he was laying siege to her innocence, or simply gratifying her lust? (*Pro Caelio*, ch. 48-49).

The sexual morality among the young men of the colony was lax and Paul considered this to be a barrier to the holiness and honour to which God had invited them.

What God wants is for you all to be holy – that each of you keep away from fornication; that each of you (*ekaston humou*) know how (*eidenai*) to acquire (*ktasthai*) a wife (*skeuos*) in a way that is holy and honourable, not giving way to the passion of lust like the pagans who do not know God; that no man transgress and wrong his brother in this matter, because the Lord always punishes sins of this sort, as we solemnly forewarned you (1 Thess 4:4–8).

These few verses in Paul's letter, in its original Greek, have proved difficult for scholars and exegetes to unravel and render intelligible in English, or for that matter, for the great scriptural scholar to translate into his Vulgar Latin. So, in an attempt to capture the true meaning of Paul's words we need to make some basic observations on a few of the critical Greek words he used.

The Greek word *eidenai*, in its perfect, active infinitive form, is best translated into English as 'to know how to do something', 'to have the ability to do something'. So the sentence would read, 'each of you (men) must learn or know how to get a *skeuos* of your own', or literally, 'every one of you men should know how to acquire his own vessel (his *skeuos*)'.

The words *ekaston humou*, being in the masculine form, mean 'everyone of you men', and while some commentators consider that women were included by implication in the masculine gender pronoun, this is not at all clear. Paul was in the habit of addressing himself to his 'brothers' in Thessaloniki and elsewhere. He wrote to the male members of his local communities – after all, they were the ones in charge and the unreflective recipients of Paul's message.

In the passage, the Greek word *ktasthai* appears in the present middle infinitive form of the verb *ktaomai*. It should not be translated as 'to possess' or 'to own', but rather 'to gain possession of', 'to acquire', 'to procure' or 'to purchase'. This word was used in the same way in relation to marriage in the Greek or Septuagint version of the Jewish Bible (Ruth 4:10; Sir 36:24, Xenophon, *Symp*. ii. 10).

But it's the word *skeuos* which has caused the most controversy among the experts and exegetes. In a literal sense, it means 'container' — 'a receptacle for containing something' — or 'utensil' or 'instrument'. It was used to refer to kitchen utensils, to the impedimenta or accoutrements of war, or to the tackle associated with ships such as sails and ropes. Some English translations render the Greek word in its literal meaning as 'vessel'. But it can also carry several metaphorical or figurative meanings. A few scholars have suggested that it might best be seen as a euphemism for the *membrum virile* or the male genitalia, as King David was reported as using it in 1 Samuel 21:4–5.

In the proper context the Greek word could mean 'body' in the sense of the container of the soul. The human body, for example, could be described as a vessel in which the soul would reside for a time. However, when the word was used as a metaphor in this sense, the figurative meaning always seems to have been made explicit in the context. In other words, it was not used to signify 'the body' unless it is presented in an explanatory context – a vessel fashioned by a potter from clay or the earth.

To avoid the difficulty this Greek word presents, many modern English translations of this New Testament passage have been content to translate the word into its pure literal meaning, 'vessel'. Other translators, however, have attempted to capture Paul's real meaning. The Catholic edition of the *Revised Standard Version*, the *English Standard Version*, the *New International Version*, the *Jerusalem Bible*, and the *New Revised Standard Version* (1989), for example, have all followed the lead of John Chrysostom, Theodoret, John Damascene, Tertullian, Pelagius, Calvin and others by rendering the meaning of the Greek word *skeuos* as 'body'. The original *Revised Standard Version*, *The Good News Translation* and the *Contemporary English Version* follow people like Augustine, Theodore of Mopsuestia, Thomas Aquinas, Zwingli and others by translating the word as a metaphor for wife or a man's sexual partner. It points to a man's vessel for begetting children or his container into which he would insert his 'member'.

It was common in the Jewish culture for a man's wife to be referred to as 'a vessel'. The anonymous author of the first epistle of Peter used the same image and the same figure of speech to refer to a wife, describing her (significantly) as the 'weaker vessel':

> You wives, be submissive to your husbands ... Likewise you husbands must always treat your wives with consideration in your life together, respecting a woman as one who, though she

may be the weaker vessel, is equally an heir to the life of grace (1 Peter 3:1–7).

This figurative use of the Greek *skeuos* to mean a man's wife is supported in several passages in the Babylonian Talmud.

The rabbinical commentary on the Mishnah records an incident involving a feast for King Ahasuerus. The men who were present began to discuss which women were the most beautiful – the Median or the Persian women.

> Ahasuerus said to them: the vessel that I use, i.e., my wife, is neither Median nor Persian, but rather Chaldean. Do you wish to see her? They said to him: Yes, provided that she be naked, for we wish to see her without any additional adornment (*Seder Moed Migillah*, Daf 12b:3)

And another example appears in the *Zohar* which was at the basis of the literature of Jewish mysticism:

> Therefore whosoever asks God, how can he fix upon a good vessel (as a wife) for this man. For whoever discharges his seed into an unsuitable vessel (*in vas non bonum*), that man fouls and dishonours his seed (*Sohar Levit*, Fol. 38, col. 152).

The *Mishnah Ketubot* was composed in Israel in the late second century and early third century of this era and is part of a treatise called the *Nashim* which deals with women. In stating the law on rape which obliged a man to marry his victim, the author of the *Ketubot* employed the metaphor of a vessel to signify his victim's genitalia and to speak of her as his wife.

> One who seduces a virgin pays for three things, and one who rapes her pays four. The seducer pays for her disgrace, deterioration in value, and for the fine. A rapist adds payment for the bodily pain he inflicted upon her. What is the difference between the punishment of the seducer and that of the rapist?

The rapist pays for the bodily pain; and the seducer does not pay for this pain. The rapist pays immediately, and the seducer only when he sends her away (i.e. refuses to marry her). The rapist must drink out of his chosen vessel (i.e. he must marry his victim) and may never divorce her, whereas the seducer may send her away.

How far does the saying 'he must drink out of his chosen vessel' extend? Even if she is lame, even if she is blind, and even if she is afflicted with boils? However, if unchaste behaviour is discovered in her, or she is not qualified to enter by marriage into the Jewish people, he is not permitted to maintain her as a wife, and it is said, 'Unto him she shall be a wife', a wife who is fitting for him (*Mishnah Ketubot*, ch. 3, sects. 4 and 5).

Finally, the Talmudic *Tractate Sanhedrin* recorded a saying of a Rabbi Samuel who was speaking in the name of a renowned commentator on the oral law, a rabbi named Abba Arikha who had lived in the late second to early third century of this era and who was referred to as Rab or Rav:

R. Samuel b. Unya said in the name of Rab: 'An unmarried woman is an unfinished vessel, and she makes a covenant with (or cares for) no-one except him who made her a vessel; as it is said (Isa 54:5) – For now your creator will be your husband [in the Hebrew text – 'your possessor'] [or 'the one who deflowers you is the one who creates you'] – Yahweh Sabaoth is his name' (*Tractate Sanhedrin*, ch. 2).

The rabbinic saying described a single woman as 'an unfinished vessel' or as it appears in another translation, 'a shapeless lump' simply because she was not married. A spinster is transformed into a 'vessel', however, by her husband who thereby becomes her creator or her owner by the act of deflowering her.

In describing a married woman as the vessel of her husband and presenting her as the antidote to a man's natural urges, Paul was simply following a Jewish figure of speech. And at least some of the early Christian writers understood this. Augustine of Hippo had had no doubt that in his letter to the Thessalonians Paul had been addressing his 'brothers', the male members of the local community, and that he had been using the common Greek word for vessel or utensil as a metaphor for a man's wife.

> This disease of concupiscence is what the apostle refers to, when, speaking to married believers, he says: This is the will of God, even your sanctification, that you should abstain from fornication: that every one of you should know how to possess his vessel in sanctification and honour; not in the disease of desire, even as the Gentiles which know not God (1 Thessalonians 4:3-5). The married believer, therefore, must not only not use another man's vessel, which is what they do who lust after others' wives; but he must know that even his own vessel is not to be possessed in the disease of carnal concupiscence (*On Marriage and Concupiscence*, book 1, ch. 9)

Being a citizen of Rome who spoke Greek, and someone educated in one of the best Pharisee schools of higher learning, Paul was familiar with the Greek or Septuagint version of the Bible and sometimes quoted from it. Though the Wisdom of Ben Sira (also known by its Latin title Ecclesiasticus) did not find a way into the official Hebrew canon of the Jewish Bible, it was often quoted in the rabbinical writings as well as by authors whose writings appear in the New Testament. This piece of wisdom literature appears to have been widely circulated during the intertestamental period – copies have been found in Cairo, at Qumran and Masada. One of its dominant themes – the beauty and wonders of creation – can be seen in a poem in praise of the acts of God in the world of nature (Sir 42:15-43:33). The author also believed that one could gain wisdom from a close observation of the natural world – a theme which appears in wider Jewish thought at the time and which can also be seen in some of Paul's writings (e.g. Rom 1:19–20 and 1 Cor11:14).

Ben Sira had been a scribe dedicated to the pursuit of wisdom and reverence for the Law, the Torah. He was a teacher of wealthy young men and his words of wisdom and advice (mainly to an audience of young men) had been translated by his grandson from its original Hebrew into Greek. Later, his translation became part of the Greek Bible known as the Septuagint. Some scholars have concluded that the material was used to train young Jewish men for positions of leadership.

Ben Sira's book of Sirach was read in ancient synagogue services and early church meetings. It reflects Jewish beliefs and societal values in Palestine just prior to the Maccabean revolt (167-64 BC) when the society was highly polarized between rich and poor, powerful and weak, male and female, the pious and the non-observant, and between Jew and Gentile. Judaism was gradually becoming more and more focused on the Mosaic Law and this law would become the central characteristic of Judaism after the Temple in Jerusalem had been destroyed.

While in his writings Ben Sira personified wisdom as a virtuous woman to be earnestly sought (4:14–15), he seems to have had a profound distrust for women in general.

At the beginning of Chapter 9, the author returned to providing advice about women. This was a topic that attracted his attention more than the other authors and composers of the wisdom books. He urged his reader not to let a woman, any woman, a wife, a harlot, a singer, get a hold on him. She would dominate him if he gave her the upper hand by surrendering to her without restraint. If she could keep her cool while he was almost off his head with passion, she could control him. Fornication was a problem in places other than Thessaloniki.

Do not look intently at a virgin, lest you stumble and incur penalties for her. Do not give yourselves to harlots, lest you lose your inheritance. Turn away your eyes from a shapely woman, and do not look intently at beauty belonging to another. Never dine with another man's wife nor revel with her at wine (Sirach 9:1–9).

The Book of Proverbs is another Jewish collection of wise sayings and aphorisms, supposedly utterances of famous people such as Solomon, Agur and Lemuel. In the opening few chapters a father is seen to be giving his son lessons on how to behave.

Chapter 5 is part of those father–son lessons and addresses the subject of how to approach members of the opposite sex. These introductory chapters were composed somewhat later, scholars suggest probably the fifth century. Since in his letter to the Romans Paul quoted a passage from Proverbs, we can conclude with some degree of certainty that he was familiar with the Jewish Wisdom literature (cf. Rom 12:20 and Proverbs 25:21–22)

> My son, pay attention to my wisdom,
> listen carefully to what I know ...
> Take no notice of a loose-living woman,
> for the lips of this alien drip with honey,
> her words are smoother than oil,
> but their outcome is bitter as wormwood,
> sharp as a two-edged sword.
>
> And now, my son, listen to me,
> never deviate from what I say:
> set your course as far from her as possible,
> go nowhere near the door of her house,
> For you will surrender your honour to others.
> Drink the water from your own cistern,
> fresh water from your own well.

> Do not let your fountains flow to waste elsewhere,
> nor your streams in the public streets.
> Let them be for yourself alone,
> not for strangers at the same time...
>
> Find joy with the wife you married in your youth,
> fair as a hind, graceful as a fawn.
> Let hers be the company you keep,
> hers the breasts that ever fill you with delight,
> hers the love that ever holds you captive.
> Why be seduced, my son, by an alien woman,
> and fondle the breast of a woman who is a stranger?
> (Proverbs 5).

The book of Proverbs and the wisdom of Ben Sira taught the same basic message which Paul addressed to his brothers in Thessaloniki.

But his pastoral advice and the language he clothed it in seem to clash against what we know of the advice Jesus offered. He spoke to men and women while the others, including Paul, spoke about women, but not to women, and addressed their advice about sex and marriage to men. And what they said was based on stereotypes hostile to women. Jesus and the others were functioning in differing worlds, pushing differing sets of values, preaching differing messages.

In the wide world where Paul was working, women were obliged to remain chaste, and faithful if married while men could sleep around without much disapproval. This social and gender divide governing sexual activity was what Paul had to contend with. According to Jesus' message (and Paul's preaching) both sexes were bound by the same law. While the contemporary Roman and Greek world tended to condone marital wanderings on the part of husbands and to view prenuptial sexual behaviour by men, especially young men, as a comparatively venial offence, Paul demanded chastity also from men. The same moral standard was required of all Christians, men and women, rich and poor, regardless of their social status.

Paul therefore had advice for male believers about how to manage their passions. His advice was to choose a wife, sleep with her and no-one else. And besides, all male believers had to behave honourably towards their wives. Marriage was not a form of legalised lust. A man's wife was not to be seen just as an object, a vessel, a utensil who was there to satisfy his sexual passions. Marriage was the antidote for unlawful sexual activity. But even so, in this relationship the male partner had to act with honour.

Paul accepted that a man's basic passions had to be satisfied. Some solution had to be found to replace the sexual excesses which normally involved other men's wives or city prostitutes, or both. They were all the same, the Thessalonians and the Corinthians.

To the Corinthians he would say, 'Because of the temptation to fornication, each man should have his own wife and each woman her own husband' (1 Cor 7:2).

To the Thessalonians he wrote that God wanted the new Christian believers (Paul's 'brothers') to keep away from fornication, and therefore that each one of them (of the men) should know how to acquire a wife (a vessel, a *skeuos*), but not in any selfish, lustful manner, like the pagans. They had to behave honourably, treating their wives with respect, not abusing them or treating them just as sexual objects, as instruments or vessels to satisfy their unnatural passions, or sleeping with other men's wives, thereby taking advantage of a brother 'in these matters'. Paul told them that the Lord always punishes these kinds of sins.

The image of a *skeuos*, a utensil, a container was a particularly explicit literary device, perhaps confronting to a modern reader who might think it to be rather crude. No wonder some of the modern translations are more discreet.

There were several dimensions to the metaphor as it referred to a man's wife. She could be the container in which the embryo was developed, a type of oven in which the foetus was cooked. Or his wife could be the container or sheath into which the husband planted his member in order to produce an offspring, or to assuage his natural, sexual drives.

Being his vessel, a type of kitchen utensil, an antidote to masculine urges, a wife belonged to her husband. When he 'acquired' her, she became one of his possessions so that by interfering with her, another man trespassed on his property. Adultery was not so much an offence against the woman. It compromised a man's position as head of the family and his property rights as a husband.

Furthermore, this image Paul used is reminiscent of Aristotle's pseudo-biological description of the process of the development of the foetus in the female body. While the male was the active principle or the efficient cause of the foetus in the procreational process, a man's wife was the passive principle, the one whom her partner impregnates. The process went on inside the female. She provided the basic materials and the space where the little person was produced, but her partner was really the source, the cause of the final product – the living person.

> The male is the active principle, the party which causes the movement to occur, whereas the female is the passive party. She receives the activity of the male and is moved by him in the act of procreation. The male is active and causes movement, and the female is passive and is set in movement. The foetus is formed by the male and female, but only in the sense that a bed is formed from the conjunction of the activity of the carpenter working on a piece of timber (Aristotle, *Generation of Animals*, book 1, chaps. 21 & 22, 729b–730b).

Aristotle considered that in the act of generation the male was like a potter or a carpenter, while the female was the timber or the clay being used – she provided the material, but her man provided the movement, the *dynamis*, the life and form. She was the receptacle, the container, the vessel – the oven.

As Paul would have it, and in the world in which he had been brought up, for a man of passion marriage was the answer: 'As a safeguard against fornication let every man know how to procure his own vessel.'

Further Pauline Ruminations about Women

Any contemporary theological library has to include at least a small collection of books and articles commenting on Paul's two letters to his mob in Corinth. And off to the side you will find a shelf of material on what he had to say in Chapter 7, being one of the earliest documents produced by a follower of Jesus. Paul's first epistle was written perhaps only months after his letter to the Thessalonians.

In Chapter 7, Paul was attempting to answer some curly questions the Corinthians had asked him about. These were questions about, amongst other things, marriage and sexual abstinence, about whether it was best for a Christian to remain married or to choose to live a celibate life without the complications that accompany intimate sexual encounters. In his reply, the author ventured into the world of human relations, into the murky world of sexual urges of men and women, conjugal rights and sexual abstinence, the power of the devil, divorce and virginity. Most of what he wrote need not concern us here. But in dealing with these issues Paul provided his readers with some insights into his attitudes towards women and how they fitted into his way of thinking about the world.

We can only guess what questions the Corinthians asked, but he began with the curious remark that, 'It was good for a man not to touch a woman.'

'Touching' was a familiar literary euphemism for sexual intimacy. At first glance, this opening statement might appear a touch heretical. It might seem to undermine the message at the heart of the creational myth of Adam and Eve. It seems to clash with the theological truth that the creator of the world designed the animal kingdom and the human species for coupling and procreation. It was a religious belief which Jesus had endorsed. And besides, on the face of it, this blunt statement offends the dictates of common sense and our daily experience of life. Paul appeared to be launching into his advice with a rather provocative observation.

Three hundred years later Jerome would adopt this unorthodox statement to support a furious drive to downgrade the institution of marriage and to establish a biblical foundation for a virginal way of life that he was keen to promote. Paul's brief opening proposition would be surgically removed from its Corinthian context, endorsed as a policy statement to support sexual asceticism, virginity and the celibate life, and presumed to apply universally to all ages. But Paul's opening gambit demands to be treated with more subtlety and respect than Jerome and many others later afforded it.

The blunt proposition that a man should not touch a woman was more than likely an extract from the letter of request which Corinth had sent to Paul. It had perhaps been included in that lost letter at the insistence of an extreme puritanical faction within the local church. If this reading of Paul's opening statement is correct, namely that it is a quotation from the letter Paul received, the authors of the Corinthian letter had suggested that in their particular circumstances it might have been better if a man did not touch a woman, better if there was no physical contact between a man and his wife. But why would they have said that?

It's possible, however, particularly in light of what he had written to his brothers in Thessaloniki, that the Christian warriors in Corinth had meant to suggest that it was better if a man had no contact with prostitutes, with the women of the back alleys and the waterfront who painted their faces and wore their hair high on their heads, or cascading over their shoulders and down their backs. The city was notorious for the services it was able to offer.

Others have suggested that Paul's opening remark had its origins in the classical debate that the Stoics and the Cynics had conducted for centuries, and which would have been the static in the background of discussions about sex and marriage in Greek cities like Corinth.

The Cynics were of the view that any male member of the species who was serious about life should not waste his time engaging in trivial sexual conjunctions with women. They thought he should devote his energies to his intellectual and personal development. For some of these Cynics, the thrill of masturbation was the obvious antidote to a man's basic sexual needs. It was always better not to touch a woman.

Whatever its origins, whether the view of Cynics or of extreme ascetics in Corinth or Paul's own opinion, this simple proposition is rather chauvinistic. Paul immediately took the side of the man. And it is at odds with what was to follow when the author began to expound his version of the intimate relationship between a man and his wife.

Once Paul had opened his remarks with this enigmatic aphorism, he took up its basic theme (men touching women) and began to play different tunes around this motif – modifying and qualifying, rejecting and enriching the message of perpetual abstinence. He told his readers what he had previously told the Thessalonians, that he understood most men needed to touch a woman, that sexual urges could flood over a man, overwhelm him and lead him astray, into the clutches of Satan. But it's hard to miss the fact that at this stage only the male of the human species was at the centre of Paul's remarks. He was dealing with a man's responses when engaging or not engaging with a woman. Women were more like the passive receptacles of a man's sexual drives.

But then the author suddenly changed his focus. He continued by saying that it was appropriate for husbands to satisfy their needs with their wives. He had already told the men in Thessaloniki the same thing: 'Because of the temptation to immorality ... each man should have his own wife', adding immediately that 'each woman should have her own husband'. In this way both men and women could cleanse the system of its concupiscence.

Total abstinence was not a realistic answer, at least for most men and women. Paul went on to develop this idea briefly before moving off in another direction, adding that what he was about to recommend was by way of concession, not a command. I imagine him thinking out loud, strolling up and down as he dictated an answer for his enquirers.

He observed that it was good if a man didn't need to touch a woman and that, as far as he was concerned, the life he was leading without a sexual partner was preferable to the marital state. And even if a man had to be married to satisfy his needs, it was sometimes good for him not to touch his wife so that he could concentrate on higher things – on praying and reflecting on the meaning of life. Perhaps we can notice in Paul's advice the same type of thinking about marriage and sexual encounters we have already seen from Aristotle's friend Theophrastus. Paul's second principle was that any sexual retreat should only be for a short time – and by mutual agreement.

Immediately following the curious aphorism that men should keep their hands to themselves, Paul advised his brothers and sisters in Corinth that to avoid the basic human urge to engage in sexual immorality, each man should have his own wife, and presumably shouldn't be driven to sleep with someone else's. Each woman should have her own husband, and again, not sleep with other men to assuage her basic urges. Nothing new here. Basic marital morality, except that Paul was not concerned only with the rights and privileges of patriarchs and husbands, viewing wives as property or lesser beings, at least as far as sexual satisfaction went. Women had their rights and privileges too.

According to him, the wife had her rights in the bedroom. Her man should pay attention to her and be ready to meet her sexual demands. And conversely, the wife should accept that her man also had his conjugal rights and she was duty bound to honour them. Each party had a mutual duty one to the other, to sleep together, to welcome one another into an intimate embrace which would satisfy and anaesthetize their sexual urges.

We read nothing so explicit from Jesus. He had only put his toe into the muddy waters of sex and marriage. According to the Gospel writers, he had spoken once about the rules governing divorce and had informed his audience on another occasion that any man who stared hard at another man's wife had already indulged his adulterous urges. That's as far as he went, though his ethical stand was pretty radical. But while Jesus had just tip-toed to the edge, Paul had stripped off and waded in over his head.

Paul was basing his marital advice on two mutual principles. First, no wife should think she was in command of her own body or that she had exclusive control over her sexuality. Her husband was the one who enjoyed power over her body.

Surprisingly, the reverse was also true. A shock to all male members, to every husband, and a surprise to their Jewish or pagan wives, was Paul's second principle, that a husband shouldn't presume that he was in command of his own body. As far as his sexuality was concerned, his woman was in charge. No sex for him wherever he wandered, whenever he felt the need, with whomsoever took his fancy. The prevailing cultural custom which favoured men and minimised their sexual misdemeanours was removed from the ledger. Men and women were equal, at least in the bedroom.

How Paul found himself writing in this way about sex and marriage is not clear, though we can assume that some of the believers in Corinth (where sex was a popular sport) had asked him a few questions which he felt obliged to answer. His general advice was that at least in the home, partners should accommodate each other. No wife or husband should turn his/her face to the wall and refuse to sleep in the embrace of her/his partner (except maybe for a short period, and only by agreement). Married couples should certainly not engage in any protracted period of sexual abstinence, and if they did, they would be giving Satan the opportunity to step in and, because of a man or woman's low level of self-control, the Evil One would occupy the vacant space and entice one of them to sneak into someone else's bed. Even if based on a rather bleak view of human nature and on a superstitious belief in the power of the devil, Paul's advice was clear and practical.

But his advice about sexual equality in the home was not a novel idea. Paul was a man of his times. The Stoics had been talking the same language for a long time. The Greek philosopher Plutarch, who followed the Stoic tradition, would be writing essays on ethical and sociological topics, including on marriage, forty years or so after the believers in Corinth had been corresponding with Paul.

> As the mixing of liquids, according to what men of science say, extends throughout their entire content, so also in the case of married people there ought to be a mutual amalgamation of their bodies, property, friends and relations (Plutarch, *Moralia, Conjugalia Praecepta* or *Advice to Bride and Groom*, para. 34)

As early as the second century BC, Antipater had written in his treatise *On Marriage* that marriages were unlike any other friendships because marriages demanded 'complete fusions, as wine with water'. According to him, husbands and wives 'not only share a partnership of property and children ... and the soul, but they alone also share their bodies.'

Musonius was a well-known Stoic philosopher who was teaching in Rome during the reign of Nero. He wrote several discourses, including *On Sexual Indulgence; What is the Chief End of Marriage* and *Is Marriage a Handicap for the Pursuit of Philosophy?* In his last essay he posed the question, 'To whom is everything thought to be common – bodies, souls, possessions – except a husband and wife?', and again, in his lecture on the principal purpose of marriage, he stated that married couples considered 'everything common property and nothing one's own, not even the body itself'.

This form of equality in the bedroom and within marriage as preached by Paul was not new, but what Paul wrote to the Corinthians was significant. It established within the Christian community the equal status of women *vis-a-vis* their husbands, at least within the privacy of the home.

Like Jesus, Paul also felt moved to make some observations about divorce, and on this subject he followed the lead of Jesus and endorsed his counter-cultural policy of equal rights before the law. He had obviously been asked a few questions about divorce and, focusing on marriages between two Christians, he relied on what had fallen from the lips of his leader. Someone had filled him in on what Jesus had said to Paul's fellow Pharisees:

> To the married I give this charge, not I but the Lord, that the wife should not separate from her husband (but if she does, let her remain single or else be reconciled to her husband) – the husband should not divorce his wife (1 Cor 7:10–11).

In the Palestinian Jewish community at the time Jesus and Paul were teaching or writing, the law on divorce set out in the book of Deuteronomy was much disputed, especially among the Pharisees. One school permitted a man to divorce his wife for silly reasons, and another school allowed it only for serious sexual misconduct. But whatever one's view, the right to divorce was available to the husband, and only to him.

According to the Gospel authors, some Pharisees had challenged Jesus about his stand on divorce, asking him a particularly chauvinistic question – at least by today's standards. They asked if it was lawful for a man to divorce his wife and reminded Jesus that Moses had allowed men to write a certificate of divorce (Mark 10.2).

Even though Paul had been educated as a Pharisee and members of that faction were in favour of some form of divorce to benefit the husband, it was Jesus' answer to the divorce question which formed the basis of Paul's advice to Corinth.

From the beginning of creation, God had made members of the race 'male and female', and for that reason a man would leave his father and mother and be joined to his wife, and the two would become one flesh. They were no longer two, but one. So in principle, what God had joined together, no-one should put asunder. However, because of human weakness and sinfulness, Moses had enacted a concession (for men only) that allowed divorce.

The important stand Jesus had made was that in matters of divorce, the wife and her husband were bound by the same rule.

> Whoever divorces his wife and marries another (woman) commits adultery against her. And if she divorces her husband and marries another, she commits adultery (Mark 10:11).

The official position within the churches to which Paul belonged was that, at least in the marital partnership, wives were on a footing equal to their men. The old Mosaic concession to human weakness had been removed. Jesus had established a new regime which had resulted in a new law. The kingdom was already present in their midst. Sin and human weakness had been conquered. There was no longer any need for the Mosaic concession. God's original plan had to be restored. In the kingdom, men and their wives were equal, and the new law was meant to reflect this reality.

In the matters of divorce, despite what the intellectuals and the Pharisees had to say, despite what the Old Law provided to favour husbands, for Jesus, wives in the kingdom were not to be at any disadvantage, and Paul was following 'the Lord'.

Paul moved on to other issues which had been bubbling away under the surface in Corinth. While conceding that his next piece of advice was his own recommendation rather than a command from the Lord, he wrote that personally he would prefer that everyone, man and woman, remain celibate, just like himself. As we have already noted, he complained that unlike the other missionaries, he and his fellow missionary, Barnabas, did not enjoy any female company on their journeys. He accepted, however, that each one had his own individual gift from God.

What Paul was driving at is not clear from this distance. Perhaps his special gift was that he was celibate and therefore able to move around, without being answerable to any partner. His body and its urges did not belong to anyone else. He had no bedroom duties to perform, and no-one but himself and God to please. On this basis, a wife was considered to be an encumbrance to a preacher who wanted to take his work seriously.

On the other hand, maybe Paul was telling his readers that he was out of Satan's reach. Unlike many of his brothers in Thessaloniki or Corinth for example, where sexual indulgence was popular, Paul had been blessed with a low libido, so that in his case, a wife was surplus to requirements. He was well able to control his sexual urges. In any event, he obviously assumed that a true missionary was a male believer – a salesman who could live on the road without the services of a female companion.

As a general policy, and contrary to what was reported of God's plan for mankind in the scriptures, Paul thought that it was better to remain single – at least for the Corinthians as they were waiting expectantly in their new heavenly condition for the second coming of Jesus and the end of the world. Whether this was a general policy to be extended to all Christian men and women down the centuries was a question that would not have entered Paul's mind. He was replying to specific questions in a particular context – a context which he identified – and unaware that men and women would be reading his words in Australia, for example, in the early years of the third millennium and trying to make sense of them.

In the beginning the members of the early churches were waiting anxiously for a second coming of Jesus. They believed that his coming was just on the other side of the horizon. Some were worried about the fate of those who had already died before Jesus' final return. What was going to happen to them? Would they be included in the rally, or had they already gone over the edge and disappeared into nothingness?

As Paul was dictating his letter to Corinth, he entertained what proved to be the fallacious belief that the shape of the visible world was passing away and the time for it to end was at hand. The period God had appointed for the world's continuance was short, and in view of the trouble facing them, it was better if a person, man or woman, remained as he/she was – if single, to remain single; if married, to stay that way. At that stage, Paul's rule for his churches was that in the brief time remaining, everyone should be satisfied with the life God had assigned to him or her. Stability at all costs. Peace and tranquility for the time left. No changes. No disturbances. They should stay just as they were. Silly to make new commitments when all is going to collapse within a few days – months at the most. Soon they would all be in heaven with the Lord.

Paul advised that 'from now on' believers should live in the world as though they were not in the world. Those who had wives should live as though they had none; those who mourned, as though they were not mourning; and those who had dealings with the world as though they had none, 'for the form of this world is passing away'.

Christians were living in a new world. Their flesh existence had been transformed by baptism. They were already heavenly, other creatures. Those who had wives should live as though they had none because that was how husbands would be in heaven, like Adam was originally, before Eve had been created as his partner.

Again, it seems significant that Paul did not think to advise the wives that in their present circumstances they should also act as though they had no husbands. His focus was automatically, unconsciously concentrated on husbands. While Jesus had taught his followers how to live as kingdom-people in the world, Paul was teaching his followers how to live outside the world, on the other side.

However, even as he and his people were waiting for the end, Paul was no crazed ideologue. He knew that humankind's sexual urges were powerful and could be destructive. When push came to shove, if a person couldn't cope, if the drives were too powerful, he/she should marry and escape Satan. It was better to marry than to be consumed by fire.

Paul provided a number of reasons for his recommendation to Jesus' followers that they should adopt the way of virginity and his reasons had nothing to do with sexual asceticism. According to him, in order to be free of any anxiety, any distraction, ideally a man should remain celibate. A man who was free of the encumbrances associated with being married could concern himself exclusively with the affairs of God – preaching, praying, journeying. The married man, on the other hand, had to please his wife, and Paul would have known that some of the apostles and many of the believers were married. And inevitably, as Christians and as married men, their interests would sometimes have been in conflict.

The married woman's heart would also be split between God and her husband, whereas the unmarried woman or virgin could attend to God's business, without restraint. As Paul saw it, a virgin's job was to discover how to be holy 'in body and spirit', rather than being anxious about 'worldly affairs' and pleasing her husband.

This concluding gloss, which was couched in rather chauvinistic terms, seems somewhat out of tune with what we know of Jesus' mentality and his way of relating to his female friends. Why was it the *virgin's* calling to be holy 'in body and spirit', and not also the vocation of a married woman? Was a married woman, by virtue of being married, having sex with her husband, giving birth to children, feeding them on her breast and attending to her family's household needs, not holy 'in body and spirit'? Had her body and spirit been compromised by living as a married woman? Did Paul think that a married woman was living a less angelic life, that she had not withdrawn from the world? Not yet transformed into a new creature. Still tied to the old world, to Adam's world of sin and sexual couplings.

Paul agreed that it was not a sin to marry, but it's hard to avoid the conclusion that people like Jerome would later draw, that he thought the married state was inferior – a step down in Christian living, involving some degree of contamination – less angelic.

Paul was of the opinion that, at least for the Corinthians and in the circumstances in which they found themselves, it was better to remain unmarried. There is nothing wrong with marriage, especially if the storms of concupiscence proved too turbulent, but the unmarried state was preferable and peaceful. 'It is well for a man not to touch a woman.'

The question is, what did Paul mean by it being 'better to remain unmarried'? Did he mean more virtuous, more pleasing to the God who created us 'male and female', more in accord with the mind of Jesus, more ethical, or more liberating? Perhaps he meant that in view of the imminent re-appearance of the Lord and the approaching end of our world, it was more prudent and practical for a man not to clutter up his life with new responsibilities(a wife, education of children, in-laws and debts), but to put his head down like an athlete and lunge for the finishing line. Maybe Paul's statement had nothing to do with the value of virginity or with any general policy of favouring virginal integrity and sexual abstinence over marital coupling. Perhaps he was merely advising that since time was limited, the Corinthians should stabilise their lives.

However, on balance, after reading this epistle and searching between the lines, it is difficult to avoid the overall impression that Paul considered marriage as second rate, as an antidote to sins of the flesh, a distraction which interfered with the work of the gospel. He appeared to think that although in principle baptised men and women were equal in the sight of God, female virgins were holier in 'body and spirit' than their married sisters. Virginity was the natural state for angels. Adam and Eve had both been virgins before their Fall into sin. In baptism, followers of Christ had entered a new, heavenly world. Virginity, not marriage, was to be a feature of their new vocation. Paul seems to have been adding a number of complex levels to Jesus' simple message as it would be laid out in the Gospels.

Chapter 7 of his epistle consists almost entirely of what Paul admitted was his personal opinion on the topic of marriage, sexual restraint, celibacy and virginity. We don't know what the Corinthians made of his letter or whether they modified their behaviour to conform to his advice. But once his letter had been read to the community, what were the locals to do with it? Archive it for future reference? Re-read it occasionally to see whether the advice had been heeded? Or perhaps share it with neighbouring communities, copying the text and circulating it.

The locals sought to pass on Paul's advice to other churches for their instruction. He was becoming a giant in the early church. He had been authorised by the church in Jerusalem to be its travelling salesman and to preach the Jesus gospel to the pagans. What he wrote had a local flavour, but behind his advice were values and attitudes, beliefs and spiritual insights, a vision of the world, an ideology – all transcending the particular, and all part of the mix which constituted Christianity for the early believers. His words became normative for the future of their faith-system.

The difficulty for all Christians, however, is how to decide what to jettison and what to salvage, how to leave aside the particular while conserving the essence of the message. To resolve the problem one has to know what the real business of the Lord was. Ritual worship, psalm recitation, building churches, administering schools, preserving a complex code of orthodoxy? Or feeding the poor, caring for the sick, supporting the elderly, comforting those who mourn and building up the kingdom? Where should a believer's preferences lie?

Living without the distraction of a wife, or the touch of a woman had not proved to be the secret to an uncluttered existence or necessarily the best way to further the spread of the gospel. And what was perhaps appropriate advice for the people of Corinth in the middle of the first century is not necessarily ideal, or practical, or relevant for the faith-people living in the twenty-first century.

In his Chapter 7, Paul was not addressing the question of finding a place for women in his ministry, or whether they should share in the power structure and be leaders in the local community, or whether they should occupy some position within the hierarchy. He was directing his remarks to questions of intimacy between a man and a woman and the question of equal rights in the process of divorce, and to questions about the lives of those, like himself, who choose to live and work as celibates. Paul was giving his slant on the relationship of a couple within their marriage and while asserting their equality within the intimacy of their sexual relationship, he was not making any comment one way or the other about a man and a woman's relationship within the family and in the community. His mind was still fixed within a patriarchal mould of family life and society.

However, being a male himself and a trained Pharisee, the author seems to have been demonstrating some unconscious preference for exploring the male side of the marital bond rather than the female. Perhaps contrary to Jesus' message about God creating men and women for each other, to live together as one unit, he advocated a celibate, virginal, angelic existence in which men and women live separate, independent lives. The question may be asked – how did this line play out in the life of the early church? And how did Paul's advice determine the position and status of young female believers?

On Paul's personal recommendation, virginity was to become a way of life for young girls, and celibacy was to be made compulsory for members of the clergy. Jesus' saying about being a eunuch for the sake of the kingdom of heaven would take on a new meaning. Whereas the Kingdom of Heaven of which Jesus spoke was a reality to be found here on earth, among men and women as they went about living their daily lives, the kingdom of which Paul and those who came after him spoke, was an otherworld reality, a new creation, over and above, and separate from the physical world of ordinary men and women.

At the conclusion of his first letter to his church in Corinth, Paul engaged in a typical Pharisaical and theological discourse about the resurrection of the dead.

> What is sown in perishable, what is raised is imperishable ... It is sown a physical body, it is raised a spiritual body ... The first man was from the earth, a man of dust; the second man is from heaven ... I tell you this, brethren: flesh and blood cannot inherit the kingdom of God, nor does the perishable inherit the imperishable (1 Cor 15:42–50).

However, being a male himself and a trained Pharisee, the author seems to have been demonstrating some unconscious preference for exploring the male side of the marital bond rather than the female. And whatever his opinion might have been about how Christians should behave as they waited for the imminent end of the world as they knew it, contemporary Christian men and ministers have to decide whether in the present age, a wife would be an encumbrance or a help, whether it is 'better' for them to live alone as celibates or live as God created them, as man and woman, husband and wife, for coupling and completing one another.

Paul's Reputation as a Misogynist

> 'As in all the churches of the saints, the women should be silent in the churches, for they are not permitted to speak. Rather, let them be submissive, as in fact the law says. If they want to find out about something, they should ask their husbands at home' (1 Cor 14:34-36).

You might reasonably conclude from this text that Paul was a rather autocratic, perhaps misogynistic leader who didn't hesitate to use his authority to keep women of the community in their place — silent in church and subservient at home. Paul the patriarch and misogynist.

If you wanted to find proof beyond reasonable doubt that Apostle Paul was an enemy of the feminist cause, that he was in fact a dyed-in-the-wool, unreconstructed misogynist, you only have to quote these two verses of his first letter to the people of Corinth. On the face of it these verses show clearly that Paul was against women's active participation in liturgical assemblies, and in favour of an inferior status for women. They paint the great man in a very poor light.

The passage seems so unambiguous. Just a plain straight-out prohibition. Paul agreed with the Greek heroes, Plato and Aristotle, and with the cultural prejudices of the day. Women were inferior beings. They had to do as they were told and accept their proper place in the scheme of things. He was issuing his last word on the topic of women in the assemblies. If any woman in the group wanted to remain a Christian, she had to be obedient. Paul was claiming that he was repeating a commandment of the Lord and that was the end of it. No further questions (1 Cor 14:37–38).

But don't go away. This is not, in fact, the end of the matter. These few verses have presented modern scholars with a multiplicity of problems. No-one can tell us, for example, what law the author was thinking of which required women to be submissive. And who were 'the women' who were not permitted to speak? All women, or just rowdy, quarrelsome ones?

But of even more concern, many scholars consider that these few verses did not form part of Paul's original letter; that even though they appear under his name, he didn't in fact write them; and that even though they are part of what is accepted as inspired, canonical literature, they do not reflect his thinking about women and their place in the liturgical assemblies of the churches he founded.

If these scholarly propositions are well-founded, this quotation is useless in any search to discover Paul's mind-set *vis-à-vis* women. It is no help in determining what Paul of Tarsus's pastoral position was on controlling women's behaviour in the liturgical gatherings, about whether he had a general policy that all women should remain silent, or only the noisy, argumentative ones, or whether all women were free to pray publicly and prophesy as the spirit moved them.

This is not to say, however, that this little passage in 1 Corinthians 14 is unimportant. Whether authentic or not, the relevant passage formed part of Paul's letter from very early times, almost certainly from sometime in the first century, and it reflected what some early believers expected of women in the assembly, namely, silence and submission.

Furthermore, while the passage is very probably not a Pauline text in the sense that it was written by Paul himself, from very early times it appeared under his name, as his words, and was accepted until very recently as bearing his authority. By inserting these verses into Paul's long letter, some scribe (mistakenly, one hopes) was demeaning the reputation of the great missionary and presenting him to the world as the authority for an ecclesiastical policy to keep women underfoot, on their knees.

Because of its anti-feminist flavour, this quotation of three short verses above Paul's signature has proved extremely difficult material to deal with. There is a team of reputable exegetes who have concluded (probably correctly) that it did not form part of Paul's letter and should be removed from the official text. It was inserted into the original document sometime after he wrote his letter, though all agree on the basis of early manuscript evidence that it was not long afterwards.

Other reputable exegetes, however, consider that, on balance, the passage did form part of Paul's original letter. Some think that he lifted it word for word from the letter he had received from Corinth asking him a series of questions and that Paul, for some reason, simply inserted it into his letter in reply.

To complicate the issue, others have concluded it is more likely that Paul wrote the verses to solve a particular problem in the Corinthian community, a problem of noisy, outspoken women, and for this reason his prohibition should not be applied, in their opinion, in any general sense to control or silence all women of whatever century.

And of course there are some more conservative exegetes who believe the text is truly Pauline and that it was meant to establish the general principle, a rather chauvinistic one, that all women should be silent in public assemblies and obedient to their husbands. Over the centuries, some of the Fathers have quoted these verses with approval to do just that.

But the overall weight of scholarly opinion now is that these few verses fit uncomfortably into the text, that they interrupt the flow of Paul's material, and that they were introduced into Paul's letter by a faceless copyist.

The solution to the problem as to whether 1 Corinthians 14:34–36 is a genuine Pauline text rests on the following basic, academic conclusions.

First, it is clear that on the face of it this prohibition negates what Paul wrote to his Corinthians in Chapter 11 verse 5 where he clearly implied that a woman could pray in public and prophesy, provided she was wearing a head-covering.

Second, none of the ancient manuscripts which include the original Greek text of Paul's first letter to the Corinthians omit these two verses. Consequently, if they didn't in fact form part of Paul's original letter, they appeared in the text at a very early stage, sometime in the first century.

Third, while some of the more ancient manuscripts have these verses positioned after verse 33 (where they stand in all our contemporary translations), other manuscripts have them tacked on after verse 40. We're not talking here about a misplaced word, a single letter or even an isolated phrase. How such a slab of text came to be positioned by a copyist in different places is not easy to explain. The raw fact which emerges from this manuscript evidence is that these verses do not appear to belong to the original version of Paul's letter.

Fourth, if you remove verses 33b, 34 and 35 (but not 36), the text flows seamlessly and logically from verse 33a to verse 36 and onto verses 37 to 40. Verses 33b, 34 and 35 have a different grammatical construction in the original Greek text, being written exclusively in the feminine form, while the two passages on either side, the passage above (verses 26–33a) and the passage below (verses 36–40), are addressed to men and women, and were constructed in the masculine form which grammatically could apply generically to either gender.

Fifth, the insertion of this passage calling for women to remain silent in the assembly and submissive can perhaps be explained by the fact that in verse 28 and verse 30, Paul was calling for silence in certain liturgical circumstances, namely in respect of a speaker in tongues if there was no-one present to interpret, and secondly in respect to a prophet if another prophet was in the process of making his or her revelation. The requirement of silence in the prayer assemblies may have inspired a copyist, on his own initiative, to insert this foreign regulation into the text.

And finally, it would seem that no scholar can provide a satisfactory answer to the question as to what 'law' (*nomos*) Paul or the author of the verses was referring to. The New Testament literature refers to the Hebrew Bible as the 'law', but no part of this 'law' required a woman to be silent or submissive, and being a trained Pharisee, Paul would have known that. Many theologians over the years have 'interpreted' Paul as referring to the law in Gen 3:16: 'To the woman he (God) said, Your desire shall be for your husband, and he shall rule over you.'

Perhaps the author's reference was to the rabbinical law, or to the Roman law, or to law in general whereby, according to the culture of the day, women had to be submissive to their husbands and demure in public. But no-one knows.

In the face of these basic, academic conclusions, some scholars have still insisted that Paul did write these verses, and that if they did not appear in his original letter, he had inserted them soon afterwards. These scholars then have to explain what he meant, how they came to be in different places in the ancient manuscripts, and how these verses can be read together with what he was writing in 1 Corinthians 11:5. Not an easy exercise.

Some of these scholars have concluded that Paul was dealing with a particular problem which had arisen in Corinth, that he was intending to control those women who were socialising, gossiping and chattering in the public prayer meetings, or that he wanted to shut down those ill-informed women who were constantly interrupting and asking stupid questions. None of these explanations, in my opinion, carry the same likelihood as the interference of a foreign hand.

Other scholars considered that Paul might have lifted these verses from the letter he had received and in his reply was quoting the words back to the people of Corinth; that they were in fact not his opinion, but it was the standard policy to silence women – a policy adopted by one or some of the factions in Corinth, and that

Paul was providing his rather sarcastic reply in verse 36 where he changes into the generic masculine form to address both males and females and dismisses any suggestion of such a prohibition: 'What! Did the word of God originate with you, or are you the only ones it has reached?'

This of course is a reasonable explanation and one which casts Paul in an even more favourable light.

Finally, in an attempt to explain these verses and preserve them as truly Pauline, Ben Witherington III, in his *Conflict and Community in Corinth, A Socio-Rhetorical Commentary on 1 and 2 Corinthians*, pointed to the ancient popular practice among pagan Greeks of consulting the oracle of Delphi. The prophetess Pythia used to provide answers to personal questions about marriage and divorce, children and death. People came to her from afar seeking answers to their personal problems. Witherington thought that some women in the community at Corinth might have been disrupting the assembly by demanding answers from the prophets and prophetesses to their personal and mundane questions. According to him, Paul only wanted to silence these women, not to silence all women.

On the evidence, it is safe to conclude that it's more than likely these critical verses do not reflect Paul's pastoral policy about the behaviour of women during the liturgical assembly, though this is certainly not to say that this passage has not been a negative and powerful force in the life of the church. It reflects the values and attitudes of some of the believers during the first century of this era. It would seem that early in the piece, some faceless scribe took the opportunity to insert into Paul's letter a solution of his own – a solution which some faction or other in Corinth was seeking to impose. But this was a cruel stab in the back for a man who was so keen to defend and preserve his reputation. From the earliest times these words have been presented to believers as those of Paul himself. They came with his authority. They have been quoted down the centuries in support of a general policy to control and silence women in the life of the church. But in my opinion, though they remain a part of the official, canonical text, they were not Paul's and do not represent his opinion.

However, in his life and ministry, and in his writings, Paul didn't do justice to Jesus' message. While Jesus had been what we would now call an enlightened feminist, Paul proved to be more conservative, more traditional in his relationship with women, and patriarchal when it came to family relationships. Unfortunately, without showing signs of a typical misogynist mindset, he nevertheless laid the foundation for the emergence of a particular variety of misogyny within the early Christian communities. Those who followed him, even those who wrote in his name, continued in a direction away from Jesus and his message, towards a mentality and culture which sought to control women, to keep them in their place, to deny them a place in the power structure of the institution, to speak of them in a disparaging manner and to regard them as inferior to men. Because of his effort to accommodate the gospel message within its contemporary cultural setting, Paul initiated the movement's slide back into a patriarchal world, into the cultural values of male superiority and female subservience. This return to old attitudes and values was further promoted throughout the Christian diaspora by the anonymous author of the Pastoral Letters. And as the local churches moved into the second, third and early fourth centuries, we can witness a downhill stumbling and tumbling into a pit of women-haters and fearers, into a witch's brew of misogyny.

The Adam-and-Eve Myth

The story of Adam and Eve was a powerful myth that functioned deep in the psyche of every religious Jew. A simple fairy story repeated to children by their mothers and fathers to 'explain' how the world started. It told of how animals came to be spread throughout the land, how men and women first appeared on the earth, and how evil had erupted and infected the world.

The opening chapters of the Bible where the first couple make their appearance are the result of a long oral process of primitive tribes telling and re-telling stories of imaginary events. These events occurred long ago, in the period of our prehistory. The stories had been passed down in oral form from one generation to the next, along a long ancestral line – stories about God, creation, our original ancestors, evil and the devil, stories that entered into the religious psyche of peoples and families.

The Pentateuch as we know it only functioned as a finished text, the Torah, from the period of the Jewish exile. It had travelled through various traditions of different ages until a complete edition of all the five books (the Pentateuch) appeared in the sixth century BC. The book of Genesis, the first book in the collection, begins with the creation narrative and the story of Adam and Eve.

The Bible stories of creation and of the significant actions of humanity's ancestors are only some of a number of versions of the same mysterious events, all of which were circulating in and around Mesopotamia at about the same period. These narratives were all tainted with the same prejudices. They were both patriarchal and misogynistic. The Bible story had told one generation after another that Eve had been inferior to Adam because, according to the fictitious story, she had been created after him and from one of his body parts. Adam had been lonely in the midst of creation and she had been given to him as a companion, to fill the gap. But she had led him astray and when confronted by the creator of the universe, Adam didn't hesitate to hide behind his partner and to level the blame at her. It was she who had given in to the evil serpent. Under the text and in the name of God, young and old were being told that women were weak, dangerous, inferior creatures who were responsible for evil in the world.

God said, 'Who told you that you were naked? Have you eaten of the tree of which I commanded you not to eat?' The man said, 'The woman whom you gave to be with me, she gave me fruit of the tree and I ate.' The Lord God said to the woman, 'What is this that you have done?' The woman said, 'The serpent beguiled me and I ate.' ... To the woman God said, 'I will greatly multiply your pain in childbearing; in pain you shall bring forth children, yet your desire shall be for your husband, and he shall rule over you' (Genesis 3:11–13,16).

We don't know whether Joseph or Mary used to put Jesus to sleep telling him the stories of creation and of Adam and Eve, of the Tree of Knowledge and the serpent. Since the story had a prominent place as the opening passage in the Torah, it would certainly have been known among the people in the mountains around the Lake of Galilee, in tiny villages like Nazareth. But Jesus' parents were unsophisticated people, maybe illiterate, members of the working class, earning their living by the sweat of their brow as God had ordained after Adam's sin. How deeply the creation myth had penetrated into Joseph's household and the subconscious religious mind of Jesus we will never know.

But Jesus didn't appear overly interested in these stories. There is only one oblique reference to them in Matthew's Gospel – to Genesis 1:27:

> Jesus answered, 'have you not read that he who made them from the beginning made them male and female', and said 'for this reason a man shall leave his father and mother and be joined to his wife, and that two shall become one flesh?' (Matt 19:4–5).

As far as we know, unlike Paul and other Jewish writers, Jesus was not inclined to breathe new life into the myth of Adam and Eve. He obviously knew the story, but he paid practically no attention to its significance. Paul, however, was different. He was a sophisticated, educated and successful Jew. He had studied the Torah. Adam and Eve and their story would have been part of his stock-in-trade, part of his religious and theological world. After his conversion, he included them seamlessly into the structures of the theological rabbinical arguments he devised to support his pastoral, disciplinary stance. He would set the theological hare running in his authentic letters, initiating a tendency among the men who followed him to trace all kinds of doctrines and dogmas, attitudes, prejudices and regulations back to the original Genesis story about humanity's first parents.

In his third, perhaps fourth letter to Corinth (the one we identify as his second epistle), Paul visited the Adam-Eve motif and injected the story with a dose of growth hormones. In 2 Corinthians 11, by a simple throwaway line, he provided a strong rootstock on which later authors would graft a branch of Christian misogyny.

Paul was worried about his little church in Corinth losing its way. Some ring-ins had arrived in the city and had begun to preach another Jesus and a different message – not the one Paul had learnt from his mystical experiences in the deserts of Arabia and from the other apostles in Jerusalem. Apparently, these mavericks were more compelling preachers than Paul. They were making in-roads and destabilising his community. Paul was experiencing what he described was 'a divine jealousy' of his little churches. As he expressed it, like any father arranging a suitable marriage for his daughter, he had betrothed his communities to Christ and presented them as pure brides to their husband. Paul was like a passionate father who was worried sick for his daughters. He was afraid that the serpent, by his cunning, would lead the Corinthians astray in the same way as it had deceived Eve – yes Eve, not Adam.

Paul obviously had had no doubt that Adam and Eve had been real, historical figures, our first parents and people of importance.

The author of Luke's Gospel would share the same conviction and trace Jesus' genealogical line back to Adam. Paul's passing reference to Eve in his letter and her encounter with the serpent are significant. He included her in his argument so causally, so seamlessly. This is an indication of the intellectual and religious world in which Paul lived and operated.

> I am afraid that as the serpent deceived Eve by his cunning, your thoughts will be led astray from a sincere and pure devotion to Christ (2 Cor 11:3).

A few years after his letters to Corinth, Paul wrote a long dissertation to the believers in Rome. In dealing with humankind's deliverance from sin and death by the power of Christ, this time he called on Adam to strengthen his argument. Sin had entered the world through Adam and as a result, death had spread its tentacles through the whole human race. This first man had prefigured the One who was to come. Whereas through one man's fall many had died, through Jesus Christ the free gift of divine grace had flooded the world. Paul went on to expand the reverse parallels between Adam and Christ. Just as by one man's disobedience many had been made sinners, by one man's obedience many would be made righteous (Rom 5:12–19). Paul shanghaied Adam, introducing him so naturally into his train of thought and at the same time giving a little hint of the discontinuity framework in which his mind operated. Jesus was not the fulfillment of God's initial plan when he created Adam and begun the story of humanity. Jesus had disrupted the flow of history and reversed what Adam had done. Two completely contrasting dispensations – before and after Jesus paralleling evil and grace, earth and heaven.

Before Paul had begun to tinker with it, the story of Adam and Eve had been expanded, interpreted and twisted out of its simple, original shape by Jewish scholars from about 200 BC. Well into the second and third centuries of the present era they were continuing to show interest in this pair from the book of Genesis. Jewish Apocrypha and the pseudo-epigraphic literature, as well as the writings of Jewish intellectuals and historians, witness to a nation's fascination with the figure of our first parents.

In the history of his people, the Jewish historian Titus Flavius Josephus (who was a contemporary of Paul and a native of Jerusalem) wrote an expanded version of the creation of our first parents and their fall from grace. He belonged to a long line of authors (all males) who blamed Eve for humanity's misfortunes. According to Josephus, the Creator had punished her for her sin by inflicting on her the curse of womanhood.

Josephus believed that after the seventh day of creation, Moses (who according to the legend was the author of the book of Genesis and of the other four books of the Pentateuch) had begun to talk philosophically about the formation of the human race. God had taken dust from the ground and fashioned a man, implanting in him a spirit and a soul. This man was called Adam.

When God saw that his man had no female companion and that Adam was wondering about the other animals which were male and female, God put him to sleep, extracted one of his ribs and formed a woman. She was brought to him and he 'knew' her (or in other words, he had an intimate, sexual coupling with her). The name of this woman was 'Eve', signifying the mother of all the living.

Josephus moved on to deal with our first parents' fall from grace. Adam had made excuses for his sin and had asked God not to be angry with him. He told God that Eve had deceived him, and she in turn had passed the blame on to the serpent. God had punished Adam because in his weakness he had given in to his wife, and he also made Eve suffer the inconvenience of monthly purges and the pains of childbirth. She had persuaded Adam to sin with the same arguments the serpent had used to convince her to eat of the tree of knowledge.

Philo was a young contemporary of Paul living in Alexandria and like him, educated as a Pharisee in the Jewish law, living and working, like Paul, with one foot in the Jewish culture and the other in the contemporary Roman world, and like him, a Roman citizen. He was a Jewish philosopher and commentator on the Jewish scriptures. He held views similar to Paul's, though more colourful. He had much to say about wives and their naturally schizophrenic, duplicitous character, leading to an amusing diatribe against female tricks of their trade, their fashions and hairstyles.

In his work *On the Birth of Abel*, Philo revealed seriously distorted prejudices towards women and plastered bright colours onto the customary female stereotypes. Identifying with his male readers, his mates, he wrote,

> Two women live with each individual among us, both unfriendly and hostile to one another, filling the abode of our soul with envy, and jealousy, and hostility. We love one of the two, looking on her as someone who is mild and tractable; dear to us and closely connected to ourselves – and this one is called pleasure. The other we detest, deeming her unmanageable, savage, fierce and completely hostile – and her name is virtue. One of them comes to us luxuriously dressed in the guise of a harlot and prostitute, with mincing steps, rolling her eyes with excessive licentiousness and desire. She entraps the souls of the young, looking about with a mixture of boldness and impudence, holding up her head and raising herself above her natural height, fawning and giggling, having the hair of her head dressed with the most superfluous elaborateness, her eyes shaded with pencil, her eyebrows covered over, enjoying incessant warm baths, painted with a fictitious colour, exquisitely dressed with costly garments, richly embroidered, adorned with armlets, and bracelets, and necklaces, and all other ornaments which

can be made of gold, and precious stones, and all kinds of female decorations.

This woman, a figment of Philo's demented imagination, was depicted by him strolling proudly in the company of her many friends, and full to the brim with bold cunning, rashness, flattery, tricks, deceit, telling lies, crazy opinions, impiety, injustice and intemperance. She was right there in the middle of them, like the leader of the company, marshalling her team, promising them that if they stuck with her, they would receive a share in the treasury of human blessings.

Philo the philosopher focused his mystic mind on the first chapters of the Book of Genesis. According to him, God had fashioned his prized creature on the sixth day, observing that the number six was, by the law of nature, the most productive number. Adam was the perfect creature, made to reflect the image and likeness of God. From the beginning, man was a pure spirit – a mind living in isolation in Paradise, in a garden free of disease and corruption. But creation was by nature changeable. Nothing lasted forever. When the creator distinguished between the sexes, transforming his original prized creature into male and female, he set in train a process of trouble and strife. Adam rejoiced at the sight of his Eve and took her in his arms. He was superior because God had given him the dominant feature in humankind's make-up, namely the mind, the soul, while Eve had been endowed with sensations. The experience of pleasure was associated with these female sensations and they clouded and overpowered Adam's mind. The serpent had concluded that the way to Adam was through Eve. By nature, she was unstable and fickle – more prone to evil than her male counterpart.

One of the more outrageous character assassinations of Lady Eve was penned by this Jewish philosopher from Alexandria. His frequent references to the original *femme fatale* were sprinkled with damning observations about women in general He saw Eve as the beginning of all man's troubles. She was the root-cause of all sexual passion, and because of her husband's powerful sexual drive, humankind has had to suffer. She ruled over death, and over all vile and putrid things. By her nature she had been less honourable than her partner. Adam had sinned by surrendering his birthright as lord and master when he had become subordinate to someone inferior; from the beginning women were meant to be subordinate and submissive to their menfolk. According to Philo, since Eve had come from Adam, women enjoyed only a secondary ontological status, and while Adam had been made in the image and likeness of God, his partner had been two steps removed from that immortal image.

Both Josephus and Philo were contemporaries of Paul and living in the same theological world as him. The myth of Adam and Eve was at the forefront of their minds, ready to be taken up to advance their worldview. Along with other figures in Jewish literature and folklore (Cain and Abel, Noah, Moses and Abraham, to mention a few), the Adam-and-Eve myth made the crossing from the world of Judaism into Christian territory.

As far as we know, unlike Paul, Jesus had not ventured into the dangerous territory of women's fashions. In preaching his kingdom message, he didn't need to waste time on such trivia. Paul, however, did not hesitate and again co-opted the myth of Adam and Eve to lend support to his pastoral stand. He was intent on establishing his churches on a firm foundation and on making sure, as far as he could, that the members were on their best behaviour in foreign lands.

Further on, in his first letter to the Corinthians, after he had dealt with the issues around sex and marriage, Paul addressed another problem which was causing some distress (1 Cor 11:2–16). Apparently, some of the female members of the community were displaying their glorious hairstyles on the public streets and in the prayer assemblies. Paul was determined that their lewd behaviour had to cease. He and others considered it was not proper for a woman to address God with her head uncovered. Only hussies and prostitutes let their hair down in public or put their hair up to attract attention and titillate their potential customers. Ladies didn't parade themselves in this way outside the home. They kept their eyes down, mouth shut, and head covered when out and about, and when at prayer in the assembly.

In Paul's time Corinth was a busy seaport and a major commercial centre – a densely populated, cosmopolitan and wealthy city – a maze of narrow streets and laneways where merchants from near and far set up their stalls. She was a city of debauchery, profiteering and eastern cults. And she also boasted a strong Jewish presence as well as a rainbow range of religions and sects from Asia Minor such as followers of Isis, Cybele, Serapis, and Aphrodite of course.

By reputation Corinth was a steamy town populated by foreigners and sailors, pimps and prostitutes. The priestess-prostitutes who spent their lives in the temple service of Aphrodite were reputed to spread their graces and blessings wide and far so that the resulting pox was popularly called 'the Corinthian disease'. Sex was a popular pastime even inside Paul's churches. Some Christians who had crossed over from pagan cults were mingling with believers of Jewish background, including factions that were fighting to preserve their Jewish traditions and beliefs.

In their former lives, some members of the Christian community would have participated in the activities of other religious sects and perhaps to some degree were still involved – in mystery cults, for example. They would have regularly eaten meat offered in sacrifice to idols. Some would have seen women leading the worshippers in prayer and behaving outrageously, as though under the influence of drugs. Paul's community was made up of men and women, married, single, widowed and virgins – all performing a variety of functions. There were apostles, prophets and prophetesses, those who 'spoke in tongues', teachers, preachers as well as simple followers – some behaving badly, even at the memorial of the Lord's Supper.

The Christian community in Corinth would have reflected the social and economic make-up of the city – the wealthy and poor, tradesmen and artisans, freed people and slaves, Jewish sympathizers and Judaizers, converts from the mystery cults and those from a Hellenistic background, pimps and prostitutes. This local community included libertines as well as extreme puritans. And there were disturbances, conflicts and chaos. According to Paul, some members of his little church were fornicators, idolaters, adulterers, sodomites, thieves and drunkards – all eminently suitable, on standards established by Jesus, to apply for membership of his Kingdom but badly suited to be members of an established organisation trying to make its way in the world.

Some of these characters with shadowy pasts had to be brought into line. Some of the more conservative members of the community were unhappy. Paul knew how he wanted his people to behave, but he couldn't just tell them. He had to argue his position.

Beginning with a play on the word 'head' – which could mean either a leader, a person in charge such as the head of a department, or the upper part of the human body – drawing on his training as a Pharisee, Paul developed an artificial rabbinical argument by exploiting the double meaning of the word. He juxtaposed man, woman, Christ and God in order to strengthen a theological proposition which some readers might have found unconvincing.

He wanted his readers to know that as far as male members were concerned, Christ was the head (the leader), that a husband was the head (the leader, the boss) for his wife, and that God was the head (the leader) for Christ. All a perfect model for a traditional patriarchal system. Paul was accepting the prevailing culturally determined gender relationship between man and woman.

I want you to understand that the head of every man is Christ, the head of a woman is her husband, and the head of Christ is God (1 Cor 11:3).

Without exploring this idea further, Paul seems to have assumed that his readers would simply accept what he was saying. It was obvious. The husband was in charge. Then he followed his now-puzzling statement involving 'heads' with what we might regard as a complete *non-sequitur*. Any man who prayed and prophesied with his head covered, dishonoured his head (his leader), referring to Christ. When a man prayed or prophesied with his head covered, he appeared to be hiding from Christ instead of allowing his open face to reflect the glory of his leader (2 Cor 3:18). With his head covered, a man would be behaving improperly, like a woman. He doesn't need to have his head covered. He is the one with the authority.

On the other hand, every woman who prayed or prophesied with her head uncovered was an affront to her head, that is to her husband, because she had removed the sign of her husband's control over her. Covering her head was the symbol of her submission and subjection. Appearing in the liturgical gathering without a head covering would indicate she was her husband's equal, an independent woman no longer under his control. As we see in verse 10, Paul thought that a woman's veil was the sign of her subjection and the sign of her husband's authority: 'That is why a woman ought to have a veil (in Greek: authority) on her head, because of the angels' (1 Cor. 11:10).

Whenever a woman was wearing a headscarf or a veil she was licensed to pray in the assembly because she was displaying the authority which came from her husband. She knew her place and was prepared to acknowledge it by wearing the veil.

Presumably, both parties, male and female, were licensed to pray and prophesy in public, but when the woman did, she had to be veiled. According to Paul, and exaggerating a little, if a woman refused to wear a veil, she should 'go the whole hog', shave her head and appear like a harlot, covered in shame and disgrace. These observations would have flowed naturally from what Paul and others were used to seeing in the streets of cities like Corinth.

And there followed another now-apparent *non-sequitur* but which, when seen in the light of the author's training in the Pharisaic school of Gamaliel, seemed so obvious. A man should not cover his head because he is 'the image and glory of God'. This is a reference to the Genesis myth of God creating his prized creature, Adam. A woman however was the glory of the man because, also according to Genesis, a man was not made from woman. The woman had been created from man – Eve from Adam – but not the inverse. 'For man was not made from woman, but woman from man. Neither was man created for woman, but woman for man' (1 Cor 11:8–9).

Then he added a puzzling observation. A woman had to wear a veil on her head 'because of the angels'. We'll come back to this reference to angels, but whatever he meant, it included a commitment to proper order and decorum at all times in the assembly. Cultural standards of dress should prevail in order to preserve man's authority over his woman.

Paul continued with his ponderous argument in favour of female veiling. As far as the Lord was concerned, women were not independent of men, or men independent of women. At the time of creation, a woman was born from a man. Eve came from Adam, while now men are born of women. The lives of men and women are intertwined. And in any event, as Paul added, 'all things are from God'.

In truth, Paul only had to issue the directive that in the assemblies women had to be veiled if they wanted to pray or prophesise. But he had to justify his regulation and argue his case. Have another look at his convoluted thought process:

But I want you to understand that the head of every man is Christ, the head of a woman is her husband, and the head of Christ is God. Any man who prays or prophesies with his head covered dishonours his head, but any woman who prays or prophesies with her head unveiled dishonours her head – it is the same as if her head were shaven. For if a woman will not veil herself, then she should cut off her hair; but if it is disgraceful for a woman to be shorn or shaven, let her wear a veil. For a man ought not to cover his head , since he is the image and glory of God; but woman is the glory of man. (For man was not made from woman, but woman from man. Neither was man created for woman, but woman for man.) That is why a woman ought to have a veil on her head, because of the angels. (Nevertheless, in the Lord woman is not independent of man nor man of woman; for as woman was made from man, so man is now born of woman. And all things are from God.) Judge for yourselves; is it proper for a woman to pray to God with her head uncovered? Does not nature itself teach you that for a man to wear long hair is degrading to him, but if a woman has long hair, it is her pride? For her hair is given to her as a covering. If anyone is disposed to be contentious, we recognize no other practice, nor do the churches of God (1 Cor 11:3-1).

The convolution of his ideas came out of the rabbinical world which Paul had inhabited as a young man. It was the result of his years of religious training. To persuade his people in Corinth that God wanted women to be veiled and socially acceptable when they were praying, Paul based his argument on the opening chapters of Genesis and the divinely established relationship between Adam and Eve as reflected in the Torah. How convinced the Gentile people of Corinth were by this mode of argumentation can be left to our imagination.

With these off-the-cuff observations involving our first parents, and their theological significance, Paul was taking up a motif that had become popular in Jewish literature and dominant in the Jewish religious psyche, and introducing it into early Christian thinking. It was destined to dominate the minds of bishops and theologians, Fathers and Doctors of the church for almost two thousand years, until in recent times people of faith reluctantly ceased believing that Adam and his companion had been real, historical figures rather than the product of a storyteller's fertile dreaming. Our first parents were mythical figures embraced by our ancestors and given centrestage in the story of creation. Now Paul was exploiting the story to justify rules about women's dress code and their inferior status.

His reference to Adam and Eve was to put a light to a long fuse which would begin to sparkle in the Pastoral Epistles and eventually light up a virile Christian misogynistic tradition. This Genesis story would be used to prosecute the central role of women in humankind's tragic unhappiness and in the emergence of cosmic chaos; to classify women as temptresses and the cause of sin in the world, with special emphasis on the enjoyable sin of intercourse; to explain the spread of original sin by copulation; and to establish Satan's power over the emotional and unstable members of the opposite sex.

The Adam-and-Eve myth would become a rich theme to be embellished and exploited by Church Fathers like Tertullian, Jerome and Augustine, explored and expanded down the centuries in what became known as the Adam-and-Eve literature. Anonymous authors would dream up crazy variations of the story involving the original couple and recount the expanded story in lengthy Latin, Gaelic, French, German or English poems and legends. The influential scholastic theologians (Thomas Aquinas, Bonaventure, Albert the Great, for example) were fascinated by our first parents, by the Genesis story of their creation and their tragic fall from grace.

In Paul's mind, and as we saw also in Philo's mind, there were two types of women. For Paul, they were divided into those who were properly veiled in public (those with their feminine glory hidden under a scarf when they were praying in the assembly) and the second category was comprised of jezebels, harridans and tarts. A woman was either dressed properly or she wasn't, and if she wasn't, she might as well be totally bald for the affront she was offering her husband and the community. Such a woman was a disgrace.

While the apostle Paul did not share Philo's explicit misogynistic ideas about women, and while these same sentiments were certainly not part of Jesus' thinking, within a few decades they would become a feature of the way leaders of the Christian communities would write and preach about women.

But returning to his argument in support of the veiling of women, Paul invited his readers to use their common sense and to judge for themselves. He said nature made it obvious that it was degrading for a man to wear his hair like a girl, round his ears and over his shoulders. While for a woman, long hair was her pride and glory. A woman's hair was created as a head covering. That's the way God had intended that men and women should present themselves – men with short hair, women with long, glorious hairstyles covered by a veil. Paul believed the natural way established by the creator from the beginning should be preserved. Societal customs should be honoured. Christians should not appear to be different. Paul was insisting on order and conformity within his communities.

Finally, by way of conclusion and again unlike Jesus, Paul simply laid down the law. He told the Corinthians that this was the way it was going to be. If any of them didn't like it, if any one was disposed to be argumentative, they would either have to accept his regulations or leave the community. Paul didn't recognize any other practice. All his other churches agreed that women had to be veiled when praying or prophesying in public. Corinth had to fall into line. 'If anyone is disposed to be contentious, we recognize no other practice, nor do the churches of God' (1 Cor 11:16).

So what can we make of what Paul wrote on this issue of women's fashions?

First, it appears to have been the norm in Corinth and in the other Pauline churches for both men and women to pray publicly and to prophesy. In the assembly, at least during Paul's time, women could do what men did. They were licensed to assume an active, public role in the liturgical gatherings. They enjoyed a new authorisation. While Christians of Jewish origins would not have been accustomed to women performing these functions, and while they would have expected the women present to remain silent and separate, in Christian circles women could participate, and actively.

However, women who were moved to participate had to be veiled, and as Paul said, the veil was their authorisation to participate. 'This is why a woman ought to have an authority or an authorisation on her head, because of the angels' (1 Cor 11:10).

The meaning of this verse is not immediately obvious. What was Paul thinking? For some obscure reason, angels were being introduced into his discussion. Obviously, Paul (and presumably his readers) knew something about angels which escapes the modern reader.

The reference may simply have been to messengers, to the visitors from other churches who would have been expecting the Corinthian church to be like all the others, with the female members demonstrating their respect and their subjection to their husbands and to the community by being veiled in the assembly. The Greek word *angelos* was commonly translated as 'a messenger' and on this hypothesis, the visitors would have reported their impressions of Corinth back to their own churches.

On the other hand, Paul might have had real angels, heavenly creatures in mind, and if this be true, there are two possible interpretations of what Paul meant.

First (and by way of background), Plato reported in his *Apology* that Socrates had developed some idea of a private inner voice which would warn him of danger, a guiding spirit which he called his *diamonion* and which would have been something like a guardian angel. The Essenes at Qumran believed that angels hovered in the air when the members of the group were together in worship. They were observers and supervisors of the created world, charged with the task of governing the world, preserving reverence and ensuring a level of order in the assembly. Worshippers were engaged in promoting God's glory – and that glory alone had to pervade the religious experience. There was to be no distraction. According to Paul, God's glory was symbolised by man's uncovered head whereas, since a woman was man's glory, and her hair was her own glory, during worship her head had to be covered with a veil to preserve order and decorum. A tortured argument which may not convince a modern reader, but Paul was talking to the members of his little first-century church community in Corinth. Today his arguments might ring hollow, but he was reasoning like a rabbi.

Second (and parallel with the popular myth of Adam and Eve, of the serpent and the fruit tree) there was another creation story involving a tribe of angels (also called 'watchers'). One hundred and ninety-nine of them had been struck by the blinding beauty of the daughters of men, had descended to earth, fornicated with these gorgeous girls and had begotten a race of giants, of Titans and supermen. Women were required to wear a head-covering in the assembly to protect themselves from rampant, sex-starved angels who were tormented by lustful demons.

We can find relics of this myth in the book of Genesis (6:1–4), but the story was told in more detail in the first book of Enoch, and particularly in the *Testament of Reuben* which was part of a Jewish-Christian document called the *Testaments of the Twelve Patriarchs*. In his testament the Patriarch Reuben was imagined addressing his sons, warning them of the dangers of the fair sex. The text was known in some form to the author of the Epistle of Jude (1:14–15), and probably Paul had come in contact with the story in his early studies, though the final version of the Testaments was not complete until the second century of this era.

For thus they (the well-endowed but showy daughters of man) allured the Watchers (the angels) who were before the flood; for as they continually stared at them, they lusted after them, and they conceived the act in their mind; for they changed themselves into the shape of men, and appeared to them when they were with their husbands. And the women lusting in their minds after their form gave birth to giants, for the Watchers appeared to them as reaching even unto heaven (4:1 & 5:1–7).

Paul wanted to insist that women should wear headgear in public and at community worship. After-all, at the time it was the prevailing custom in Corinth and elsewhere, both among Gentiles and Jews. To have done otherwise, to tolerate adult women appearing in public without their headwear would have made the Christian movement like a group on the fringe of society, and the women themselves like harlots or hippies. Paul wanted his communities to appear part of society – serious, substantial, properly ordered and well controlled, not unhinged like some of the popular mystery religions.

In order to buttress his pastoral position, and like any trained theologian, Paul was calling on every trick in the book. He was arguing from every angle. He was throwing everything at his readers – Genesis, Scripture, nature, common sense, and the final punch – authority.

Traditionally, this has been how theology develops. Arguments have often been confected, like the arguments marshalled by the church in Rome in defence of her policy on female ordination or against artificial birth-control. Arguments in support of a basic pastoral position often emerged from the way a particular culture thought, from the fashions of the times, from typology, for example, or from what was described by the scholastics as *convenientia*, or from the mystery of numbers, from literal interpretations of some mythological or poetic passage. In the end, arguments come and go, moving in and out of fashion. The practical, pastoral position was what was important to preserve, namely, order, harmony, orthodoxy and peace, and it was preserved by considerations that varied from age to age.

In his first letter to his brothers and sisters in Corinth, Paul had released the myth of Adam and Eve from its cage, setting it free to roam in the dense forest of Christian literature. He had enlisted the ancient fable to buff and polish his pastoral policy that women were naturally inferior to men and that somehow the biblical story of Adam and Eve was related to the status of women within the community. A woman had arrived late on the creation scene, after Adam. She had been born from his flesh and created as his companion. Consequently, women were the glory of their husbands. They were secondary, subservient and inferior.

Later, when he dictated what Christians came to refer to as his second letter, he penetrated further into the shadows of the myth and, leaving to one side any role the male partner might have played in the tragedy, Paul simply asserted that a cunning serpent had deceived the woman.

Paul felt himself consumed with a 'divine jealousy'. He saw his position and authority in Corinth being undermined. People were speaking ill of him, boasting about themselves and Paul wanted to defend himself: 'But I am afraid that as the serpent deceived Eve by his cunning, your thoughts will be led astray from a sincere and pure devotion to Christ' (2 Cor 11:2).

There is the story of Adam and Eve and the serpent in the forefront of Paul's mind – an image and an argument ready for him to use so spontaneously.

We can be confident from reading his letters that Paul was not a woman-hater of any colour. Nowhere in his authentic letters can be found a poisonous word addressed to any woman or about women, abusing or demeaning them as some of the Fathers would later do. He had many female, as well as male, companions and regarded them all as his co-workers. He engaged on a daily basis with women, accepted their hospitality, enjoyed their company, greeting them in his letters (sometimes affectionately) and accepting that they could pray and prophesy in the liturgical assemblies. He regarded his female companions as important members of his team. He does not appear to have been frightened or dismissive of women in general and certainly did not speak disparagingly of them.

While Paul was clearly an alpha male figure in the early church, thin-skinned and somewhat paranoid, he was still able to work with women and acknowledge their contribution to the mission he had set himself – to preach the message of salvation which Christ had accomplished by his death and resurrection and to establish communities of believers throughout the Greco-Roman world. And he was not loath to express his emotions – his affection for his fellow workers, men and women.

Nonetheless, he believed women were inferior to men. They were the descendants of a woman who had been created for Adam, after Adam and from his sleeping body. They were the glory of their husbands and needed to know their place and show submission to their husbands in all things, except maybe in the bedroom. He wanted his church members to be accepted as part of the mainstream, and this meant that Christian women had to behave themselves properly in public places and within the faith gatherings. They had to dress modestly and not present themselves like madams and flighty street women. Women had to conform to the standards of society.

Paul showed himself to be patriarchal, chauvinistic and somewhat anti-feminist – not a radical revolutionary like Jesus, but a social conformist who was intent on preserving order, authority, established structure and the social norms.

From what we can divine, from comparing what Jesus is reported as saying and what Paul wrote in his letters, the apostle of the Gentiles was more cerebral than Jesus, more intellectual, more ideological, and more strategic. The thought-patterns he had acquired in the school of Gamaliel where he had learnt his theology, would determine how he would argue a case and muster his points of reference. He did not write as Jesus tended to speak. He did not preach in parables, or talk to his churches about his dreams and visions of a kingdom or a world which was not predicated on power or wealth. He did not speak to his audience in aphorisms and puzzling epigrams as Jesus had done. Paul tended either to deal with practical, immediate issues of pastoral concern, or else with grand theological questions about God and his plan, about salvation, liberty and the law, death and resurrection. And in dealing with both of these areas, the practical and the ideological, he drew on his knowledge of the Bible, on the myth of Adam and Eve, on his traditions and on what he considered reasonable, appropriate, obvious and in accordance with the prevailing culture norms. His letters show his mind working both as a practical administrator of an expanding organisation, and as a man with formal education trained in law and theology to argue a case. Jesus was not a lawyer or a theologian who was interested in mounting an argument based in Scripture' or tradition, to defend a pastoral decision or a theoretical teaching. He was more down to earth, more grounded in the moment.

But it is plain from comparing the Gospel narratives and the letters of Paul that Jesus had never talked like Paul the theologian. No twisted rabbinical arguments to justify a ruling or support a practice. Jesus was not an academic or a professionally trained teacher. He spoke simply, directly, in homespun parables, without frills and flourishes, without torturous analogies or sinuous pleadings. But it didn't take long before his Kingdom message was on the wane and Paul was in the ascendency.

The relationship which Jesus had enjoyed with his female followers and with other women, and the role they had played in his life and mission, were not replicated in the life and mission of the early communities. None of the apostles seem to have followed Jesus' lead. The female atmospherics within Acts, and for that matter within Paul's letters, are of a different order to those pulsating throughout the Gospels as the authors described the life and work of Jesus.

Faced with the profile of women in the early apostolic churches, their involvement in Paul's missionary work and their prominence in the house churches spread around the Mediterranean communities, it is a shock to come across a number of passages in his authentic letters which provided both practical and theological grounds for the subordination of women within his churches: the headship of man over women in the hierarchical structure of God – Christ – man – woman.

Paul's Alter-Egos

The most problematic passage for those who seek to protect Paul's reputation is in the first letter he was supposed to have written to his friend Timothy. Paul's uncomfortable literal interpretation of the Adam-and-Eve myth and its application to support the traditional and conservative status of women was further exploited by the author of the Pastoral Epistles. He expanded the basic Genesis story to enhance Eve's role in the drama. She became the primary transgressor of the law and the one Satan had deceived. She bore the blame for everything that had gone wrong in the world, and this was the principal feature which the author of the Pastorals added to the story.

In his first epistle, the anonymous author pretended that the great apostle Paul was telling Timothy that he wanted women to dress conservatively, in seemly apparel, 'not with braided hair', not ornamented with gold or pearls nor dressed up in costly attire. Women should learn to be silent and submissive.

> I permit no woman to teach or to have authority over men. She is to keep silent. For Adam was formed first, then Eve; and Adam was not deceived, but the woman was deceived and became the transgressor (1 Tim 2:12–14).

With this reference to the Genesis myth, misogyny was off and running. The movement that Jesus had initiated was on its way to turning away from his approach to women, to their central role in his religious world, and on its way to developing a woman-hating, woman-fearing tradition in which Eve (and all women except the mother of Jesus and a few others uncontaminated by sex) would be forever linked to Satan, to evil and sin, to sex and damnation. The message was that men were superior to woman. This was because a woman's position in the community of faith was to be governed by the mythical-theological fact that the original woman had consorted with the Evil One and had broken the covenant God had established with his creation.

In this brief reference, the early church gatherings were confronted with a misogynistic interpretation of the Genesis myth. This interpretation associated women with Satan. It blamed the female member of the species for the appearance of malice and evil in the world and for generating a radical disruption at the heart of creation. The myth had been patriarchal from the beginning, but now it was being re-interpreted to support a general policy of exclusion, debasement and stereotyping of women. In these few verses attributed to Paul, we can find the beginning of an ugly tradition which would bedevil women, blacken their reputation and hold them shackled in an inferior, dependent state. This theological 'truth' involving women was to be repeated and further developed over the centuries. The next step in the evolution of the tradition was to associate women and all things evil, with the ugly, awkward act of sexual coupling and its associated urges. These dark themes would be mined by many of the Fathers (Jerome and Augustine among them) and would prove popular throughout the Middle Ages among the celibate theologians and monastic poets.

The Pastoral Epistles (1 and 2 Timothy and Titus) and the epistles to the Ephesians and to the Colossians, are in the same category as the few verses in 1 Corinthians 14 we have already looked at – verses 34 and 35. Though for two millennia they have appeared under Paul's name, scholars have come to accept that he was not the author, though in its official documents the Vatican persists to this day in quoting the Pastoral Epistles as Paul's personal material. If he has had a reputation as a chauvinist, that reputation was largely based on someone else's material. He might have been annoyed to learn that these late epistles (as well as a particularly hostile passage introduced by a foreign hand into his letter to the Corinthians) were published worldwide and for so long, bearing his seal of approval. His name and authority make these letters particularly important in the study of Christian misogyny.

Paul's letter-writing concluded some years before 70 AD. The story of his missionary work recorded in Acts was completed after that, maybe ten or twenty years before the end of the century, sometime between 80 and 90 AD. At about the same time, two of the letters we have classified as the deutero-Pauline letters made their appearance, the epistle to the Colossians and the one to the Ephesians. Based on the differences in literary style and theological content, many scholars are in general agreement that these two epistles were not written by Paul. In view of the marked similarities between them and his authentic works, the same scholars have also concluded that the author or authors of these two important epistles had a deep knowledge and appreciation of Pauline literature and had probably been a member of one of the communities established by him. They had more than likely been composed after Paul's authentic letters had been collected and bound into a corpus, probably towards the end of the first century. The three Pastoral Epistles (also attributed to Paul) appeared sometime after the four Gospels and Acts, also towards the end of the first century.

If these two thin bundles of pseudo-Pauline letters present a trustworthy picture of what was occurring in the early Christian communities at the end of the first century, the recently improved status of women and their involvement in the life of the church, was beginning to teeter on the edge.

While we can find in Paul's authentic letters occasional indications of classical chauvinist prejudices mingled with a wish to include women at least in middle-management roles, it is beyond doubt that within two or three decades of his death, at least some of the churches of the diaspora had begun to speak of their womenfolk in ways inconsistent with Jesus' revolutionary, counter-cultural *modus operandi*. The church was drifting away from Jesus into a new paradigm. His teaching about the Kingdom and his attitudes towards women, for example (as portrayed in the Gospels), had passed through Paul's world, through his theological mindset, and was coming out the other side fundamentally changed. Then towards the end of the first century, the variations and adjustments that Paul had fashioned underwent a further metamorphosis. The intellectual grid behind these post-Pauline letters was considerably more conservative than Jesus' mindset had been and more reflective of the values of the society at large.

From a cursory reading of these post-Pauline epistles, the deutero-Pauline letters (Colossians, the Ephesians, and 2 Thessalonians) and the Pastorals (1 and 2 Timothy and Titus), we can conclude that the leaders of the Christian communities were anxious to encourage a code of behaviour which conformed with the social mores of the time, which reflected the values and attitudes of society at large, and particularly the Greco-Roman ethics and customs. The code of behaviour incorporated into these later epistles dealt with three types of relationship within the household – the wife/husband, children/parents and slave/master relationships. Each of these household relationships was based on a paradigm of superiority and submission, of authority and obedience. These social and familial codes were deeply rooted in the cultural values of the times and were seen by the authors of the post-Pauline epistles as a reflection of the relationship between Christ and his church.

The author of the letter to the Colossians, for example, advised wives, husbands, fathers and slaves, in Paul's name:

> Wives, be subject to your husbands, as is fitting in the Lord. Husbands, love your wives, and do not be harsh with them. Children, obey your parents in everything, for this pleases the

Lord. Fathers, do not provoke your children, lest they become discouraged. Slaves, obey in everything those who are your earthly masters, not with eye service, as men-pleasers, but in singleness of heart, fearing the Lord (Col 3:18–22).

This same code involving male dominance and female submission was repeated by the author of the epistle to the Ephesians, again presenting it as reflecting the wishes of the Lord, but now with an added twist. The author linked the code with the Pauline idea of headship which we examined earlier in 1 Corinthians 11.

> Be subject to one another out of reverence for Christ. Wives, be subject to your husbands, as to the Lord. For the husband is the head of the wife as Christ is the head of the church, his body, and is himself its saviour. As the church is subject to Christ, so let wives also be subject in everything to their husbands. Husbands, love your wives, as Christ loved his church and gave himself up for her, that he might sanctify her, having cleansed her by the washing of water with the word, that he might present the church to himself in splendour, without spot or wrinkle or any such thing, that she might be holy and without blemish. Even so husbands should love their wives as their own bodies. He who loves his wife loves himself (Eph 5:21–28).

Again, the author goes on to address children and parents, slaves and masters in the same vein, adding to the advice he addresses to masters about treatment of their slaves: 'Masters, don't threaten your servants, knowing that he who is both their Master and yours is in heaven, and that there is no partiality with him' (Eph 6:9).

Ultimate equality in all things before God – slaves equal to their masters, children to their parents, and wives equal to their husbands. But as far as the author of this epistle was concerned, and unlike Jesus' Kingdom policy, this equality and divine partiality was not part of a believer's daily experience in society. A Christian's code of behaviour was to be the same as that of the rest of society. It was based on the accepted paradigm of superiority/inferiority, of authority/obedience, and bound into the great mystery of the relationship between Christ and his church.

While we don't find these admonitions in the authentic letters of Paul, we do hear him telling his people that they need to conform to the standards of the day, that they should not draw attention to themselves in the public forum by their unconventional behaviour, that they should not be seen to be scandalising non-believers. Paul wanted his communities to be generally accepted in the towns and villages where they were living. He claimed that in his own missionary life, he was anxious that his behaviour was seen to conform to the generally accepted norms of society. This was obviously not a consideration which had defined Jesus' relationships with those in authority, with non-believers, lepers, sinners or with women.

The institution had moved on since the days of Peter and Paul. Though some of the old problems were still bubbling away, the administrative structures of the churches had stepped up a notch. The author of the Pastoral Epistles found himself addressing a church, probably in Asia Minor, maybe in Ephesus, which had the basic elements of an ordination ritual and an established set of guidelines for appointing bishops, deacons (or 'ministers-servants') and widows. He was writing in a language that was drawing more deeply on a Greco-Roman philosophy than Paul had done, or for that matter, the authors of the Gospels. The local board of 'elders' or 'presbyters' which had earlier been in charge within the community was replaced by 'the bishop' or 'the overseer' – a single male person who was exercising a controlling authority. Those with special spirit-gifts (men and women) had become less visible than they had been in Paul's churches. Power was now concentrated in the hands of a male hierarchy. Almost within living memory, within about seventy years, the movement that a gifted charismatic leader had launched was mutating into an established institution.

But the problems were the same, perhaps even more intense. If the Pastoral Epistles present us with a reasonably accurate picture, a turbulent storm of ideas and practices was battering the Christian communities throughout Asia Minor. Ephesus was a cosmopolitan city and a hotbed of religious activity – mystery cults; strange Gnostic sects; false teachers spruiking their wares and hostile currents of thought circulating. Add to this sexual misbehaviour among young women; some female believers involved in peddling myths and endless genealogies, useless speculation and dualistic mythological visions; idle chatter and venomous gossip; and some women renouncing their beliefs. Then others still were making their appearance in the prayer gatherings with extravagant hairstyles similar to those worn by rich wives and courtesans, adorned with braids and curls, plastered with make-up, heavy with pearls and gold trinkets. Some of the women were boisterous and badly behaved. They would talk incessantly, refusing to listen and trying to take over the assembly. The author of the Pastoral Epistles had focused his attention on women – on wild women.

Assuming the persona and the authority of the Apostle Paul, the faceless composer of these epistles saw it as his role to identify the steps necessary to restore order within the assembly. It seemed his mission to move away from the fervour of charismatic outbursts, spirit-filled gifts, the confusion of prophecies, the 'babbling' of tongues – from unbridled freedom and undisciplined spontaneity. He sought to restore order in the ranks. Like Paul before him and the author of the letters to the Colossians and Ephesians, he wanted the Christian communities to look good in the public domain and fit into the mores of the times. He wanted these communities to be socially acceptable out there in the marketplace. Proper order and decorum couldn't be achieved without prohibitions and regulations, solid advice, discipline and proper authoritative structures – without clamping down on those women who were stepping out of line.

The author's solution was obvious. He insisted that the female members should present themselves modestly in the assembly as well as outside on the streets. They had to be properly dressed and covered so that they would not generate the wrong sort of attention. They had to be quiet – ready to listen and learn. The foreign hand that had inserted his tuppence worth into Chapter 14 of Paul's first epistle to the Corinthians was becoming the closed fist of authority. There was no learning without listening, and no listening without silence.

Furthermore, women had to be content to stay in their allotted place. They were not supposed to rule over their husbands or order them around. The author's remedy to women spreading false doctrine or betraying the true faith was to make sure they were under control by reaffirming their traditional role within the family. Men were in charge. Men were superior. Women had to be submissive.

Pretending to be the apostle from Tarsus, the author wrote to Titus whom, according to the letter, Paul had left in Crete to address urgent problems and to appoint elders or bishops 'in every town as I directed you'. Among his instructions was a direction to warn the older women to behave properly and not slander others or spend their days drinking. This advice would not have been offered without some reason. It was undoubtedly based on what the author's impression was as to how some senior women were spending their time. Furthermore, these older women were responsible for training their younger sisters to love their husbands and children, to be sensible, chaste and good homemakers, kind and submissive to their husbands, so that the message of Jesus would be respected in the city and not discredited within the general community. The author was anxious to create a good impression. The church was becoming part of the establishment, or at least that was its goal.

But we don't hear the Jesus we meet in the Gospels proffering any of this type of conservative advice. His followers were beginning to travel backwards into the territory of traditional values. Jesus hadn't seemed to care much about the impression he was making on society or about telling women how to behave as women. He was more interested in advising human beings how to live a life of love and inclusion. According to the Gospel writers, Jesus spoke from time to time about bad examples, but never in the context of making a good impression on potential converts to his message. That seems to have been a consideration quite foreign to him. In fact, one can say with some confidence that Jesus behaved as though he couldn't have cared less what impression he was leaving in his wake. He was not establishing any organisation or setting himself up as the CEO of a large multi-national corporation. No PR department was required. He was preaching his ideal world for human beings to live in – his vision of a heavenly kingdom on earth.

Then, in his first letter to Timothy the author warned the young bishop of Ephesus to treat the older men with respect like a father, the younger men like brothers, old women like mothers and younger women like sisters, adding that Timothy had to approach these younger women 'in all purity'. The young bishop had to be careful dealing with nubile females. They could prove troublesome if he wasn't on his guard.

The author then went on to offer advice about how the local widows were to be treated, thereby providing convincing evidence of the emergence of an order or sodality of widows within the community. He identified three categories of these women – those who had no need of support because their own families were looking after them; real widows who were alone and needed social services; and finally, enrolled widows who were commissioned to perform some official functions within the church.

An enrolled widow had to be a woman of a certain age (over sixty) and well-known for her virtuous life. Underage widows were not eligible for enrolment. Instead, the author thought they should marry and provide children for their husbands. (It's a view not too popular among young women today.) He seems to have had a jaundiced opinion of younger women. If they were enrolled too soon in the association of widows, they might be inclined to renege on their promises. Young widows tended to be capricious and wanton, untrustworthy and unstable. According to him, they became gossipers and busybodies, gadding about from house to house doing nothing and saying things they shouldn't. Again, we don't hear similar pejorative comments coming from the Jesus of the Gospels. There is no record of him uttering a word of criticism of women in general or of any woman he came in contact with.

The final step in the flowering of a women-hating tradition among the leaders of the churches was to defame women of all sizes and contours. And this final step in the process was one which the author of the Pastorals didn't hesitate to take. He was leading the way into the toxic bog of Christian misogyny. After warning Timothy about men who were lovers of themselves, proud, arrogant, abusive, ungrateful, greedy for money, slanderers, treacherous, reckless lovers of pleasure and swollen with conceit, the author turned his attention to feckless women. He advised the young bishop to avoid those men who were able to worm their way into households and who strangled 'weak women' who were weighed down by sin and swayed by 'various impulses', women who would listen to anybody and who were incapable of discerning the truth.

The 'impulses' which were haunting the mind of the author and which gathered like storm clouds around his female sisters would undoubtedly have included all the negative stereotypes associated with being a woman – scatter-brained giddiness, irrationality, unreasonableness, hysteria, capriciousness, skittish wanton behaviour, charming sensuality, bewitching seductiveness. After only a very short time many Christian writers would happily dip their quills in gall and indulge their contemptuous view of women. The story of Christian misogyny is crowded with willing satirists, venomous critics and unstable celibates anxious to vilify womenfolk by describing them in demeaning language.

The storyteller from Nazareth would have been horrified to learn what was being written about women in his name.

Supercharging the Myth of Adam and Eve

It is no surprise that the early Christian writers took up Paul's lead and continued to reflect on the theological significance of the classical Genesis story. Over the years these writers bent and twisted the story and its characters to reflect and strengthen their theological worldview.

In the south of France, in the back half of the second century, the second bishop of Lyon exploited many parallels between the Jewish and the Christian dispensations – Adam, for example, as the first man and Christ as his counterpart in the new world. Bishop Irenaeus was clearly fascinated by patterns woven into the history of the world by the Creator.

In Book V of his *Adversus Haereses*, Irenaeus returned to his well-worn theme, contrasting Eve with Jesus' mother. The virgin Eve had been espoused to a man (Adam); she had been deceived by the word of an angel in the same way as the Virgin Mary, also betrothed to a man, had received her glad tidings during a visitation from an angel. The author's mind was full of parallels and counterbalances, contrasting and comparing the old with the new. From the beginning, God had laid out his plan with meticulous care. As he saw it, in God's plan for the world, the Virgin Mary would become the patroness and the advocate of the virgin Eve.

> As the human race fell into bondage to death by means of a virgin, so is it rescued by a virgin; virginal disobedience having been balanced in the scales by virginal obedience (*Adv. Haer.* 19:1).

Somehow early in the life of the church, this mythical Eve, the mother of the human race, had taken on the elevated status of a virgin. Someone's creative imagination had been at work to expand and modify the original myth and record the original asexual purity and physical integrity of Mother Eve.

Some years later, maybe in Rome (though scholars are not sure), Hippolytus was making his own contribution to the myth. In his commentary on the Canticle of Canticles, he drew an imaginative parallel between the bride of the Canticle who was seeking her lover in the garden (Cant. 3:1), and Martha and Mary who were seeking Jesus in the tomb. As 'apostles to the apostles' (*quae apostoli ad apostolos*), they had been responsible for announcing the good news to the other apostles and thereby becoming the redeemer of Eve's sin. These two friends of Jesus were not liars as Eve had been, and as the male apostles had presumed. They had been commissioned by Jesus, against Jewish custom, as witnesses to the truth and to destroy the power of evil which Eve had unleashed so long ago.

Hippolytus was unknowingly beginning to explore themes which were to become familiar motifs in the literature of the Western exegetical and theological tradition: the female redeemer, women as the first witnesses to the Resurrection, and the parallels between the image of the bride, the Jewish synagogue and the church.

In an early Christian tradition, the mother of Jesus was presented as a second Eve and as a figure of redemption, and other women who had been involved in Jesus' life and ministry, Mary Magdalene, Martha and her sister Mary, as 'apostles to the apostles', as 'the apostle of the apostles', as witnesses of the Resurrection and messengers of the risen Christ.

Hippolytus must have known some 'alternative historical facts' involving Martha and her sister Mary, facts which had escaped the authors of the Gospels as well as modern biblical scholars, or he was repeating a rumour involving these two women from Bethany.

In any event, he saw them as apostles of Christ, untangling the mess which Mother Eve had left the world in. And he portrayed Jesus as a supporter of the Resurrection-women and as someone intent on enhancing their status in the eyes of his male apostles.

> In case the female apostles should doubt the angels, Christ himself came to them so that the women would be apostles of Christ and by their obedience rectify the sin of the ancient Eve ... Therefore the women announced the good news to the apostles ... In order that the women should not appear to be liars but rather truth-bearers ... Christ showed himself to the (male) apostles and said to them: 'It is I who appeared to these women and I who wanted to send them to you as apostles.' (The commentary of Hippolytus survives only in a Gregorian version, *Corpus Scriptorum Christianorum Orientalium*, vol. 264 [1965], pp. 43–49).

Other Christian authors, including Augustine of Hippo, for example, would later take up the female redeemer motif. 'Death through a woman and through a woman, life – *per feminam mors, per feminam vita*' (Sermon 232) was to become a popular theme applied to Mary, the virgin mother of Jesus.

Clement of Alexandria was another Christian writer and teacher who adopted the theme Paul had passed on to those coming after him. As a convert to Christianity and as an educated Alexandrian, he had been schooled in the works of the classical poets and philosophers. He was familiar, for example, with the works of Plato and Aristotle. Echoing the macho sentiments of his fellow-citizen Philo, he made his contribution to the Christian stream of anti-feminist consciousness. And based on the theories of Aristotle, he expounded an original theological position on beards and body hair. He recommended men to take pride in their hairiness, their toughness, their ruggedness and body warmth. But, as Clement pointed out, this position wasn't adopted by contemporary hairstylists in the backstreets of the port city of Egypt.

Clement believed that in creating Adam as he did, God had determined that men should be superior to women, and that their beards were a mark of their manhood and a token of their superior nature. God had deemed it right and proper from the beginning that men should excel. Consequently he had planted hair over Adam's entire body – chest, legs and arms, shoulders and back. The unmanly smoothness and velvety softness which had originally formed part of the male make-up had been removed when Eve 'had been drawn from the side of his body'. She had been fashioned like an oven, to receive and cook Adam's life-giving semen. Adam had been a shaggy man. Because he was covered in hair, head to toe, he was naturally drier and warmer than his smoother, weaker, softer partner. With more hair on their bodies, men were able to generate more heat. They were as a consequence more complete as animals and therefore more perfect than their female partners.

Clement considered that women (his mother, of course, and other men's wives and daughters) were emasculated animals, with literally nothing between their legs, lacking the equipment which their menfolk possessed. For this reason, they were imperfect. Following this logic, Clement was convinced it was virtually an act of desecration for a man to shave, or cut his hair, or to have his body hair removed by tweezers and warm wax.

Clement's intellectual life had predated his conversion to Christianity. He had been familiar with the works of the pagan poets and philosophers. In his writings which praised male hirsuteness, men's toughness, their ruggedness and body warmth, we can detect traces of Aristotle's prescientific ideas on the subject of the human biological processes – ideas we have already examined which had later been taken up and developed by the notorious Greek surgeon, Claudius Gallenus.

At about the same time as the bishop of Lyon and the Alexandrian catechetical scholar had been broadcasting their ideas,

Theophilus was putting his pen to papyrus in the Syrian city of Antioch. In his *Apology to Autolycus* he shared a view of Mother Eve similar to Irenaeus and Clement. A wicked demon (also called Satan) had spoken to the first woman through the agency of a serpent. She had been deceived and had become 'the author of sin'. Such a simple view of the world, from a man.

But not all the early Christian writers shared this bleak image of our primeval mother. While most available documents conspire to present Eve as Adam's inferior partner and blame her for sin and death in the world, this interpretation is not reflected in an ancient fragment which was found appended by some faceless monk to one of the manuscripts preserving the works of Irenaeus. This fragment was attached to the manuscript because it was presumed to be an excerpt from a work of Irenaeus which had been lost. It had been extracted from Book X of the *Anagogicarum Contemplationum*, composed by a seventh century monk from Egypt, Anastasius the Sinaite. He had included the fragment in his commentary on the Genesis creation narrative entitled *Hexaemeron*.

The author had drawn on various commentaries on the Genesis creation story by Clement of Alexandria from the second/third century, for example; from Origen and the works of the Cappadocian Fathers from the fourth century; and presumably from Irenaeus. Though Anastasius claimed the excerpt could be traced to Irenaeus, scholars are now agreed he was not the author. When Wigan Harvey published his two-volume English translation of Irenaeus's *Adversus Haereses* in 1857, he expressed his doubts concerning the authenticity of this fragment. In her article published in 1978 in the Journal of Biblical Literature (vol. 92/2) Jean Higgins entertained no such doubts. She observed that neither Irenaeus in the second century nor Anastasius in the seventh century had demonstrated a pro-feminist tendency in any of their works. Knowing what she knew of him, it was difficult to imagine Irenaeus composing such a surprisingly fresh interpretation of the figure of Eve. For guidance as to its origins, she pointed to the Nag Hammadi Gnostic-Christian documents which had been discovered in 1945 in Egypt and which contained material involving strong female religious figures. The fragment was more than likely an extract from one of the works of an opponent of Irenaeus – some Gnostic source from the second-third century.

Writing in the late fourth century, the historian Epiphanius spoke of a heretical Christian movement from Phrygia in Asia Minor. The Quintillianists were followers of the prophet Montanus and his female colleagues. These heretics also had a favourable view of Mother Eve. They used to praise the first man's consort, giving thanks to her because she had been the first one to taste food from the tree of wisdom. Using her as their example, this Christian sect used to 'ordain women as bishops and presbyters' (*Panarion*, 49:2-3).

Nowhere in the early period of the church's development of theology and exegesis, however, do we find such a spirited argument in favour of Eve's superiority as appears in the 'Irenaean' fragment. It would be nice for the modern feminist to know how widespread this pro-feminine opinion was, especially among women, but the chances of finding out are slim. The author's works were not preserved by the monks and episcopal secretaries who were in charge of the ecclesiastical libraries. We are fortunate to have a fragment available.

The author of this fragment stated that in the tragic story of Genesis, Eve had shown that she was stronger than her partner, Adam.

> Why didn't the serpent prefer to make its attack upon the man instead of the woman? And if you say that it attacked her as being the weaker of the two, [I reply that], on the contrary, she was the stronger, since she appears to have been the helper of the man in the transgression of the commandment.

She had stood up against the serpent. Although she had eventually eaten the forbidden fruit, it was only after she had put up some spirited resistance. Without a word of contradiction or even a simple enquiry, however, Adam had accepted the fruit Eve had handed him. He had shown no independence of spirit. He demonstrated his weakness and cowardice, 'an indication of the utmost imbecility and effeminacy of mind'. While Eve had wrestled with the demon and had eventually been pinned to the ground, Adam had shown no moral backbone. And he had had no excuse. He had personally received the commandment from God while Eve had been excluded from the meeting. She had been judged unworthy to converse directly with God. The author suggested that she might have sinned because she suspected that Adam had made up the whole story and was misleading her.

The author of this fragment was showing a surprising originality in his interpretation of the myth, arguing Eve's case rather than Adam's. But his views would not prove attractive to future theologians and exegetes, or at least to those in charge of the scriptoria throughout Europe and beyond, who chose to copy and preserve only 'orthodox' versions of the myth.

In about the third century, an even more esoteric version of the myth of Adam and Eve made its appearance. In 1945, a Christian-Gnostic document telling the story of creation and the Fall came to light in Upper Egypt, at Nag Hammadi, and gave an original twist to the basic version narrated in the book of Genesis. According to the *Hypostasis of the Archons*, Adam and Eve (and all creation) had been the product of a conspiracy that had been hatched by lesser heavenly beings called Archons or the Rulers of darkness. These were semi-hostile powers or inorganic beings which were the last and the lowest emanations seeping out of the Godhead – servants of an inferior creator god known as the Demiurge.

According to the bewitched theological and spirit-filled worldview scrambling the minds of the members of this Christian-Gnostic sect, the ineffable, transcendent Father of all things had had a female consort-companion known by the attractive, feminine name of 'Incorruptibility'. Lower down the heavenly hierarchy were powerful female figures – Pistis Sophia and her daughter Zoe, for example, and other females with catchy nicknames such as Sagacity and Understanding. As it turned out, the Father of all things and his consort had not been involved in the creation of the material world, or in the birth of Adam and Eve. The evil Rulers of darkness had carried out this inferior work.

In the creation process described by the author of the *Hypostasis*, two Adams had been fashioned from the earth – one version had only a soul, but the second had a spirit which had eventually given him life. Two females emerged from Adam's side – a spiritual woman and a carnal one.

As servants of the Demiurge, the Rulers (or the Archons) had hypnotized Adam into a deep sleep of ignorance. They opened his side ('like a living woman' giving birth), and from this opening a creature like a living woman appeared. The Rulers closed the gap in Adam's side and a spirit-endowed woman came into being. In this process of delivering a woman, tragically, Adam had lost his spirit and was thereafter endowed only with a soul. His state of excellence had been compromised. The status of both members of the initial couple had been diminished.

When the woman roused Adam from his sleep of ignorance, he uttered a puzzling proposition that didn't seem to reflect the mysterious reality behind his existence, 'It's you who have given me my life. You will be called "Mother of the living". For she is my mother, my physician and the woman.'

The hostile powers of darkness had been disturbed as they witnessed the process unfolding. The Archons fell hopelessly in love with the woman. Being anxious to plant their seed inside her, they begun to stalk her. But she mocked them, ridiculing their stupidity. Eventually, as they grabbed hold of her, she turned herself into a tree and left a shadowy reflection which these evil Rulers proceeded to sexually defile.

The author went on to narrate the story of a snake that had swallowed a female power – another interesting twist to the myth. The serpent had begun enticing the carnal Eve to pick some mythological fruit from a mythological tree. She fell for this serpent's trick and in turn she enticed her man to do her bidding. When the leader of the Archons confronted Adam about what he'd done, of course he blamed the wife: 'The woman that you gave me, she gave the fruit to me and I ate it.'

According to the story, Eve passed on the blame and shame of her sin to the feminised snake and in the final scene of the tragedy the head Archon cursed the snake, expelled Adam and Eve from the garden and condemned them to a life of toil and worldly affairs.

The author then moved on to the great flood where we meet Eve's daughter, Norea, in deep conversation with the cruel Archons and their leader. They had planned to seduce Norea and invited her to their beds, to ravish her as they had done her mother. However, she rejected their sexual advances.

In brief, the author of the *Hypostasis* followed the same basic storyline involving some of the original Genesis characters (including the snake, now a female snake), but God had been written out of the script, and many more women appear on the Gnostic stage in this unorthodox Christian play.

The *Hypostasis of the Archons* presents an ambivalent mythical picture of the role of women in the creation of the world and in the terrifying fall from grace which was visited on Adam and his female companion. The heavenly, invisible world, as well as the material world, was peopled with a number of female figures. Lady Incorruptibility, the companion of the Father of all things, was female, as were her daughter Pistis Sophia and her grand-daughter, Zoe – all divine female figures from the upper realms. In the lower spaces, Norea, who was a spirit-filled person and a virgin, was the daughter of Eve. And there were two Eves – a carnal woman and a spiritual one – the first with a soul but no spirit, while the second was blessed with a spirit. The carnal Eve was the woman whom the snake tempted, and she had led Adam astray. She had fallen headlong into sin when she encountered the female power in the guise of a snake. In this story the reader was introduced to two worlds – a heavenly one, and an earthly one – both full of mythological women. None of these divine, heavenly female figures scored a role in the orthodox Christian version of the Godhead. In the official version the principal occupants of heaven were male – God the Father and God the Son accompanied by legions of male angels.

Now let's cross the waters from Rome to the north of Africa, to where Roman officials and citizens were speaking and writing in the Latin language.

Quintus Septimius Florens Tertullianus was probably the son of a Roman army captain serving his emperor across the sea in the wheat-belt of the empire. A trained lawyer, a gifted scholar, a bitter conservative and a fiery layman, he is the first Christian author writing in Latin available to us. The Scottish historian Diarmaid MacCulloch described him as a talented and bad-tempered high-class journalist – a maverick Roman intellectual who indulged in offensive outbursts, often against women. It seems that towards the end of his life his fanatical attraction to harsh religion led him into the ranks of the 'heterodox' followers of Montanus, which meant that he was forever smeared as a heretic. One cannot help wondering what his wife must have thought of him. Perhaps he didn't care. Or perhaps she didn't care!

When her husband picked up his quill to draw on his extensive knowledge of *haute couture* in Carthage, of female cosmetics, hairstyles and jewellery, he began by letting his readers know what he thought about women in general, and perhaps about his wife and mother-in-law in particular. As an experienced journalist he searched for an attractive opening sentence, a paragraph to capture his readers' interest and entice them into his world. Addressing the women of Carthage and drawing on the Adam-and-Eve myth, Tertullian's opening gambit proved a *tour de force* which would echo down the centuries.

> You ladies should accept that all of you is an Eve. The sentence of God on your sex continues to be lived out in this age: the guilt must of necessity also continue. You are the devil's gateway. You are the one who broke the seal on that forbidden tree. You are the one who originally abandoned the divine law. You are she who persuaded the man the devil was not strong or courageous enough to attack. With such ease you destroyed the one who bore God's image – man. On account of your rebellion and its consequences, namely death, even the Son of God had to die (*De Cultu Feminarum*, I.1).

The author was clearly striving to persuade his readers, perhaps even his female readers, that women should wear appropriate clothes. His wife may have been reading over his shoulder as he wrote, or stretched out on a reclining chair under the Carthaginian sun, covered in sunscreen, unrolling the scroll as she savoured her husband's advice to the members of her book club.

According to Tertullian, Eve had a lot to answer for. She had been the gateway, the entry point for the devil to get at humanity. This ordinary, domestic image will appear again in other places – in the twelfth century poem of Bernard of Cluny, *De contempt mundi*, for example. Unable to entrap God's Superman, Satan had got at his perfect creature through Eve and exploited her feminine weaknesses. She had been the first one to abandon God's law, the person who had destroyed God's image imprinted on Adam; she was the source of corruption in the world. She had broken the good-and-evil seal on the tree of knowledge. Her act of rebellion had meant that the Son of God was doomed to die. This is a notorious

Tertullian passage which, to bolster their sour view of the world, has been much repeated by theologians, monks and bishops of the church.

The North African author saw Eve as the primordial figure of womanhood. He considered that every Christian woman in Carthage was identified with her and duty-bound to reflect on the tragic story of their sister. She had to conduct herself in public as though she was herself an Eve, wearing a garment of penitence, of mourning and repentance. In this way she could rid herself of what she had inherited from the first woman, namely the ignominy, the humiliation of the first sin, the putrid stench that followed her as the cause of human perdition. Mrs Average from Carthage was condemned to share in Eve's sinfulness. Every woman was tainted by Eve's fall from grace. Every woman was polluted by the whiff of her forebear's evil act.

In his ultra-conservative mindset, Tertullian conflated every woman with the mythological first female. If Eve had been living at the time Tertullian was writing to his female readers, and if she had wanted to live again, he thought that she should have turned her back on all pagan objects of distraction. Eve had not possessed any feminine baubles and trinkets when she was alive, so no Christian woman should allow jewels and bangles to dominate her life. Tertullian argued his case: 'Accordingly these things are all the baggage of woman in her condemned and dead state, instituted as if to swell the pomp of her funeral.'

The Pseudo-Clementine literature is a series of writings which are of a mixed Christian-Gnostic character. It purports to deal with the life of Clement of Rome and names him (falsely) as its author. In this work of fiction the narrator tells Clement's story. Disillusioned with listening to the pagan philosophers in Rome, he had sailed for Judaea in search of 'the Son of God' and had come into contact with Peter and followed him on his missionary journeys in and out of the cities of Syria. The various chapters which make up the whole Pseudo-Clementine corpus are a romantic account of these journeys, of Peter's message and the people he and Clement had met along the way.

The history of the composition and of the circulation of this strange work is tortuous, but the details don't need to delay us, except to say that the *Kerygmata Petrou* (or *Kerygma of Peter*) forms a substantial part of the series.

The author of this *Kerygma of Peter* was writing in a mixed Jewish-Christian Gnostic milieu, probably in the middle of the third century (maybe even as early as the second century), almost certainly in the eastern region of the Mediterranean, probably somewhere in Syria, but certainly not in Rome. The author was composing his work at a time when the turbulent interaction between Judaism and Christianity had not yet settled. The Christian world was still in a state of intellectual, spiritual and theological turmoil. It was a time before the Christian churches had finally separated from those sects that were peddling 'heretical' and divisive ideas, before the tenets and structures of Christianity had hardened.

For those for whom the author of the *Kerygma of Peter* was writing, the Christological problem which would later be settled by the bishops who attended the Council of Nicaea in 325 had not yet been clarified. Jesus' death on the cross, for example, had little or no religious significance for the members of this community. The major figure underpinning the author's worldview was not a saviour or a redeemer, but 'the true prophet', the authentic voice of the Creator, the source of divine revelation and the author of the eternal law. The *Kerygma* reflects a basic Gnostic dualism which had infected the mind of the author – a dualism which can be reduced to a simple view: while man represented goodness and truth, woman controlled the dark regions of evil and error.

> The world that now is, is temporary; that which shall be is eternal. First is ignorance, then knowledge. So also had he (the

creator) arranged the leaders of prophecy. While the present world is female, like a mother bringing forth the souls of her children, the world to come is male, like a father receiving his children *from their mother*. Therefore in this world there is a succession of prophets. They are sons of the world to come and have knowledge of men. And if pious men had understood this mystery, they would never have gone astray, but even now they should have known that Simon, who enthrals all men, is a fellow worker of error and deceit (*Homily* II, ch. 15).

The dominant figure in the *Kerygma* is 'the true prophet', the bearer of divine revelation to the world. From the beginning of time and through a series of different characters, this true prophet has continued to manifest himself (*Homily* III. 20:2). Adam was his first incarnation, and like all true prophets, he had been anointed, by the oil of the Tree of Life (*Recognitions* I. 47). He was the first to be possessed by the Spirit of God (H. III.17:3).

The popular story of our first parents, the story recounted in Genesis, needed to be amended. According to the anonymous author of the *Kerygma*, Adam had committed no sin. Instead, he had been the original true prophet (H. III. 17:21.2; II. 52:2). Moses had been another figure of 'the true prophet' in the flesh (H. II. 52:2), and Jesus had also been part of the continuous line of those prophets entrusted with the mission of proclaiming the 'lawful knowledge' which showed the way forward towards the future aeon (H. III. 17-19 and XI. 19:3).

In the *Kerygma*, the female prophet is the enemy of the true prophet. During the passage of the true prophet through the dimension of time, the female prophet was at his side as his negative, left-handed syzygy-partner (H. II. 15-17). Her first appearance in flesh was in Eve, the mother of mankind, who had been created at the same time as Adam, the first true prophet (H. III. 22:25). But Eve had only pretended to be the agent of redemptive knowledge.

In fact she had led all those who followed her to their death (H. III. 24:3ff).

> But a companion was created along with him (Adam), a female nature, but very different to him, as quality is different to substance, as the moon to the sun, as fire to light. As a female ruling the present world, she was entrusted with the role of being the first prophetess, announcing prophecy to those born of woman ...

There were two kinds of prophets. The true prophet was male; the other was a woman, and she was the superintendent of this present world. She had wanted to be accepted as masculine, so she had stolen the life-giving seeds of her companion, sowed them mingled with her own seeds of flesh and presented the fruits (her words, her revelations) as wholly her own. She had announced that there were many gods, and that she was one of them. She had polluted all who touched her. In brief, her life had been a pretence.

The author went on, as the author of the book of Genesis had done, to explain human tragedy and sinfulness through the figure of this primeval prophetess. She had given birth to earth-bound kings, and through them she had stirred up wars and shed oceans of blood. She had told her devotees a series of lies and had led astray those who desired to discover the truth. From the beginning she had been the progenitor of death to those men who had followed her blindly, and by prophesying nothing but deceit, ambiguities and obscenities, she continued to deceive those who believed in her.

From his statement that this female figure had named her son Cain, we can conclude that the author was recording his own supercharged version of the Adam-and-Eve myth. At the same time, he was revealing some features of the central female figure in the story – the original false and deceitful prophet Eve. Her son had proved to be a murderer and a liar. Cain was unwilling to live at peace and accept the rule of law. As the author said, the prophetic line of Cain's descendants became adulterers (H. III. 23-25).

The author told his readers that the manifestations and revelations of the true prophet in his different guises had been adulterated and contaminated by the female prophets preaching a message of error and death – a message the evil *syzygoi* had spread among the community. In the beginning, Eve had twisted and falsified the message of the prophet Adam. The history of the world was to be seen as an unfolding drama reflected in the struggle between good and evil, between the true male prophet and the evil female prophet.

The female was the dominant figure in the dark world of visible reality and at the centre of the cosmic tragedy. She was a Lady Macbeth spreading her poison through the cosmos, and her various subsequent personifications carried out her foul mission.

The story of Adam and Eve that Paul had introduced so gently into the Christian message proved a powerful weapon in the hands of women-fearers and women-haters, of those who sought to keep women in their place, to stereotype them as fickle, brainless and associated with sin and sex.

The Transgenderisation of the Female Believers

Gradually, as the theological thinkers and spinners began to find their length, the Adam-and-Eve myth was promoted into a new dimension. The story of creation and of man's return to the stars after his trials on earth, the story as recounted by Plato to his pupils, was re-told in a different form for Christian consumption. Only men, God's perfect creatures, were destined to return to Paradise. If women wanted to participate, they would have to undergo a process of transgenderisation.

As far as Tertullian was concerned, women had no public role to play within the orthodox Christian gatherings in North Africa. They were excluded and forbidden to teach or baptise. However, again according to Tertullian, God had planned that women would share in the resurrection on the last day. Eve would enjoy the same forever life as her Adam, but Tertullian had his own ideas as to how Eve would advance to the promised land.

> For you too, (women as you are) have the self-same angelic nature promised as your reward, the very same sex as men: the Lord promises you the very same promotion to the dignity of judging (*De cultu feminarum* I. 2:5).

While Plato and Aristotle (and many inhabitants of the ancient world of faith and superstition) would have easily understood what Tertullian was driving at, this is a curious statement for a modern believer or reader. As their reward, women could receive the same angelic nature as men. They were destined (presumably by God) to advance to the dignity of judges and have 'the very same sex as men' – '*idem sexus qui et viris*' – or literally 'the same sex which also belonged to men'.

Did Tertullian mean what he seems to have said? That women would participate in eternal life only after they had been transformed into men? Or both had been transmorphed into sexless (or asexual) beings? Was a final transgendering an inevitable precondition for Christian women? Was heaven to be populated by men only? This may explain why Jesus was supposed to have said that there was no marrying or giving in marriage in heaven: 'For in the resurrection they neither marry nor are given in marriage, but are like angels in heaven' (Matt 22:30).

This notion of women being transformed into men before they could re-enter Paradise can be traced to the theological world of the thirteenth apostle and further back to the mystical-philosophical world of Plato. In his letter to the Galatians Paul was writing about the significance of baptism, and about the life of any baptised believer, and (it has been assumed) about the equality of the sexes:

> For as many of you as were baptised into Christ have put on Christ. There is neither Jew nor Greek, there is neither slave nor freeman, there is neither male nor female, for you are all one in Christ Jesus (Gal 3:27–28).

In the new reality created by baptism, in the world of angels and the Spirit where believers live, there was no distinction drawn between the citizens. All were equal. No-one was more pre-eminent than anyone else, slaves or free.

But his pithy observation to the Galatians has been given some unwarranted attention. Because of a mistranslation of Paul's saying (as it appears in the English above), those who have a radical bent in their theology have regarded the aphorism as a knock-out blow to all the conservative voices frozen in a pseudo-tradition, an explosive little box of incendiary devices to put fear into the hearts of patriarchs who support the policy of female invisibility in the church, and a rallying cry for those who persist in their longing for change. According to the translators, Paul was in favour of gender equality and would perhaps have voted for female ordination.

But we have to look again, and this time more closely, at Paul's aphorism.

The translators of the Revised Standard Version (published in 1946 and reprinted twenty years later as the official Catholic Edition) has Paul telling his Galatian readers that in the past they had been subject to the law, living in legal chains in the period before the coming of Christ. But with his coming and by the power of their faith, they had all been released to live in freedom – everybody, no-one excluded. Whoever was baptised had entered into a saving relationship with Christ the Lord. Equality before the Lord was the hallmark of the new dispensation. A radical, existential equality. In one simple abstract statement, Paul was giving expression to the essence of Jesus' kingdom message.

However, while Paul was saying that because of their baptism, God did not distinguish or discriminate between Jews and Gentiles, between slaves and freemen or women, Paul was not necessarily adopting the position that under the new law of the Kingdom, women were equal to men in any way we would understand. The short passage from Paul's letter has generally been mistranslated and then misquoted. In his Vulgate, the exegete *par excellence* didn't get it right either, or the translator of the Revised Standard Version of the Bible, or the English or French version of the Jerusalem Bible. For example:

'Non est Judaeus neque Graecus; non est servus neque liber; non est masculus neque femina' (The Vulgate).

An accurate translation of the original Greek text should read, 'Now *for those who have been baptised in Christ* there is neither Jew nor Greek; neither slave nor free-man; *there is no longer male and female ...*'

Some commentators have seen in the phrase 'male and female' an allusion to the account of the creation of Adam and Eve in the book of Genesis. In Genesis we read 'male and female he created them'. These commentators observed that in this passage from Galatians, the author was saying that the old regime which God had inaugurated at the beginning of creation – the whole Genesis regime involving sex and marriage had ended. There was no longer 'male and female', but only a believer who has been baptised into Christ. A loss of one's identity as a Jew or a Greek, a slave or a free person, and as a human being, was replaced by a new identity as a baptised being. No longer was it 'male and female', but heavenly, spiritual beings, whether a man or a woman. No gender differentiation in heaven. Gender differences become irrelevant by baptism. Being baptised 'in Christ' meant that all believers, previously divided into male and female, were like God's original, perfect creature, a sex-less, unaccompanied but perfect male as Adam was before Eve had been fashioned from his rib.

If this interpretation is what Paul had in mind it would provide a basis for future writers developing a theological view suggesting that when a person, man or woman, was baptised, by living as a celibate, as a virgin, and withdrawing from 'the world', he or she was called to an angelic life. Called to become angels and judges of angels (as Jerome would later claim), to be perfect, heavenly creatures, new Adams all of us, male and female alike.

Angels were male. All perfect human beings were male. All women should have been male and would have to be transformed into males before they could be allowed entrance into Paradise. Now no longer 'male and female' as God the Creator had created humankind when he saw that his perfect creature was alone in the Garden, but now transformed by Christ, elevated into a new realm, into a completely different world. And in this new world were only angels, only the baptised, only perfect human beings. And therefore if a person wanted to enter into glory, he had to be a male, a man like Adam.

However, this was not Jesus' way of thinking, at least as we have come to know him from the Gospel stories. He had lived in the real world with his feet on the ground. The kingdom he had inaugurated was present among us here on earth. A new way of thinking and behaving here in this world. Paul, however, took his readers into a world away from Jesus. He had the believer living in a new dimension, in a new world, as a heavenly creature, in the clouds and removed from the earth.

There was a popular belief at the time of Tertullian that before catastrophes such as the great flood or the destruction of Sodom, the human race used to eat and drink (to excess), buy and sell, plant and build, carrying on living a normal life, marry and 'give in marriage' as though nothing was going to disrupt the flow of daily life. But then, suddenly, mundane existence would end and a new, radically different world would erupt into existence – or else, the old, original world would be reconstituted. Tertullian believed that as a logical consequence there would be no women in heaven – only men – angelic men, and of course no possibility of sexual entanglements.

At about the same time, further round the Mediterranean coast, Clement was dealing with the same general question – the transgendering of women – but in the context of the Adam-and-Eve myth which had also infected some of the current schools of Gnosticism. Dealing with the Gnostic school established under the name of Valentinus, Clement wrote,

> The Valentinians say that the final emanation of Wisdom is spoken of in the passage, 'He created them in the image of God, male and female he created them.' Now the males from this emanation are the 'election', but the females are the 'calling'. They call the male beings angelic, and the females themselves, the superior seed. So also, in the case of Adam, the male remained in him, but all the female seed was taken from him and became Eve, from whom the females are derived, as the

males are from him. Therefore the males are drawn together with the Logos, but the females, becoming men, are united to the angels and pass into the Pleroma. Therefore the woman is said to be changed into a man and the church here on earth into angels (*Excerpts from Theodotus*, Sect. A. 21:3).

It's difficult to make much sense of this passage, I agree. But, putting to one side the twists and knots a modern reader may detect in Clement's brain, the overall message emerges that, according to this Christian-Gnostic sect (the Valentinians), males were perfect and females weren't. Further, Adam had originally been a mixture of male and female. While the female seeds in him had been removed to form Eve, he remained male. Males were really angels, and females would eventually become males before they passed into the pleroma.

In this Gnostic world, the female represented all that was earthy, fleshy, worldly, material, and subject to decay. The male, on the other hand, was associated with the spirit, the mind, truth, perfection and the world above and beyond. Women, Eve, sin, flesh and sex were associated in the Gnostic mindset, as well as in the minds of more orthodox thinkers, and even in the mind of the great philosopher Plato and his followers.

Many of the Gnostics of the second and third centuries believed that salvation would be achieved when the distinction between male and female was erased. Their radical dualistic system involved the final dissolution of the female world. The female dimension of reality was merely temporary. It was that part of the divine world which had become involved in the created world, in human history and it was therefore associated with sin and suffering.

Ultimately, as Plato had taught in his *Timaeus*, the female would be absorbed back into the male where it had come from, into the spiritual, into the eternal, and ultimately into the Logos.

Femininity was doomed to extinction. Or as Aristotle had taught, the female was inferior. She was a misbegotten male. Something had gone awry in the process of her conception and birth. He would have agreed with the idea that when all was restored to perfection, when the world was finally complete, it would be populated by perfect creatures only – that is, by men.

Writing in Rome around the beginning of the third century, the firebrand and divisive theologian Hippolytus (whom some thought had been a pupil of Irenaeus) was informing his readers that those arriving at the gates of heaven had to cast off their clothing and become, all of them, bridegrooms, changing into males under the influence of 'the virgin spirit'. As men and women arrived in the heavenly world, they all had to undress and show that they are all bridegrooms, not brides – all males, with their sexual parts neatly arranged or rearranged on the outside of their naked bodies (*Refutation of All Heresies* 5, 8:44).

The Passion of SS Perpetua and Felicity recounts the story of two girls named Perpetua and Felicity who had been martyred in North Africa during the Severian persecution. Perpetua was a young woman of noble birth who was facing death with her recently born child at her breast. Felicity was her prison companion, a slave and pregnant at the time. They were executed together at local military games which were being staged in 203 AD to celebrate the birthday of the emperor.

Although it was later heavily edited (some have suggested by Tertullian who was also from Carthage, but in any event, certainly by a man, and most probably by a monk), some scholars believe that this story was originally written by Perpetua herself. The account of her visions and death was written in the first person and reads like a personal diary she had kept in prison. If this is true (and putting the authorship of the *Gospel of Mary* to one side), the imaginative and rather surreal account of a mother's prison dreams and martyrdom is the first and only surviving document from before the fourth century that we know to have been written by a female author.

In *The Passion*, Perpetua is telling her story and in the middle of a description of one of her spiritual visions, she is recounting the life-and-death contest she was condemned to fight against an Egyptian warrior 'horrible in appearance'. She tells her readers that she was assisted in her struggle by a group of 'handsome youths'. In preparation for this fight, and without explanation, she said she 'was stripped, and became a man', and her helpers began to rub her with oil 'as is the custom for a contest.'

For some obscure reason known to the ancients, her femaleness, her femininity had been an insurmountable barrier to martyrdom. Women were too weak, too fickle to be confronted with a life-and-death challenge like that. So Perpetua had to be transformed into a male before she could face martyrdom and be transported immediately to heaven. Christians believed that martyrs were taken up straight to heaven. But they also believed that in order to be eligible to enter heaven, the entrant had to be like Adam. He had to be a genuine male. The problem was, how were females facing martyrdom going to be accommodated within this system of belief? A neat solution to a troubling theological problem was to transgender them before they met the ultimate test. Like Perpetua, the martyred mother, they had to become men, and all would be well.

The *Gospel of Thomas* is a collection of the hidden sayings of Jesus that were put together during the second century (some think maybe even towards the end of the first century). The author pretended that the text had been dictated by Jesus to his brother, Thomas the Twin, who had recorded some of the original sayings of Jesus. But this Jesus is a universe away from the Jesus we meet in the narratives of the four canonical Gospels. The mysterious figure we find in this Thomas Gospel is of someone who had come under the influence of the Sophists, of people such as Diogenes, Plato and Socrates.

In the saying numbered 114, a tension had arisen which involved Mary Magdalene and Peter – a tension which was probably part of the life of the Christian communities of the period. In a brief interchange, if the author is to be believed, Peter displayed an impatient, chauvinist attitude towards women and revealed a sexist view of the world – a view contrary to the attitude of Jesus as portrayed in the four canonical Gospels. Far from correcting Peter, Jesus answered with some quite strange remark. He would assist Mary to become a man like the other apostles. As the story was told, Simon Peter, as leader of the apostles, had said to Jesus and his followers, 'Mary should leave us, for females are not worthy of life'.

As far as he was concerned, Mary shouldn't have been present as part of Jesus' inner-circle. She was after-all only a woman and not worthy in the life Jesus had come to share with mankind. But Jesus replied,

> Look, I shall guide her to make her male, so that she too may become a living spirit resembling you males. For every female who makes herself male will enter heaven's kingdom (*Saying* 114).

Peter appeared hostile to Mary Magdalene because, being only a woman, she was like all women, 'not worthy of life', that is, of a life beyond the grave.

How can a modern reader make any sense of what Peter was saying, and perhaps appreciate where he was coming from? Hadn't he been with Jesus and witnessed how his Master had turned his world upside down and included women in his life and ministry? But, according to the text, Jesus didn't correct Peter's view of the world, namely that women should be excluded. In fact this Jesus seems to have shared Peter's view. He sought to put Peter's anxiety to rest by assuring him that he would guide his special friend so that she would be transformed into a male, into a living spirit resembling

Peter and his brothers. Remember, to enter the Kingdom, every woman had to make herself a male.

What world did this second-century anonymous composer of Jesus' sayings imagine Jesus and his friend Peter had inhabited? What did he think was going on in Jesus' mind as he was putting words to his version of Jesus?

Some Christian Gnostics believed that through some secret *gnosis*, some mysterious knowledge revealed from the world beyond, humans could transform the earthly, perishable, passive and sense-perceptible elements in their make-up and become rational, heavenly beings. In order to participate in the life of the Spirit, in order to be liberated from the world and float freely among the angels, earthly female characteristics had to be absorbed and transformed into the rational and spiritual features of masculinity.

This transformation of the female into the male (and sometimes the reverse process of male into female, as well as a metamorphosis of men to animals) was a theme which had been explored from time to time in ancient literature. While the change- over was sometimes viewed in a metaphorical sense, some authors understood it as a literal transformation. Some authors, Ovid for example, had told fantastic stories of women developing male genitalia. This was probably a throwback to Aristotle's and Galen's pseudo-scientific analysis of the human body where the difference between males and females was that in males, the genital organs which men and women had in common were outside the body. Basically, as we have seen, women were the same as men, though badly formed (or badly 'cooked'). Plato had also indulged in dreams of this kind, in his *Timaeus* dialogue.

The Christian-Gnostic composer of the *Gospel of Thomas* was in good company believing that women had to become men before they could enter the Kingdom. A Sethian Gnostic writer from the early third century, Zostrianos, at the end of his treatise, advised his readers that in order to avoid death they should not entrust themselves to inferior beings but to 'those who are better'.

> Flee from the madness and the bondage of femaleness and choose for yourselves the salvation of maleness. You have not come to suffer; rather, you have come to escape your bondage (131).

The *Dialogue of the Saviour* was one of the many Christian-Gnostic documents discovered in 1945 as part of the Nag Hammadi library. The text is principally made up of a series of conversations and speeches of Jesus and, as Helmut Koester and Elaine Pagels have observed, traces of some of the words of Jesus which appear in the manuscript can be found in *The Gospel of Thomas* and in three of the canonical Gospels (Matthew, Luke and John). Scholars generally agree that this document appeared in its final, redacted form in about the middle of the second century, though Koester and Pagels see signs of a somewhat earlier appearance, sometime towards the beginning of the second.

A number of features of this document have led scholars to the conclusion that the composer or composers (all of whom remain anonymous) drew on a variety of written sources to produce the version which we now have in Coptic. The bulk of the contents consists of conversations Jesus had with a few of his disciples – with Judas Thomas, Mary Magdalene and Matthew. The other source-material consists of a creation myth that was based on Genesis 1–2; in a cosmological list interpreted in the wisdom tradition and in a sequence involving an apocalyptic vision. We need not delay over this material. The main source on which the composer(s) relied, and which interests us, was a collection of what was thought to be the sayings of Jesus, though sometimes the disciples' questions and the Saviour's answers were expanded into longer units discussing a particular topic.

In one section of the document Jesus appears in conversation with three disciples, including Mary Magdalene, and Matthew who was questioning him about death and life.

Matthew said, 'Tell me, Lord, how the dead die, and how the living live.'

The Lord said, 'You have asked me about a saying ... which eye has not seen, nor have I heard it, except from you. But I say to you, when what moves a person slips away, that person will be called dead, and when what is living leaves what is dead, it will be called alive ...'

Judas said, 'Why else, for the sake of truth, do they die and live?'

The Lord said, 'Whatever is born of truth does not die. Whatever is born of woman does die' (*Nag Hammadi Codex* III, 5: 140).

Perhaps we can conclude that the author is telling his reader that Jesus had revealed to his followers that there is a fundamental divide between what is 'born of truth' and what is 'born of woman', and while one aspect of reality survives, the other simply dies.

A little later, Mary Magdalene was asking Jesus to tell them about the mustard seed (which was one of Jesus' images of the kingdom he was preaching): 'Is it something from heaven or is it something from earth?'

This was a good question, and one we would like Jesus to have answered. I have concluded that Jesus' kingdom was meant to be 'something from earth', an earth-bound reality, and that Jesus was not thinking in terms of a contrast or distinction between heaven and earth. That dualistic thought-pattern was not typical of the Semitic mind. It made an appearance in the letters of Paul who, although he had been a Jew and an educated Pharisee, had been a man of the Greco-Roman world – the world of Plato and his followers, and of various Gnostic schools of thought and mystery cults.

But as happens sometimes in the original four Gospels and regularly in these Gnostic texts, the answer Jesus was reported as giving seemed to bear no relation to the question or supply any useful information. Jesus' answer to Mary's question was obscure:

> 'When the Father established the cosmos for himself, he left much over from the Mother of the All. Therefore, he speaks and he acts.'

It is difficult to know what Jesus meant, or who 'the Mother of the All' might have been, though she clearly was a Gnostic figure. The Gnostic mind worked on a dualistic motif or pattern.

Judas interrupted the conversation with a Delphic observation – and a request about prayer that we can read also in the canonical Gospels: 'You have told us this out of the mind of truth. When we pray, how should we pray?'

This time Jesus gave a clear answer, but one charged with an attitude that was atypical of the Jesus we meet in the four Gospels:

> 'Pray in the place where there is no woman.'

This was not a politically correct answer, and Jesus gave it in the presence of one of his disciples, the woman with whom he was supposed to have had an especially affectionate relationship. But we must ask, where would such a place have been? What was Jesus thinking of? A monastery? That area of the Saturday or Sunday assembly reserved exclusively for men? Or in heaven, perhaps?

According to the Gnostic author, Matthew repeated Jesus' direction, interpreted it and explained it for the reader:

> 'Pray in the place where there is no woman,' he tells us, meaning, 'Destroy the works of womanhood,' not because there is any other manner of birth but because they will cease giving birth.

Again, this 'explanation' is puzzling to any modern reader. These Gnostic Christians saw their mission as a drive to destroy 'the world of womanhood', the visible, material world, the world of emotions and sensations, because according to God's plan, while women were initially created to procreate and to populate the earth, at the end of time her work would be done and she would be redundant.

But returning to the conversation, Mary was apparently not convinced:

'They will never be obliterated.'

While Jesus was not so sure, Judas' mind was clear on the subject. Jesus said:

'Who knows that they will not dissolve and ...' [unfortunately two lines are missing in the manuscript].

Judas said to Matthew:

'The works of womanhood will dissolve ...'

According to the author of this dialogue, when there was no further need to continue the human race, when all mankind was on its way to heaven, this birth role for women would be superfluous. They and their work would naturally disappear. At that time we will be praying in a place where there is no distraction, no temptation, no sex and no women – namely, in heaven.

Another document from the Nag Hammadi library witnesses to the same theme. In the *First Apocalypse of James* (41:15–19) the author observed that when the perishable had ascended into the eternal, 'the element of femaleness has attained to the element of this maleness'. And females would merge into this superior element.

Clement in Alexandria, writing at the turn of the second century or the commencement of the third, shared the same peculiar view of some orthodox Christians and some Gnostics – that in the end women would disappear.

For example, in an early second-century document written between 125 and 150 AD, the *Greek Gospel of the Egyptians*, as reported by Clement, we read that God had appeared to Salome and revealed that death would retain its power as long as 'you women' bear children (*Stromata* III:6,45). Elsewhere in the same document, we learn something new – that the Kingdom would come when the male became one with the female (but not in any sexual encounter), when there is no masculinity or femininity:

> When you have trampled on the robe of shame and when the two shall become one, and the male with the female, and there is neither male nor female (*Stromata* III:13,92).

Though it might come as a shock to careful readers of the canonical Gospels, Clement claimed that Jesus had said,

> I have come to destroy the works of the female – by the 'female' meaning female lust, by the 'works', birth and corruption" (Stromata III:9,63).

As far as we know, Jesus never said anything like this. Although very little of his writings have survived, Theodotus had been an important figure in the Gnostic Valentinian School flourishing in Alexandria. The *Excerpta ex Theodoto* is a collection of notes compiled by Clement. They deal mainly with the teachings of Theodotus, though it also addresses other Valentinian and 'orthodox' speculations. In this collection, Theodotus quoted one of the Gnostic sayings:

> For as long as we were children of the female only (as though the product of a base intercourse, incomplete and infants and senseless and weak and without form, brought forth like abortions), we were children of the woman, but when we have received form from the Saviour, we have become children of men' (*Excerpts from Theodotus* 68).

And presumably as 'children of men' we become children of reason and of perfect balance since these were the qualities associated with God's perfect creature.

As long as the seed is still unformed, they say, it is an offspring of the female. But when it is formed, it is changed into a man and becomes a son of the bridegroom. It is no longer weak and subject to the cosmic forces, both visible and invisible, but, having been made masculine, it becomes a male fruit (*Excerpts from Theodotus*, 79).

For some Gnostics and some more 'orthodox' Christians, salvation for women was a process of 'transgenderisation'. To enter heaven, women had to return to their original form. The primordial balance had to be restored. God had created his perfect creature in the Garden of Paradise – a man after his own image and likeness. It was only at a later stage that he created Eve, from the body of Adam – 'male and female he created them'. But at the conclusion of a woman's earthly life, and before entering heaven, when she was of no further use in producing offspring, she had to become again part of God's original creation and return to where she had come from – back to the image and likeness of God in the form of a man.

This sexist view of the world was common among Christians and others, and much later even found expression among the theologians of the Middle Ages.

However, in the face of this strange view that women would have to return to their origins and change into men before entering the Kingdom, Tertullian seems to have had an even more radical view. He thought that both men and women would have to be transmogrified since both were destined by God to enjoy an angelic existence in heaven. Both would become 'as angels'. Human flesh would be 'angelified' (*De anima* 26:7), or would receive an angelic covering – '*habitum angelicum*' (*De anima* 42:4). 'They will be like angels. They will be transposed in an angelic state.' (*Similes enim erunt angelis transituri in statum angelicum*)' (*De anima* 36:5).

At the beginning of his treatise on women's fashions, Tertullian's vision for the end of time became clear. He saw 'us', men and women, seated on 'that future judgment-seat' and pronouncing a sentence on all the fallen angels whose gifts had been bestowed from the beginning of creation on women – the gifts 'we all seek after'. Addressing women, Tertullian told them that as their reward they had been promised a truly angelic nature, given the same sexual nature as men, and a promotion to the dignified status of judges.

As the years passed (and to step out of our time zone for a moment) the doctrine of transgenderisation of female believers became more popular. Jerome was persuaded that once a woman could liberate herself from her body, from her sexuality, her passions and dreams, she would enjoy a truly spiritual existence as a male. In a letter to Lucinius and his wife Theodora who had both taken a vow of chastity, he told them that Theodora had once been a woman, but that she was now a man – once inferior, but now equal. She was a wife who had become a sister – a woman who had become a man (Ep. 71).

In his *Commentary on the Epistle to the Ephesians*, Jerome would take up this Platonic theme of female transgendering:

> As long as woman is for birth and children, she is different from man as body is from soul. But when she wishes to serve Christ more than the world, then she will cease to be a woman and will be called man (*vir*). (*Sin autem Christo magis voluerit servire quam saeculo, mulier esse cessait, et dicetur vir*). (*Comm. in Ep. Ad Eph.* III 5:28)

And further on, commenting on Ephesians Chapter 5 verses 28–29:

> Husbands should love their wives as their own bodies. He who loves his wife, loves himself. For no man ever hates his own flesh, but nourishes and cherishes it, as Christ does the church, because we are members of his body.

Jerome invited his readers to cherish their wives so that 'wives might be converted into men, and our bodies into souls'. (*Foveamus igitur et viri uxores et animae nostra corpora, ut et uxores in viros, et corpora redigantur in animas.*) (*Comm. in Ep. Ad Eph.* III).

In his *Exposition of the Gospel of St Luke*, Ambrose of Milan (a contemporary of Jerome and Augustine), who would become one of the four Doctors of the Latin Church, expressed similar views. In order to be saved, a woman had to surrender her femininity to become fully human, that is, to become a male:

> She who does not believe is a woman and should be designated by the name of her sex, whereas she who believes progresses to perfect manhood, to the measure of the adulthood of Christ. She then dispenses with the name of her sex, the seductiveness of youth, the garrulousness of old age (Book X n. 161).

An interesting gloss on the same theme (to return the female to her original male form) would appear later in Asia Minor around the middle of the fourth century. The bishop of Ancyra wanted to advise the virgins under his pastoral care about what they had to do to conserve their gift of virginity. He was one of those rare ecclesiastical leaders who were worldly-wise enough to appreciate the blinding power of the sexual drive – in women.

Just because a young woman had consecrated herself to a life of virginity didn't mean she was not open to experience the eruptions of sexual desires deep within her body. The sexual drive was not the exclusive domain of man. The bishop realised that, like everybody, a river of sensuality cascaded through every consecrated virgin. A touch, a glance, a simple kiss could create ripples in her flesh just as the touch of a snake could cause the entire body to shiver and shake (*De virginitate tuenda*, PG. 30: 677, 681 & 700). According to him, there was no such thing as sexual innocence, even among children or eunuchs.

In his treatise *On the Preservation of Virginity*, the bishop advised his virgins that they had to adopt a strict code of sexual avoidance – and that meant they had to develop the firm, muscular body-contours of a man. This was the only effective way for a virgin to protect herself from unwelcome advances while she was on earth. She had to take on the characteristics of a man and suppress her femininity. She had to walk like a man, speak like one and adopt an unnatural, masculine brusqueness (PG. 30:708).

Here on earth virgins had to protect themselves by pretending to be men. On the way to the next world they would need to be transgendered back into their primordial state as God's perfect creatures. Jesus' message had travelled far from an oasis in Palestine, out into the desert areas of Asia Minor and beyond.

A Toxic View of Women

The early Christian writers (Paul, the author of the Pastoral Epistles, Tertullian, Irenaeus, Origen, Clement and others) were not at home in the world in the same way Jesus had been. Each of them, in his own way, was a stranger in his society, frightened by the devil, by the power of sexual urges, governed by a deep fear of women and their power to destroy. Their attention was not focussed on the kingdom Jesus had preached but on a future existence somewhere else. They saw themselves surrounded by the works of the devil whose aim was to tempt a man to commit the predominant sin of fornication. While Jesus had lived in the world as a member of society and of the human race, and seems to have related with ease and grace to all kinds of people, these men were surviving in an alien world, living as critics of society, relating mainly to members of their own sect.

In the post-apostolic period, during the second and third centuries, the Christian authors – at least, the ones whose writings have been preserved by the monks of the middle ages – were full of cautionary advice to men, especially young men who might be inclined to give into temptation. These authors were bishops, exegetes, theologians and polemists. Some of them seemed to be particularly interested in the world of women's fashions and beauty products. Some showed themselves curiously well-informed on the subject, keen to pay close attention to the ways of women, and ready to condemn them. The faith movement had travelled many miles from the simple dictates of Jesus as recorded in the Gospels. Jesus' visionary message of service to all, of care for the poor and oppressed had become obscured behind the controversies, the power struggles, the rules and guidelines to regulate behaviour, maintain standards, keep men safe and sinless – and keep women in their proper place.

The Testament of Reuben

The Testaments of the Twelve Patriarchs purports to record the dying wishes of the twelve sons of Jacob, and was eventually recognised as part of biblical apocalyptic literature. It is obvious that as a matter of historical fact the testaments had nothing to do with the original twelve patriarchs. The earliest Christian reference to these testaments can be traced to Origen who quoted from a Greek version of the text in about 200 AD, so they come from an early period.

The literary form of a testament (or a farewell discourse) was well known both in Jewish circles and in the Greco-Roman world. It came in the form of a speech which was delivered by a famous personage (always a man) addressing his children or his followers before his death and giving them the benefit of his life-experience. It was often a constructed oration by some imaginary admirer. A well-known example of such testaments would be Jesus' Last Discourse in the Gospel of John, Chapters 13–17.

The Testaments of the Twelve Patriarchs was modelled on Jacob's blessings of his twelve sons in Genesis 49. The anonymous author or authors of the collection imagined each of the twelve patriarchs addressing his blessing, his last discourse to his son.

While these twelve testaments had reached their final written form in the second century AD, scholars are divided as to whether they were originally Jewish documents which Christian writers later retouched to give them a fresh, Christian tone, or Christian documents from the start, written in the first or second century, originally in Greek but based on some earlier material in the Semitic language. Since the text was made up of both Jewish and Christian elements, its origin could swing in either direction, though no Semitic original of the document as we have it has as yet been discovered. Suffice to say that this religious text was circulating among Christians as early as the second century.

One of the testaments, the *Testament of Reuben*, is concerned with the sinfulness of one of the patriarchs and with the universal human passion of lust. Reuben had engaged in an illicit sexual relationship with one of his father's concubines. According to his testament, Reuben had been perving on his de-facto mother-in-law as she was bathing naked in an enclosed garden and he had been smitten with lustful desires.

This *Testament of Reuben* witnesses to the twisted attitudes and anti-feminist prejudices found in some of the Christian literature of the second and third centuries and which were presumably infecting the spiritual and social lives of its readers. Many of the contemporary authors whose works have survived portrayed the daughters of Eve (women in general) as the cause of the downfall of the angels and of mankind in general. The flesh, illicit sex, pleasure, original sin, evil, the devil, Eve and women were all caught up in a vortex of male anxiety and misogyny. Women were defined by their sexuality, associated with concupiscence and portrayed as temptresses. Because of their sexual nature, beauty and voluptuousness, because of the hidden parts of their body which sent a man's mind and imagination into a spin, they were thought of as the source of evil in the world. 'For evil are women, my children.'

The *Testament of Reuben* comes in the form of an extended metaphor. In the story, Reuben is seen talking to his boys, telling them not to look at women, not to associate privately with married women or meddle in their affairs. He tells them that he would never have sinned had he not seen his father's concubine bathing alone. Once he had glimpsed her naked body, he couldn't sleep peacefully until he'd taken possession of her. Consequently, while Bilhal was intoxicated, naked on her bed, Reuben tiptoed in, gazed at her nakedness and ravaged her while she slept. As he told his sons, he paid the price of his abominable act for the rest of his life.

Based on his bitter personal experience, the patriarch was anxious to advise his sons how to behave honourably. He warned them to pay no heed to the beauty of women or get involved in their affairs. Young men had to learn to wait patiently until the Lord provided a suitable wife for each of them. Fornication destroyed the soul by separating it from God, by clouding the mind and condemning a man to the worship of a false god.

Young men should realise that women are dangerous, that since they had no physical superiority over their men, they plotted to find secret ways to entice them into their clutches. The author had Reuben tell his offspring of a terrifying revelation he had received – that the angel of God had informed him that women were dominated by a spirit of fornication which was more powerfully embedded in them than in men. The Alexandrian theologian, Clement, would agree with Reuben. He regarded women as having 'strong propensities to lust'. By beautifying themselves, according to the imaginary Reuben, women led men astray and put their minds into a dizzy spin. By the way they fluttered their eyes, like spiders they injected poison and took their prey captive.

Basing his advice on the myth of the fallen angels (or as they were known, 'the Watchers'), Reuben continued the story told in Genesis 6 (a story retold later by Enoch), that before the flood, women had been responsible for the tragic fate of the fallen angels. He said:

> Pay no heed, therefore, my children, to the beauty of women, nor set your mind on their affairs; but walk in singleness of heart in the fear of the Lord, and expend labour on good works, and on study and on your flocks, until the Lord give you a wife, whom He will, that ye suffer not as I did.
>
> For a woman can't force a man openly but by looking like a harlot she beguiles him. Flee, therefore, fornication, my children, and

command your wives and your daughters, that they adorn not their heads and faces to deceive the mind: because every woman who employs these wiles hath been reserved for eternal punishment. In this way they also allured the Watchers who were before the flood. While they continued to stare at them, they lusted after them and conceived the act of intercourse in their mind. They changed themselves into the shape of men, and appeared to them when they were with their husbands. Lusting in their minds after their forms, the women gave birth to giants, for the Watchers appeared to them as reaching even unto heaven (ch. 5).

The author of the *Testament of Reuben* addressed his advice to young men, warning them of the dangers involved in allowing themselves to stray close to women and to become victims mesmerised by what they had to offer. It is significant that no document from the period exists which provides a similar warning to young women about the dangers men presented to their virtue or virginity. Men were the focus of attention. At that stage, authors were speaking to men – about women. In the overall scheme of things women were the ever-present danger, the temptresses, the sexual aggressors. They were agents of the devil and relatives of Eve.

Tertullian had also been familiar with the creation myth of raunchy angels who had fallen out of the sky, fallen in love and had become sexually entangled with the beautiful daughters-of-men on earth, and who were paying the price for their lusting. Their sinful co-habitation had produced a mythical tribe of giants.

In the author's theological worldview, women had been responsible for seducing the angels and since they bore the shame of the angels' tragic fall from grace (*De cultu feminarum* I. 2:1 and *De oratione* 22:5–6), he thought they had to hide themselves within a safe fortress, and redeem themselves by making sure they were never again a cause of temptation either to men or to angels.

'Those angels who rushed from heaven on to the daughters-of-men have been condemned to death, and their ignominy also taints all women.'

In a dark age of faith and superstition, when ordinary people, bishops, scholars and lay-folk were less informed, it was believed that angels had revealed to the daughters-of-men the power of certain hidden substances and had taught them a number of secret 'scientific arts'. They had uncovered the natural properties of herbs, revealed formulae of enchantments and disclosed the mysteries of the heavens and the stars. They had brought to earth and gifted to women the instruments of feminine adornment, medicines and dyes for clothing, black powder for eyelids and lashes. They had dressed the ladies with jewels such as necklaces and gold bangles. All these gifts had come down to them on the wings of fallen angels, from illicit lovers, from renegade spirits.

The book of Genesis (6:1-8) had recorded the basic story of these rebellious angels. The 'sons of God' ('the Watchers') had been enchanted by the daughters-of-men down below. These earthly creatures had been fair and extremely desirable. Naturally, the smitten angels had 'gone into them' (or 'rushed onto them' as Tertullian would say) and bore children who were known as 'the mighty men'.

The same myth of male angels and glorious, earth-bound females was recorded in the *Book of Watchers*, which had appeared in written form before about 170 BC. The same myth would be expanded and retold in the *First Book of Enoch*. The author of this first book claimed to have received revelations (which he committed to writing) about the origin of evil, about angels and their invasion of the terrestrial world, and about other apocalyptic events.

This Jewish literature was known to members of the early church. A passage from *First Enoch* (1:9), for example, had been quoted in the Letter of Jude, which in turn would later become part of the New Testament canon. Another passage had been quoted in the *Epistle of Barnabas* which was in turn falsely ascribed to the apostle by Clement of Alexandria, but which was more probably written between 70 and 100 AD by an anonymous Christian from Alexandria. Justin the Roman Martyr, Irenaeus of Lyon, Clement and Origen from Alexandria, were all familiar with the *Book of Enoch*. Although other Christian writers didn't share his opinion, Tertullian regarded the document as part of Sacred Scripture (De Cultu Feminarum I. 3:1).

The beginning of Enoch's story about the fallen angels had been virtually identical with an earlier version in the book of Genesis, but it was destined over time to blossom into a fully embellished myth.

At one stage (now buried in the distant past) the sons of man had produced a sodality of 'fair and beautiful daughters' – so beautiful indeed that when the angels caught just a glimpse of these young girls, the besotted heavenly creatures had lusted after them. They had descended to earth. Each had chosen a wife (all angels of course were males) and generated a tribe of stunning offspring. But before these events had unfolded, when the leader of the bewitched angels had realised that he and his followers had been planning 'a great sin' with these beautiful, earth-bound virgins, he had insisted they join wings and agree that they were all in the venture together, that no-one would break ranks, desert the team and return to heaven.

Everything went to script. The angels engaged the daughters in conversation, folded them in their wings and shared their secret charms and spells with them. The promiscuous angels 'went into' the beautiful daughters-of-men. As a consequence, the daughters had given birth to giant offspring who proceeded to devour whatever mankind was producing on earth, and when they had exhausted the supply of nature's produce, they had turned on men to satisfy their hunger.

This was an ugly story about the world. When these rampaging giants had sinned against the birds and animals, reptiles and fish, when they had begun to devour each other and drink blood, Mother Earth had complained bitterly about these lawless angels and the evil daughters-of-men. In the story, one of the terrorising angels, Azazel, had taught men how to make swords, daggers, shields and breastplates, and had instructed women how to fashion bracelets and ornaments, how to paint their eyes and beautify their eyelids, how to identify precious stones and use different coloured dyes. Evil was hard at work.

The whole world was in turmoil – creation had become twisted and corrupted. Fornication was rampant. The angels were teaching their stunning wives the hidden art of casting spells and removing them, the secrets of astrology and the occult art of reading portents and the movements of the moon, as well as magic and fortune-telling.

These fallen angels and the daughters-of-men had taken the world on a journey into hell. By revealing the eternal secrets from heaven, Azazel had trained men and women in the ways of iniquity. The angels had made themselves unclean by 'going into' the daughters-of-men. The whole earth had been filled with blood and sin, and the souls of the dead could bear it no longer.

In the end, God commanded his elite troops, led by Michael, Gabriel, Suriel and Uriel, to clean out the stables and to rid the earth of oppression, injustice, sin, and wickedness – to heal creation. 'The souls of lust', the angels and their womenfolk were destroyed together with their children. A great cosmic tragedy had taken place, one in which good and evil had wrestled for supremacy and in which God had eventually triumphed. This was a myth that was more powerful and more dramatic than the Adam and Eve story in Genesis.

Reflecting on this myth, Tertullian wondered out loud why the fallen angels had been so generous in their gifts to women, why they had bought so many of their baubles to earth.

> Was it that women [even though they were unadorned and raw, and – let's be frank – crude and rude], had moved the

passions of angels, but couldn't please their men without employing artificial means of beautification, without ingenious contrivances of grace? Or was it that the angelic lovers might have appeared sordid and mean if they had arrived with no gifts for the women whom they had enticed into connubial connections with them? (*De cultu feminarum* I. 2)

But, as Tertullian wrote, there is no answer to these questions. He thought that the women who had angels as their husbands and lovers could have desired nothing more. Total bliss and heavenly contentment had taken over their lives. However, perhaps they might have suffered moments of doubt. Maybe they had reflected from time to time on how they had fallen from their original state of simplicity and had distorted their natural, simple beauty. At times after their 'heated impulses of lust', these women must have looked up towards heaven and realised that God's gift of unadorned beauty had proved an enticement to evil. They must have realised that their crass ostentation, their lipsticks and powders, potions and spells, their ambition and love of carnal pleasure were all displeasing to their Creator, and that in the wings of the fallen angels they had become offensive to him. Women were never satisfied.

When he is in full flight, it takes an inordinately long time for a gifted advocate to find his landing-strip. Finally, however, Tertullian came to the pith of his argument. The angels who had enticed women under their wings, who had slept with them, who had taught them magic formulae and given them potions and incantations, were the very angels, according to the myth, whom 'we', men and women, were destined to judge; the angels whom in baptism 'we' had renounced. The trivial possessions they had brought with them to earth and which had beguiled the women were the very reasons why the fallen angels deserved to be judged and condemned.

In an oratorical flourish, Tertullian asked what possible link there could be between the *things* that belonged to the angels, their trivia, their *impedimenta* and their judges, with Christian men and women. What connection linked the believers, who were to sit in judgment and pass sentence, with the wayward angels whom they were to condemn? How could a Christian, in all conscience, sit in judgment of the angels and at the same time accept gifts from the accused? It was as though angels had bribed the judiciary. Judges should never have accepted what the angels were offering, and of course, as Tertullian would have it, any decent woman would have nothing to do with them – no powder, no necklaces, no sensual oils or bangles.

> Unless we begin here on earth to prejudge, by pre-condemning their *things*, which we are hereafter to condemn in *themselves*, these things will rather judge and condemn us (*De cultu feminarum* I.2).

We can only hope that the matrons and virgins of Carthage found Tertullian's closing submission more persuasive than it appears today – otherwise, in the end, their judges might enter a finding that the lecherous angels are 'Not Guilty'.

In an act of exquisite marital diplomacy, in a work he addressed to his long-suffering wife, Tertullian observed that women were propelled by a sense of greed and selfishness to trample underfoot all their human feelings (*Ad uxorem*, II.8.3). It was an act of courage to inform his wife and her friends that ambition, greed, and sensuality were the principal forces urging women like themselves to marry. Wives only wanted to control someone else's house, to appropriate their husbands' wealth, to extort whatever they needed to beautify themselves, to say nothing of spending money without the least care (*Ad uxorem*, I. 4:6–7).

Tertullian did not reveal to his readers the price he had paid in his household for this courageous stand.

Female Fashions and Accoutrements

The Jesus we meet in the Gospels was not the type of man to waste his political capital talking about women's fashions, policing women's social activities, or telling them how to behave. The apostle Paul, however, was prepared to offer some limited advice to the female members of his communities about their dress and to discuss where they stood in their domestic hierarchy. In general terms, on the subject of fashions, Paul had insisted on long hair for women, short hair for men and veils for women in public places.

With his few scattered remarks about women's dress, Paul was unintentionally launching a Christian literary genre, composed by men, giving advice to women about their fashions and accoutrements, and regulating their social lives. These publications began to appear in various centres around the Mediterranean – Carthage in North Africa, Alexandria in Egypt, and in the churches of Syria. Authors such as Tertullian and Clement became fashion writers of the second century and in the process, in the sub-text, they tell us a good deal about the private lives of women of their times, how women were seen in society and what some church leaders thought of them.

From his lofty male position as a commentator and essayist, Tertullian was of the view that a woman was lucky if she was truly ugly for she had been specially blessed by her Creator. Unlike some of her associates, she didn't have to make any moves to dampen lustful advances from desperate men. If her friend happened to be pretty, however, if she was cursed with a beautiful body, an attractive face, full sensual lips, a wobbly rear, shapely legs or firm breasts, she had to hide her features to avoid arousing men's appetites.

> 'If a girl is naturally beautiful, let a holy woman give no cause to arouse carnal appetites. She should certainly not display her beauty, but take steps to hide it.' (*De cultu feminarum* II. 3:1-3)

In his treatise on women's fashions and dress sense, *De cultu feminarum*, Tertullian advised the women of his community, presumably his readers (including his wife), to resist the temptation to deck themselves out in decadent, Carthaginian fashions. They had to present themselves to the world in all modesty, without trinkets or facial creams. 'No' to painted toenails, to false eyelashes or spray-on body-tans – or the equivalent fashion *du jour*.

In Tertullian's mind, a truly Christian woman was obliged to 'go about in humble garb'. She should adopt a grey, drab appearance and put on a pale face and assume an awkward, haggard demeanour rather than hide behind some gaudy, ostentatious affectation. A woman's role of women was to please her husband – and no one else. They must not pander to a male lust-fullness by dressing up and behaving badly. They had to avoid extravagant baubles and material adornments. No high-heels. No *décolletage* or bottom-wobbling. It was the duty of all serious-minded women to take steps to maintain good order and social mores by ensuring they were not leading men astray. He himself had fallen prey. At one stage he had strayed into the embrace of a woman not his wife, and had had sex with her (*On the Resurrection of the Dead* 59:3).

As Tertullian warmed to his task, he saw mother Eve in a vision, looking at herself in a mirror, fussing and preening, her dresser cluttered with fine fabrics, vegetable products, dyes, embroideries, pearls, onyx-stones and gold necklaces – all available beauty products, pagan ornaments, fripperies, bangles and spangles which the fallen angels had gifted to the daughters-of-men. 'She (Eve) would have coveted all these things, I imagine,' he thought.

After all, she was only a woman. That was what they were all like. Self-absorbed and scatter-brained.

Tertullian accepted that he had a special duty to advise women – about their dress, their hairstyles, their diamonds and pearls, rings and necklaces, their beautification and behaviour. No self-doubt in this social commentator. Prohibitions. Condemnations. An expert in his own mind, full of confidence and witnessing to a surprising familiarity with the secret world of women. It is amazing how much one man could know about a world he didn't inhabit or approve of. Like most men with unruly hormones, he obviously kept a close eye on the shape, the gait, the conduct and the style of the women strutting around him in the street or moving about near him in the church. He was observing all before him as he wandered the streets of Carthage at night.

However, albeit unwittingly, he provides a useful service to historians of the ancient world and to Christians of all complexions. In addressing his subject so enthusiastically, he painted a tableau (perhaps a little exaggerated) of the lives of some of the women of Carthage at the end of the second and the beginning of the third centuries – and in the process, he reveals some unconscious insights into his personal, hidden world. Women were clearly one of his preoccupation.

Women were a public nuisance. In his mind, they were naturally vain, sensual and erotic, frivolous and flirtatious, vacuous and silly – but cunning. Left without proper guidance, they were interested only in style and trivia. And since the Carthaginian women were a constant temptation to men, the only way to deal with the ever-present danger was to keep them, as far as possible, in a place of subordination – at home and in the church.

In his mind, the best protection a young girl or a woman of mature years could have was to live her life behind the veil. He wrote a treatise *On the Veiling of Virgins* to encourage women, virgins especially, to accept to hide themselves behind the veil. He addressed his reactionary advice to mothers, sisters and virgin-daughters and told them to 'veil your head' for the sake of their male relatives.

> If a mother, for your sons' sakes; if a sister, for your brothers' sakes; if a daughter for your father's sakes (*De virginibus velandis* 16:4-5).

It didn't matter how old she was, any woman, young or old, was in danger if she didn't wear the veil. She had –

> to dress herself in a steel suit of modesty; defend herself by building a protective moat around her shyness; construct a wall to conceal her feminine body, one which would not allow her own eyes to wander or permit strangers' eyes to invade her privacy.

Virgins had to conceal something of their inner being 'in order to display their true selves to God alone.' And he was contemptuous of those mincing females who thought they were satisfying the obligation of wearing the veil by fluttering a small handkerchief high up on their hair-buns so that everyone celebrating the Eucharist could appreciate the beauty of their glorious hair (*De virginibus velandis*, 17:1).

Focusing his attention on those women who had 'fallen into marriage' and taken on what he referred to as the second degree of chastity, Tertullian invited his readers into his erotic world, to observe how closely he had scrutinised the flutterings of women. He had seen women reluctantly wearing the compulsory veil, but with little regard for it. They were wearing it in such a way that, as far as he could see, they might as well have been going around naked. Some were wearing turbans and woolen bands which didn't even cover their heads. They protected their hair in the front but left most of their head bare. Others covered the top of the head, the brain region, with small linen coifs, but they weren't covering their dainty feminine ears. This item of clothing was not part of the female's boudoir box of cunning tricks. A real veil was a serious and essential component of any modest woman's wardrobe. It had to reach down as far as the neck-line where the robe begun. In fact, Tertullian would have preferred his women-folk to be walking the streets in the full burqua, completely shielded from the prying eyes of lustful men.

> The terrain which the veil should cover is co-extensive with the space covered by the hair when unbound – the whole of the neck has also to be encircled. Arabia's heathen females will be your judges. They cover not only the head, but the face also, so entirely, that they are content, with one eye free, to enjoy rather half the light than to prostitute the entire face (*De virginibus velandis* 17).

Apparently, in the midst of some private revelation the Lord had provided the measurements for the particular veil he had had in mind. An angel had been the Lord's messenger, speaking in uncharacteristically offensive and sarcastic tones.

> By revelations, the Lord has measured for us the space for the veil to cover. For a certain sister of ours was addressed by an angel, beating her neck, as if to congratulate her: 'Elegant neck, and deservedly bare!' he had said. 'It is well for you to unveil yourself from the head right down to the loins, lest this freedom of your neck profit you not! (*De virginibus velandis* 17:1).

Apparently, God had revealed that it was better for a female to be nude than to be half-dressed in a veil which didn't conform to regulations.

The author was a genuine fanatic. He kept returning to the same topic and drawing on his special expertise. One might think that he had a sexual fetish or an obsessive disorder – or else he was dealing with what could only be considered as a major problem among the women of Carthage. His advice to his women readers was that if they wanted to be seen and appreciated, if they wanted to attract attention, they shouldn't stop at the nape of the neck, in the hope that it might make some men crazy, but they should strip off altogether and put beyond doubt that they were attracting the attention they wanted.

According to Tertullian, some women had been able to prove that Jesus' Gospel saying was incorrect, namely that no one could add an inch to the height with which the Creator had endowed her. But women could achieve the impossible. By attaching bundles of false hair to the back of their heads rather than on top, they sought to increase both their elegance and their stature (*De cultu feminarum* II. 7:2). Some were keen to tangle their hair into curls, others to let their locks hang loose. Some styled their hair in a mass drawn backward over the neck; others in the shape of a helmet. Women added to their weight by installing rolls or 'shield-bosses' of hair piled up over their necks, all constructed from hair harvested elsewhere. Some engaged the services of a most skilful wigmakers. But, as Tertullian rather ungallantly told his readers, none of this artificial coiffure would rise up out of the tomb on 'that day of Christian exultation' and be transported into paradise because all these trivial feminine adornments were unclean, unholy and destined for the rubbish-heap.

Further round the rim of the Mediterranean, in the city of Alexandria, and also towards the end of the second century, Titus Flavius Clemens was also offering unsolicited advice to his female readers as well as to a contingent of what he described as effeminate male citizens.

For some time, until Pope Sixtus V de-canonised him in 1586, Clement of Alexandria had been revered as an official saint of the church.

This teacher observed to his students that horses and birds, in fact all animals other than men and women, gloried in their natural, unadorned appearance, resplendent in the colours nature had handed them. It was ridiculous that women would think themselves so plain and unattractive in their natural state that they needed to purchase beauty products from shopkeepers. The cosmetics and hair dyes women were using demonstrated that their souls' interior life had been corrupted. Women who painted themselves were nothing but courtesans and prostitutes – certainly not serious-minded human beings. Those who paraded around wearing gold bracelets and pendants, those who spent their time curling their locks, oiling their cheeks, painting their eyes and dyeing their hair, practising the pernicious arts of luxury, such women were wasting their lives trying to infatuate their lovers. If you removed the headdress, the diet, the clothes, the gold, the paint, the cosmetics and searched for the true beauty within these individuals, you would find 'an ape smeared with white paint'. Some might think Jesus' simple message about the birds of the air and the lilies of the field was being mangled into a form of puritanism.

Clement's writings were poisoned with toxic stereotypes of women. He observed, for example, that some women devoted the whole day, morning till night, to performing their toiletries and that in the evening, these 'spurious beauties' crept out from their hole to paint the town red. A female who took any pride in her chastity would never dye her hair yellow, or stain her cheeks, or paint her eyes. Women who do these things were not made for domestic life (as women should be). They were lazy housekeepers, sitting around like stuffed and painted objects to be admired. It is clear that the sector from which Clement was drawing his material was, at least in part, among the elite of Carthage.

And he had a few ideas he was willing to share about the value of what in modern jargon is known as cosmetic realignment – enlarged breasts, redesigned vulvas, liposuction of the bum, inflated lips and stomach stapling – though the methods available to women of his day were considerably more primitive. A woman who was unhappy with her short stature could stick some cork on the soles of her shoes. A tall, lanky lady could wear shoes with thin soles and walk around like a turkey, with her head lowered into her shoulders. If she had no bottom to wobble, she could sew some bulk into her bloomers to attract admirers. A woman with a protruding stomach could hold her breath and stabilise her flab with a tight girdle. Those with ginger eyebrows could stain them with soot. If a woman was unhappy because she was too pale, she only had to powder herself with rouge. If she was fortunate enough to have a feature which was especially attractive, she couldn't resist displaying it – naked. The female members of the human species had proved themselves very inventive.

> Women who use crocodiles' excrement, those who anoint themselves with the froth of putrid humours and stain their eyebrows with soot, and rub their cheeks with white lead, deserve to perish (*Paedagogus*, 3. 2).

Clement thought that powder and lipstick, extravagant clothes and elaborate head-dresses, re-modeling the body which God had created, belittled women and converted them into women of the night.

And the men of Alexandria didn't escape the sharp edge of Clement's scalpel. He thought that unless you're able to see some of these men stripped naked and could catch a glimpse of the region below the belt, 'you would suppose them to be women' – and that was a horrible fate.

> Not only are the female sex deranged by frivolous pursuits, but men also are infected with the same disease (*Paedogogus*, 3. 3).

The author invited his readers into the decadent world of the elite. He believed that it was unworthy of men to shave their beards, or to smooth and soften their bodies; that oiling their grey locks and dyeing them blond was simply a mark of 'crude effeminacy'.

There must have been other men, however, men we don't read about, walking the streets, drinking in coffee-shops, smoking the shisha on the foot-paths, hard-working labourers, family men, travelling salesmen who were not spending their money on barbers and beauticians, who were paying no attention to their body hair or body odour – no combs, or hair-oil, or perfumes, rings or bracelets. Clement tells us nothing of these men, many of whom would have been members of his worshipping community – just ordinary citizens. These were not on his radar. He saw it as his role to discourage the youth, male or female, teenagers, the girls and boys who were struggling with their hormones, from dedicating their young lives to trivia, acting like giddy girls and dandies.

The Creator had intended women to be sleek, smooth creatures. Like a horse which gloried in its flowing mane, they were meant to rejoice in the natural beauty of their hair. God had also adorned his male creation, like a lion, with a strong beard and 'shaggy breasts' as a mark of true manhood. His beard and the fact that his body, back and front, top to bottom, was covered in hair was a sure sign of his superiority. It was sinful, by shaving, cutting or plucking, to desecrate and emasculate God's creation.

Jesus might have been surprised to hear himself quoted by Clement as an authority against barbers and in favour of man's shaggy, manly appearance. It is true, according to the Gospels, that he had said that God had numbered the hairs of our head – and perhaps also the hairs on our chin, those on our body and in the creases. As a trained exegete, and extending the message somewhat, Clement drew the obvious conclusion.

> Lions glory in their shaggy hair, but are armed by their hair in any fight; and boars are made imposing by their mane – hunters are afraid of them when they see them bristling their hair (*ibid*).

The exegete, theologian and social commentator, took his readers further into the decadent world of the gold coast of Egypt at the turn of the second century and revealed some of the scandalous behaviour of society women. He told them that in many households (rich households, not hovels or inner-city squats), wives were carrying on as if they were spoilt princesses, refusing to do any manual work, employing slaves and servants – to cook, to lay the tables, to guard the gold and silverware. Male and female assistants were employed to help with the lady-of-the-house's toileting – one to adjust the mirror, another to take charge of the headdresses, others to manipulate the combs or apply the grease-paint. Because it was commonly believed that fruitful erections were beyond them, many of these slaves were eunuchs. Without the usual repercussions, they could service the personal needs of their mistresses who were keen to enjoy the private pleasures they were entitled to.

Perhaps Clement was keen to entertain his readers. Maybe he was simply indulging his own sexual fantasies. Perhaps he was recording how the elite lived in his home town. How he came to know how they were behaving is not revealed.

The wives of rich husbands who were anxious to be seen in public, were being carried around the streets of the city under a canopy, on the shoulders of their domestics. They were floating about near various temples, offering sacrifices, practising divination, spending their time with fortune-tellers, with begging priests and disreputable old women, peddling old wives' tales over their cocktails, learning charms and incantations from soothsayers. According to Clement, some of these women were supporting their male lovers, some were being supported by ladies' men, while others were relying on assurances from their personal fortune-tellers that they could see rich, handsome admirers in the cards and that they were about to appear and ravage them.

These were the type of women who were enjoying the delights of sexual intercourse on the couches and in the beds of their boyfriends. They surrounded themselves with crowds of 'abominable creatures' (*kinaides*), effeminate men with loose tongues and filthy bodies, who whispered dirty language into the ear of their rich mistresses. Clement was not as tolerant or understanding of human weaknesses as Jesus had been. If these women were real and living in Alexandria, they were at the top of the social scale – high-fliers and clearly not active members of the author's local communities of believers.

The Alexandria of his day, at least as Clement saw it, had an endless supply of men to carry out whatever lewd duties their female acquaintances required – ministers of adultery, giggling and whispering, shamelessly making nasal sounds of lewdness and fornication – grunts and snorts to provoke lust, making every effort to arouse erotic fits of laughter and to satisfy a lady's needs. Sometimes, when on fire and swollen with lust, these fornicators make a sound in their nose like a frog, as if they had fits of anger dwelling in their nostrils (*Paedagogus* 3. 4).

The author was well informed and, for a celibate, not short on colourful details. Like Tertullian, he had done his homework. Both provided an invaluable glimpse into the lives of the rich and famous of the second century, and a penetrating X-ray insight into of their own minds.

Women's Sodalities in the Post-Apostolic Period

The local communities which the apostles and their colleagues had established around the perimeter of the Mediterranean began to assume a more permanent, hard-edged shape in the post-apostolic period, at the end of the first century and the beginning of the second. From the beginning, these little groups had been structured around a wide variety of personal charisms – apostles (envoys or delegates) who had received a commission directly or indirectly from the elders (or presbyters) in Jerusalem, male and female prophets, miracle workers, male and female servants (or deacons) and teachers. The early Pauline communities (about which we know a great deal more than about the other communities) had organised themselves on the basis of these special, spirit-filled gifts (1 Cor 12:4–11).

By the turn of the century Christian leaders had lost confidence in their belief, after the fall of Jerusalem and the destruction of the Temple by Titus's troops, that the world was on the verge of a catastrophic implosion. They were busy establishing structures to ensure the future growth and stability of their communities. Over time, probably before the end of the first century, the original structure of some of the local communities morphed into an organisation under the supervision of one leader or overseer known as an *episcopos* (a bishop). He was supported by a group of elders (or presbyters) and a team of servants (or deacons) – all men. This structure appears for the first time in the Pastoral Epistles (1 Tim 3:1–7 & Titus 1:7–9) and a few years later in the letters of Ignatius of Antioch, which were written between 108 and 117 AD.

Though they were excluded from the ranks of those in charge, from among local bishops and those who presided with them (his presbyters and deacons), women were not entirely invisible within these local communities. Groups or orders of holy widows were active and prominent from an early stage, and at a later period these associations probably morphed into orders for deaconesses, especially in the eastern empire. An order of women dedicated to virginity also became an identifiable part of the community of believers. And from the earliest times, from the middle of the first century, female prophets were actively exercising their charism – and causing trouble. At different times and in different places, associations of widows, of deaconesses or female servants, of virgins and of prophetesses, took shape and began to take part in the daily, religious life of the followers of Jesus.

A Sisterhood of Widows

Widows had been singled out for attention by the authors of the canonical Gospels. There is the widow of Naim, for example, who was burying her son when she met Jesus, and the impoverished woman whom Jesus had observed dropping her pennies into the Temple collection boxes. These were just several of the marginal women to whom Jesus had paid special attention and who were destined to be privileged in his kingdom. At one stage, focussing his sights on the contemptible scribes who had a reputation for praying ostentatiously in marketplaces, he condemned them for preying on widows and robbing them of the scraps that sustained them (Mark 12:40).

In the society in which Jesus had operated, unlike in our modern society, widows were not elderly women whose husbands had passed away and who were in receipt of a pension or who had inherited their partner's superannuation payout. They were women who had been abandoned by their family and by society – living outside the normal social structures which sustained other women – not in their homes, with their family, under the control and protection of their husbands. Death or a male-dominated divorce system made some women responsible for their own welfare. On their own, alone in the world. In those days a widow was either the responsibility of her male in-laws or she had to survive as best she could, on her own. In Jesus' world, on the death of her husband, the wife was often condemned to live on the scrap-heap surviving as best she could – often by prostitution.

In the apostolic church, many of the female converts who had lost their husbands, by death or divorce, would have inevitably lost contact with their Jewish relatives. They would have turned their back on the extended family and their religious traditions, and become the equivalent of heretics. Their decision to join the movement established by the preacher from Galilee would have had some family repercussions. And then there were the widows from outside Palestine. We meet them in the Acts. They were being discriminated against and receiving short rations in the daily distribution of bread. They were complaining that the native Palestinian Jews were neglecting them.

At an early stage, the leaders of the primitive church in Jerusalem and surrounds had assumed the responsibility of sheltering and feeding these women. The community had set up a food distribution system. When the burden of this service became too heavy and some widows began to complain, the leaders established a special ministry of service and commissioned a group of male members (whom we now call 'deacons') to care for those who were being neglected (Acts 6:1ff).

Later, a special order (a kind of religious guild for widows) was established in various local communities. In Ephesus for example. As we have seen, the anonymous author of the First Epistle to Timothy provided some details of how the system worked. As he told it, there were three kinds of widows: the ones whose husbands had died but who were being cared for by their families; younger widows whom the author judged as unstable gossips and busybodies (women who couldn't be trusted to settle down); and the 'real widows' – the ones who had had only the one husband, who were all alone in the world, and who were spending their time, night and day, in prayer.

When a real widow was over the age of sixty, and provided she could produce favourable character references, her name would be enrolled in an official list of widows. A woman was eligible to have her name on this list if she had a reputation for her good deeds, if she had already reared her children, if she had proved to be hospitable, washed the feet of the saints, relieved the afflicted and was generally regarded as a good woman. These enrolled women were expected to spend their time in prayer – that was their special ministry – and in return the community accepted the responsibility of looking after their material needs.

Perhaps this reference to a list of approved widows in the letter to Timothy was only a list of those women who were eligible for financial support. However, at least by the second century, there was in place an order of widows commissioned to carry out specific religious functions. These women had a visible status, and eventually they would prove quite assertive and troublesome in some places.

In the early years of the second century, in a letter to 'the colony of God's church at Philippi', Polycarp gave advice about how widows were expected to behave. But before focusing his attention on widows in particular, he made a few general comments about women. And like all the early Christian writers, Polycarp was a man talking to men.

> After schooling ourselves to conform to the divine commandments, we can go on to instruct our womenfolk in the traditions of the faith, and in love and purity, teaching them to show fondness and fidelity to their husbands, and a

chaste and impartial affection for everyone else, and to bring up their children in the fear of God.

Polycarp had a good old-fashioned stereotypical view of the place of women in society. But turning to the topic of widows, he wrote that they had to observe discretion 'as they practise our Lord's faith'. In their prayers, they had to intercede constantly for the other members of their community. 'Knowing that they are an altar of God', they had to be careful to avoid spreading gossip, spiteful tittle-tattle, false allegations, and any over-eagerness for money or misconduct of any kind (*The Epistle of Polycarp to the Philippians*, 4). Polycarp was either anticipating problems which he thought women were likely to cause, or addressing real tensions that at least some widows were already causing within the community. These widows had to be kept under control.

At more or less the same time, on his way to Rome to face martyrdom, the bishop of Antioch wrote a letter to his fellow-bishop Polycarp in which he was giving him and the believers under his charge some advice on a number of topics (marriage and chastity included). In passing, Ignatius mentioned that the bishop or overseer of the faith community was responsible for his widows:

> 'Take care that widows are not neglected; next to the Lord, be yourself their guardian.'

A similar brief reference to widows appeared in a document from about the same period, the *Shepherd of Hermas*. In this allegorical work the author managed to capture, unlike many authors of the period, the particular evangelical spirit which had inspired Jesus' life and message. In Mandate 8 he wrote,

> First of all, there is faith, fear of the Lord, love, concord, words of righteousness, truth, patience – nothing is better than these in the life of men. If a man keeps these, and doesn't hold himself back, he becomes blessed in his life.

And the author tells us what ministries 'these' virtues inspire – to minister to widows, to visit the orphans and the needy, to ransom the servants of God from their afflictions, to be hospitable, to revere the aged, to observe brotherly feeling, to endure injury, to be long-suffering, to bear no grudge, to exhort those who are sick of soul, not to cast away those that have stumbled from the faith but to convert them and to put courage into them, to reprove sinners, not to oppress debtors and indigent persons et cetera.

Ministering to widows came first in this author's long list of the corporal works of mercy which Jesus had recommended and which was at the centre of the Christian life. This author was still inspired by Jesus' message of the kingdom of heaven here on earth, looking after the little people on the margins of society. At this early stage, Jesus' fundamental message had not yet entirely disappeared under the weight of 'more important' matters.

A federated union of widows was active in North Africa in the second century and Tertullian was far from happy with the way its members were behaving. In his essay *On the Veiling of Virgins* (*de virginibus velandis*), he voiced his disapproval of the enrolment of an underage virgin in the order reserved for widows. A young virgin of less than twenty years of age had wormed her way into the sodality – or at least that's what he thought. Like the author of the Pastoral Epistles, he was of the view that membership of the exclusive sorority should be reserved to mature matrons whose first and only husbands had died.

Besides his opposition to one particular virginal member, Tertullian also complained that branch membership had been stacked with married women, mothers and infant teachers and that they were not properly dressed. He wasn't happy. Women should remain veiled in public, away from the roving eyes of men. He was convinced that women should not be allowed to teach, or baptise, or exercise any male function, and especially not fill any sacerdotal office. And in his mind, he was confirmed in his inflexible view by Paul's alleged but spurious prohibitions to the Corinthians (1 Cor 14:34–35). But like Paul, Tertullian had a fight on his hands in Carthage. It seems the association of widows had become too large, too powerful and its members were flexing their feminine muscles.

An order of widows had been established in Carthage before the end of the second century and, as far as Tertullian could see, it was in turmoil. As a lawyer, he was horrified that hard-edged rules of acceptable female behaviour were being flouted. Women had become too visible and ill-disciplined. They were allowed to visit other women in the homes where cultural practices prohibited men, even bishops, from entering – sick women, female catechumens, expectant mothers and poverty-stricken women. For obvious reasons of modesty, deaconesses or female ministers were allotted the role of anointing the bodies of the female converts receiving the sacrament of baptism, thereby relieving the bishop and his presbyters from the dangerous duty of laying their sacramental hands on naked female flesh. Women could also perform some minor tasks for other women without giving scandal. Reflecting the strict segregation of the sexes which was part of the cultural mores, their role had become gender specific. Even so, these women had to be tightly controlled. For the most part, it was better for widows to remain indoors, out of the way, and to devote their days to praying for their benefactors.

Until recent times, the accepted orthodoxy about an early Christian document known as *The Apostolic Tradition* was that it had been composed in approximately 215 AD by a difficult presbyter of the Roman church named Hippolytus, and that his reactionary views were meant to counter the innovating practices of his former friends, Popes Zephyrinus and Callistus. His treatise was meant to preserve those traditional second century practices which he believed were in danger of disappearing. Recent scholarship, however, does not support these basic historical facts.

We don't know, for example, that the treatise had originally been entitled *The Apostolic Tradition*, or that it was composed by a presbyter called Hippolytus, or that it reflected the liturgical practices and customs in Rome. However, the document was composed in the early years of the third century and has proved to be an important source for scholars who seek to reconstruct some of the liturgical practices, probably in Alexandria, perhaps in Rome, maybe even in the later part of the second century. In any event, an order of widows was obviously an important feature in the community where this document was composed. The author of the document provided some idea of the ceremony surrounding an induction into the order, as well as the criteria for assessing a widow's suitability.

Widows were not ordained, but they were appointed as prayers. There was no laying-on of hands of authority. They were not members of the clerical caste.

> When a widow is appointed, she shall not be ordained but she shall be appointed by name. The widow shall be appointed by the word alone, and in this way she shall be associated with the other widows; hands shall not be laid upon her because she does not offer the oblation nor has she a sacred ministry. Ordination is for the clergy on account of their ministry, but the widow is appointed for prayer, and prayer is the duty of all (*The Apostolic Tradition*, 11.3).

Even if a widow was of mature years, not all of them were to be trusted. If her husband had been dead for a long time, she could be appointed without delay. But if her husband had died only recently, she should not be trusted, even if she was ancient. Recent widows had to be tested with time. The author thought that passions could continue into old age in those who have tended to yield to them. Women were thought of as fickle by those who ran society. They could still do stupid things, like marrying again. They needed to be tested over time to guarantee their virtue and stability, and then they could be 'associated with other widows'.

As in other centres, the church in Syria had developed an established order of widows for whom the bishop was responsible and whose members received financial support. These women were required to spend time in prayer and to conduct themselves honourably so as to avoid scandal in the eyes of non-believers. In this region, these matrons had to be over the age of fifty – not sixty. A young widow could re-marry, but only once. If she re-married more than once, she was to be classified by the community, according to the *Didascalia*, as a 'harlot'.

In Chapters 14 and 15 of the *Didascalia* the author dealt with widows and their association. In the latter chapter we read what the community expected of them.

> Every widow ought to be meek and quiet and gentle. And she should be without malice and without anger. She shouldn't be talkative or loud, or too pushy, or quarrelsome. And when she sees anything unseemly done, or hears it, let her be as though she saw and heard nothing. A widow should have no other care except to be praying for those who give, and for the whole church.

A typically patronizing stereotype of women – passive, submissive and invisible. A widow was expected to remain silent when she was asked a question. She had to refer the questioner to someone who would know the right answer – to 'the rulers'. No widow or layman was free to talk about important subjects – subjects like punishment and reward, or the kingdom of Christ and his dispensation. Being ignorant, whatever they might say would amount to a form of blasphemy. Any woman who presumed to instruct another person in the faith would incur a heavy judgement for her sin. It wasn't right or proper that women should be teachers, especially if they were teaching in the name of Christ, talking about a redemption achieved by his passion. It was thought that if a Gentile under instruction in the faith, for example, heard the word of God being abused, that is, not spoken about in a fitting manner as it ought to be – and particularly if it was being explained by a woman – instead of applauding what was being taught, he would only mock and scoff.

> For you have not been appointed to this, O women, and especially widows, that you should teach, but that you should pray and entreat the Lord God.

Widows had to know their place. They had to stay at home, and not wander around, going from house to house in the village. Those who gossiped, who were bold and shameless, only stirred up arguments and discord. They weren't serious members of the community. They fell asleep at the common Sunday assembly or prattled on about nothing. They didn't listen to the readings or to the homily. According to the author,

> Instead of doing good works and giving (money) to the bishop for the entertainment of strangers and the refreshment of those in distress, they lend out on bitter usury.

The *Didascalia* provides a jaundiced view of what senior women were like in the Syrian communities in the early third century.

Widows were obliged to be obedient to the bishop and his deacons who acted only on instructions from above. They couldn't go to anyone's home for a meal, for example, or receive a gift, or lay hands on somebody and pray over anyone 'without the say-so of the bishop or the deacon'. Those in positions of power had to maintain an iron-grip on the behaviour of these senior women.

> Know then, sisters, that whatsoever the pastors with the deacons command you, and you obey them, you obey God.

But unfortunately, as you would expect, human nature being what it is, some of these senior women were attending to their personal wealth. Others were pretending to be sick so they wouldn't have to minister to the disabled, or endure long fasts, or pray over members of the community, or lay hands on them.

Some of the widows participated to some limited extent in the pastoral life of the community (praying, fasting, visiting, laying on of hands), but only under the supervision of the bishop and his deacons. They were well down the pecking order, towards the bottom of the hierarchical structure. They were forbidden, for example, to conduct the sacrament of baptism since that would constitute 'a transgression of the commandment' and place both the baptiser and the baptised in peril. The argument went that if it had been lawful for a woman to baptise, 'our Lord and Teacher himself' would have been baptised by his own mother, not by John the Baptist. And similarly, if Jesus had wanted women to teach or preach, he would have commanded them to do so – but he didn't – or so they claimed. Women were definitely second-class.

And it appears that some of the widows were in fact difficult to control.

> You ought to be ashamed; for you wish to be wiser and to know better, not only than the men, but even than the presbyters and the bishops.

As we have seen, in his sixth satire Juvenal has given us a good picture in verse of the annoying, opinionated woman who knows everything and won't keep quiet in public.

> I detest
> The sort who are always thumbing, and citing – some standard grammar,
> Whose every utterance follows the laws of syntax,
> Who with antiquarian zeal quotes poets I've never heard of:
> Such matters are men's concern.

Apparently, these women also existed in Syria in the third century and needed to be kept under the thumb. Perhaps sometimes they were wiser and knew better than their male colleagues. At least it was a possibility. But we will never know.

From a study of the *Didascalia*, a reader might get a bad impression of the female members of the Syrian community. Young married women and senior widows were a problem. They needed constant supervision to ensure they did not disturb the peace and well-being of the local church. Some of the younger women spent their time on trivial pursuits – on beautifying themselves and leading men astray, or at least deliberately trying to tease them into sinful, sexual liaisons. Some of the widows were super-critical, undermining the established system of social services and the authority of the men in charge. They were forever plotting, like shop-stewards, to obtain a better deal for themselves, some seeking to gain an advantage over their fellow widows, claiming to be more in need, more naked, more hungry, more entitled than those who were being showered with alms. They were constantly finding fault, murmuring, and even cursing other men and women in their community. Thus, 'Do you therefore (O bishop) admonish and rebuke those widows who are undisciplined.'

From this handbook of rules and regulations, it is clear that there was trouble in paradise and some of the female members were at the centre of this trouble. The author's advice was addressed to men, to men in charge, as to how they should deal with the many daily problems created by women. But we don't hear a balancing word from any female. They remained silent or their voices have been removed from the libraries.

The overall picture drawn is either an accurate depiction of the place women occupied in that early community, what they were like and the disruption some of them were causing, or it was a result of the author's twisted attitude to his sisters in the faith. Maybe some of the women at that time were unstable troublemakers who needed to be kept in check and who enjoyed an inferior status, devoid of any semblance of power or authority. Or perhaps the author's view was jaundiced and the male leaders felt unreasonably threatened by a few strong women. From this distance it is difficult to determine whether these passages in this ancient document present an accurate image of the female in Syria early in the third century, or whether they reflect a Christian leader's biased view of how society functioned, how women fitted in, what trouble they were creating and what advice should be offered to the bishop to regulate and control his people.

Whatever the truth, inside the Christian communities from a very early stage there were organised groups of widows who enjoyed a special status and who were entrusted with a number of ministries or services – praying, visiting the sick, caring for the needy and generally being as invisible as possible.

Powerful and Troublesome Female Prophets

In the latter half of the fourth century, the historian Epiphanius recorded the story of a strange event that had occurred sometime in the second half of the second century. A prophetess called Priscilla (though he wasn't certain, perhaps it was another prophetess named Quintilla) – had been sleeping in a town called Pepuza, somewhere in the province of Phrygia. She had claimed that Christ had come to her in her sleep and had slept beside her in her bed. He had appeared to her 'in the form of a woman', 'dressed in a white robe' and had revealed that the New Jerusalem would descend from heaven to the spot where they were sleeping together (*Panarion*, Book II, Chapter 49).

Priscilla and her best friend Maximilla and other women had been colleagues of the subversive prophet Montanus. They had founded a charismatic movement which became known as the New Prophecy. Even as Epiphanius was writing his *Panarion* some fifty years after the Council of Nicaea (325 AD), initiation rites were being conducted on the site where Priscilla had slept beside Christ. Men and women were waiting to see Christ on his return, and the movement included 'women they call prophetesses'.

The followers of Montanus appear in the pages of history under a variety of names such as Phrygians, Priscillianists, Artotyrites, Pepuzians and Tascodrugians (or 'nose-pickers' because, by repute, they used to put their 'licking finger' on their snout or in their nose when they were praying). Who knows what was true and what was spin? Enemies like Epiphanius or Irenaeus might have said anything to put their foes off-balance.

As we have seen, the storyteller of Acts reported that towards the beginning of their third missionary journey, Paul and his travelling party had landed at Philip's place in Caesarea and stayed there with him and his family of four unmarried daughters who, as the author reported, 'prophesied'.

> Among those that were celebrated at that time was Quadratus, who, report says, was renowned along with the daughters of Philip for his prophetical gifts. And there were many others besides these who were known in those days and who occupied the first place among the successors of the apostles. And they also, being illustrious disciples of such great men, built up the foundations of the churches which had been laid by the apostles in every place, and preached the Gospel more and more widely and scattered the saving seeds of the kingdom of heaven far and near throughout the whole world (Eusebius, *Eccl. Hist.* III. 37).

Prophets and prophetesses were important people in the life of the early church – and there were many of them.

Philip 'the evangelist' had been commissioned, second in line, as one of the seven servants or ministers to care for the Greek-speaking widows who had joined the church. He and the others were expected to serve these widows in place of the apostles (Acts 6:1–6).

The early encounter Paul had with the daughters of Philip was later expanded by the author of the *Acts of Paul and Thecla*. These Acts comprise part of an apocryphal book entitled *Acts of Paul*, a document which was probably written by an 'orthodox' believer and which was circulating in Asia Minor in the latter half of the second century. This would have been at about the same time as Tertullian was writing his grim treatises in North Africa and Irenaeus was composing his lengthy polemical work in Gaul. This collection of independent works under the title *Acts of Paul* had been composed to honour the apostle's missionary achievements and was modelled on the canonical Acts of the Apostles and on Paul's letters. Written in the style of popular, devotional essays for pious believers, the stories were never meant to be an historically factual version of events, but they can provide a picture of what life was like and what church people believed at the time they were written.

The *Acts of Paul and Thecla* describes the fictitious adventures of Paul and Thecla, a young girl who had fallen under his spell and his message. In the story, Paul had journeyed to Iconium. While preaching there on the exquisite beauty of virginal chastity, he had inspired Thecla to reject the man she had promised to marry and as a consequence, she had suffered a tragic death – the ultimate glory of martyrdom. It also records other incidents in different parts of Asia Minor where the Spirit of God had been active and where prophets and prophetesses had been dominating the scene.

According to these Acts, on Paul's return to Corinth, a prophetess named Myrta had spoken as the agent of the Spirit, advising him that his future was to be found in Rome. One of the classical duties of any prophet was to foretell the future as revealed to him/her by God.

The Spirit came upon Myrta, so that she said ... Paul the servant of the Lord will save many in Rome and will nourish many with the word ... so there will be great grace in Rome.

Myrta was not the only female prophet the author of the *Acts of Paul and Thecla* mentioned. He recounted various incidents involving Theonoe, Stratonike, Eubulla, Phila, Artemilla and Numpha – all women known to the community and who used to prophesy. From a very early period, Asia Minor (or modern Turkey) had been the focus of the Spirit's presence, of its inspiring activity, and often the focus of wild, supra-normal conduct.

But the story of prophets and prophetesses goes back a long way into the great religions of antiquity. From when the Torah was composed, and undoubtedly well before, prophecy had been an officially recognised institution in the Jewish system of religion, and probably formed an integral part of the nation's liturgical celebrations in their centres of worship. Prophets exercised a powerful political and religious force in Jewish society, particularly at times of crisis. Along with the Torah or the Pentateuch and the Wisdom literature or the Writings, the sayings of the prophets formed an integral part of the Jewish scriptures.

In their dreams and visions, both male and female prophets enjoyed an immediate and personal experience of the divine. They believed that they had received a divine calling to communicate God's revelations to others, though they were only the bearers of these messages, acting only as the mouthpiece of God. They were driven by some irresistible interior force to speak and act as a providential instrument for the guidance of God's people.

Their revelations, their visions and mystical experiences were often accompanied by some abnormal, extravagant behaviour, by ecstatic outbursts, for example, when he or she was possessed by a supra-normal psychological force. They were driven to communicate their divine message in a variety of ways – in story or narrative form, in poems, parables, proverbs, sermons, diatribes, outbursts of abuse, in lamentations, sometimes by a symbolic action. The messages were often confronting, sometimes threatening, taking their listeners by surprise, confusing them perhaps, frightening them and challenging the status quo.

Isaiah, Jeremiah and Ezekiel, Jonah, Amos, Micah and Daniel are all names which are well known in Jewish and Christian circles. Less familiar are the names of female prophets such as Deborah (Judges 4–5), Huldah (2 Kgs 22:14 ff), Miriam, sister of Aaron (Exod 15:20), Noadiah (Neh 6:14) and of course, Anna, the prophetess who appears briefly in the Gospel of Luke (2:36). The prophet Isaiah also referred to his wife as a prophetess (Isa 8:3).

In one of the Talmudic tractates (*Megillah*, 14a), the Jewish rabbis claimed that there were 48 male and 7 female prophets who had ministered to Israel as Yahweh's inspired witnesses. The seven prophetesses included Sarah, Hannah the mother of Samuel, Abigail and Esther. Though none of these four are identified as a prophetess in the Hebrew scriptures, each of them was, in her own way, graced by personal revelations from on high.

Because of the erratic nature of prophecy, false revelations were often part of the overall religious experience. People of faith were easily led astray and manipulated by evil men and women for sinister purposes, and it was often difficult to distinguish between the true and false prophets. In Chapter 13, Ezekiel spoke of this phenomenon as one touching both men and women. Speaking as the mouthpiece of God, he told his audience to set their face against the daughters of Israel who were prophesying 'out of their own minds'. He called down terrible curses on the women who by lies to those who listen to lies, put people to death who should not die and, 'who sew magic bands upon all wrists, and make veils for the heads of persons of every stature, in the hunt for souls!' (Ezek 13:18).

Prophecy was a dangerous profession, for the prophets themselves and for their listeners. It was a ministry from on high (or from elsewhere) which was difficult for those in authority to manage.

Joel (a man about whom we know almost nothing) was working as a prophet to Israel about 400 BC. He addressed his people in the name of The Most High,

> It shall come to pass afterwards, that I will pour out my spirit on all flesh; that your sons and daughters shall prophesy, your old men shall dream dreams, and your young men shall see visions. Even upon the men-servants and maid-servants, in those days, I will pour out my spirit (Joel 2:28–29).

And this stunning revelation was taken up by the author of Acts (2:17–21) to explain the extraordinary events surrounding Pentecost.

According to Paul, prophets and prophetesses enjoyed a high status in the local churches at Corinth. They were ranked just behind the apostles in his list of ministers. Towards the end of his first letter to his brothers and sisters who lived there, he had tried to set out various ways of dealing with the revelations of local prophets in an orderly manner. He wanted to encourage and at the same time regulate the spontaneous prophetic outbursts of the Spirit as well as the garbled outpourings of those who were speaking in weird tongues. Some order and decorum had to be preserved. No noisy babbling, undisciplined turmoil or wild utterances could be tolerated, at least in the assemblies.

> If a revelation is made to someone sitting nearby, let the first be silent. You can all prophesy one by one, so that all may learn and all be encouraged – and the spirits of prophets are subject to other prophets. For God is not a God of confusion but of peace (1 Cor. 14:30–33).

It would appear that from the earliest times women were free to prophesy in the official assembly, provided of course they were wearing their veils. A man could pray or prophesy in public provided he did this in a manly manner, with his head uncovered: a woman, on the other hand, who prayed or prophesied in public with her head unveiled, shamed herself, her husband, the whole community – and the angels (1 Cor 11:4 ff). The clear implication was that if a female believer had her head covered, she could participate actively in the prophetic ministry.

The followers of the Way believed that the inspired utterances of prophets and prophetesses came directly from the Spirit of God, though, according to Paul, it had to be a disciplined and sober ministry. They had to share their dreams and revelations in an intelligible and orderly manner. The male or female prophet who was pretending to be overpowered by some frenzied ecstatic convulsion from beyond, uttering nonsense in wild outbursts, was abusing a divinely inspired ministry. The babbling of tongues (and their interpretation) was different to sober prophetic speech. As the interests of good order and harmony demanded, a prophetess had to be prepared to restrain her impulse to speak out and show off.

Because false prophecy was a real and present danger in the early communities, Paul developed a process of enquiry in an attempt to distinguish genuine prophets from charlatans. To make sure the prophets were not simply indulging themselves, their utterances had to be tested by recognised experts in the field – by other exponents of the art.

> If anyone thinks that he is a prophet, or spiritual, he should acknowledge that what I am writing to you is a command of the Lord. If anyone does not recognise this, he is not licensed to speak (1 Cor 14:37).

Because of the continuing and real danger of spiritual fraud, and because of the difficulties of discerning valid revelations from the malevolent force of pretentious messengers, the important ministry of prophets, and particularly of the female prophets, began to lose its impetus inside the mainstream communities. Those blessed with the gifts of the Spirit began to cede their place to more regulated and institutionalised ministries – leaders, bishops, deacons, teachers, lawyers, catechists and later, monks, theologians and exegetes. The emergence of more controllable ministries began to predominate as the charismatic ministries started to wane.

As the years grew into decades, the Christian churches found themselves further separated in time and geography from Jesus and the explosive origins of their faith in Palestine. The leaders were concerned to assure some type of authoritative line of tradition. They wanted a sure and stable link with the founding apostles, and through them to Jesus. The managers and CEOs had assumed the responsibility of preserving order in the assembly and securing some basic continuity with the past. The gifted outbursts of prophets and prophetesses were not going to fill the ever-widening gap between the confusion of the present and the security of the past. Their revelations and dreams were not the answer. Their gift was too available to fraudsters and magicians, too uncertain and disruptive. The institution was calling out for more certainty and stability than prophets and prophetesses were able to provide.

The male prophet continued to be a dominant figure in the post-apostolic churches well into the middle of the second century and beyond. We find them featuring in the *Didache*, for example, grouped with apostles and teachers, carrying out what appears to have been an itinerant ministry, probably in the rural areas away from the large cities – all men, no women. This ancient text which was composed around the turn of the first century and which some had even accepted as part of the canonical collection of sacred books, had disappeared for many centuries, and reappeared in the late nineteenth century in Constantinople. Though his claim is certainly an exaggeration, and almost certainly false, the author asserted that the *Didache* was a collection of the basic Christian teachings which had been handed down by the twelve apostles. Establishing an honorific status for a document by asserting apostolic authorship was a popular strategy in those days.

The second section of the *Didache* is a kind of church manual providing rules and regulations for the general administration of the local community and its liturgical assemblies. The institutional hierarchy was made up of prophets, teachers, bishops and deacons, with no mention of women in the ranks. The whole mood of the manual is male-oriented and undoubtedly reflects accurately the patriarchal orientation of the community.

The prophets of the *Didache* were like high priests. They enjoyed an elevated status in the community. For example, they could recite the Eucharistic prayer. If there was no prophet or apostle present to proclaim the solemn prayer of thanksgiving, the local ministers (the bishop, presbyters and deacons) were entitled to take their place. And being Spirit-filled believers, unlike the others, the prophets were not restricted to the recitation of any set liturgical formula. They could give thanks freely, spontaneously, as the Spirit moved them.

It is clear from the *Didache* that while prophets were visible and active within the particular community for which he was writing, the author was nevertheless deeply suspicious of false prophets. He felt the need to set down a number of strict criteria to help the leaders and overseers distinguish the true prophet from his false relative.

In the middle of the second century, in Rome, the author of the *Shepherd of Hermas* was also concerned about false prophets who were pretending to receive fake messages from God, causing scandal and discontent, and undermining the authority of those in charge.

The author of the Book of Revelations (also known as 'the Apocalypse') recorded an imaginary announcement which the angel guarding the church in Thyatira had dictated to him, criticising the members of that church for tolerating 'the woman Jezebel' who was claiming to be a prophetess.

The original Jezebel, a native of Tyre and wife of King Ahab – the Jezebel mentioned in the Old Testament – had been a foreigner who had led the Jewish people astray into idolatrous practices and encouraged them to join in disgusting immoral acts. She had been intimately involved in the worship of Baal. She had been able to summon 450 false prophets to her side and had promoted promiscuous sexual practices associated with idolatrous rituals.

The self-proclaimed prophetess in Asia Minor also gloried in the name 'Jezebel'. She regarded herself as a member of the sorority of those female prophets who had been active during Old Testament times and in the early Christian communities.

The Christians of Asia Minor would not have been surprised to see women sprouting their revelations and visions in the assembly and prophesying in public. Apart from the Jewish tradition of female prophets, women occupied major roles as priestesses in the Greco-Roman world, particularly in the eastern cults of Asia Minor.

At the beginning of the Apocalypse (which was composed at the end of the first century or perhaps early in the second and which, after some hesitation and disputation, would become part of the canon of the New Testament), the author addressed his special revelations to each of the seven churches of Asia – to Ephesus, Smyra, Pergamum, Sardis, Philadelphia, Laodice and Thyatira. He described each of the revelations he had received from on high and called on his readers to proclaim 'the words of the prophecy', the words that the angels of the various churches had dictated to him. 'Now write what you see, what is and what is to take place hereafter.'

The author had seen the figure of Christ in a dream, holding seven golden lampstands and seven stars in his right hand. The stars represented the angels and the stands stood for the seven churches of Asia. The angels were commissioned to deliver a special revelation to each of the seven churches.

The fourth of these prophecies was addressed to the church in Thyatira – a city situated near the west coast of Asia Minor, in the Roman province of Lydia. The angel offered a modicum of praise to encourage the faithful, and followed it with his solemn warning. The Son of God was critical of the local church for tolerating a woman named Jezebel who had described herself as a 'prophetess'. She was teaching Jesus' followers, encouraging them to engage in illicit sexual activity, and trying to get them to eat food that had been sacrificed to idols. When given a chance to repent, she had refused.

This wanton female prophet had taught some of members of the local church about 'the deep things of Satan', about potions and magical formulae that could summon evil spirits. Her followers were known as 'her children' (Apoc 22:15, 18–19, cf. 2 John 1:4, 13). By naming her Jezebel, the author wanted his readers to understand that this woman was like the Old Testament queen – a prostitute prophet who had promoted idolatry among her subjects – a beautiful, malevolent seductress.

Despite Jezebel and her school of prophetesses in Thyatira, however, the institution of prophecy and the role of female prophets continued to flourish for a time, even in the more conservative and 'orthodox' communities. There were good prophets, male and female, in the ranks, and bad ones.

Thyatira was a city in the same area of Asia where the founder of the Spirit-driven Montanist movement would appear a century or so after the composition of the Apocalypse. In the late second century Montanus would launch his religious fireworks from this location. He had come originally from a neighbouring province, Phrygia, and according to his followers his hometown, Pepuza, was destined to become the site where the Holy City would descend from heaven. This cataclysmic event was destined to occur when a dramatic outpouring of the Paraclete (similar to what had happened at Pentecost) would envelope the prophet and his friends, Prisca and Maximilla.

With the help of these two female colleagues, Montanus established a vibrant prophetic movement which would spread rapidly throughout Asia as well as to other parts of the Roman world, including the south of France. It would also put down deep roots in the soil of North Africa. Even though it was condemned by a number of local synods in Asia Minor and by Pope Zephyrinus, its extreme ascetical practices and beliefs were destined to appeal to the religious sensibilities of that moody, reactionary man from Carthage by the name of Tertullian.

As a movement Montanism was more or less orthodox in its theology. But like other Christians groups of the period, the founder and his followers were preaching harsh ascetical practices which were linked to a mangled understanding of sexuality and sin. The principal reason the church leaders condemned the founder and his movement was not because it was heterodox but because of its excesses – extreme fasting, mortifications and long vigils. It was also because, in place of the standard institutional authority conferred on individual bishops, they claimed to rely on a higher authority that was founded on the Spirit and divine inspiration.

The adherents of the Montanist movement sought to validate their religious system by establishing a prophetic line of succession. This would be similar to the 'orthodox' church's apostolic line of succession such as Bishop Irenaeus had traced for the Roman church in his *Adversus Haereses* (III.3:3). Their line of prophets included Agabus (who had been mentioned in Acts), Silas (who had been a companion of Paul and described as a prophet in Acts 15:32), Judas, the four unmarried daughters of Philip from Caesarea, Ammia of Philadelphia and Quadratus (Eusebius, *Eccl. Hist.* V. 17).

Well before the Spirit had gone to work on Montanus and his female friends, throwing them into convulsions and delivering novel revelations from heaven, prophetical practices had become popular throughout Asia Minor and beyond. As far as the more 'orthodox' churches were concerned, Montanus, Maximilla and Priscilla belonged to the dark side of the profession. In their rather exotic congregations, young women enjoyed equal billing on the liturgical stage and inside the movement. They also claimed that the Spirit was speaking directly to them through the fog of their ecstasies. Their messages were coming to them directly from the other side and these revelations were proving impossible for those in authority to control.

The Montanists asserted that their team of prophets enjoyed a status above Jesus' apostles, that they had been blessed with a special aura of perfection. The pronouncements of Priscilla and Maximila, and those of their partner Montanus, were being recorded and collected as sacred texts on a par with the sayings of Jesus and the letters of Paul the Apostle. The conservative authorities couldn't allow their rebellious beliefs to spread. These women had to be silenced. They could have ruined everything.

Hippolytus (d. 235 AD) was writing, probably in Rome, at the beginning of the third century. In his *Refutation of All Heresies* he provided a critique of Montanus and the 'two wretched women'.

> There are other people who themselves are even more heretical in nature and are Phrygians by birth. These have become victims of error from being captivated by two wretched women, Priscilla and Maximilla, who they suppose to be prophetesses (VIII. 12).

The Phrygians had been claiming that the Paraclete-Spirit had taken possession of these two women. According to Hippolytus, swamped in a wetland of their own dangerous publications, these 'heretics' had been eaten up by delusional thinking. They were not judging their weird messages against the dictates of reason and common sense. They weren't paying heed to those who were competent to make appropriate decisions (presumably, the bishops). Instead they had been following imposters who claimed to have learned some secret knowledge from the leaders of their community. They saw their knowledge as above the law, more powerful than the utterances of the true prophets, and even more persuasive than the Gospels. They had been elevating these 'wretched women' above the apostles and every gift of grace. Some even presumed to claim that their women possessed a grace superior to Christ.

Origen (d. 254 AD), a contemporary of Hippolytus, had a reputation as a serious scholar who was much appreciated as a teacher of repute in the suburbs of Alexandria. Like Hippolytus, he also knew of the followers of Montanus and of his female co-workers. He disparaged these followers, giving them the contemptuous title of 'disciples of women', and condemned them for choosing two females as their master rather than Christ. These female followers of Montanus felt confirmed in their prophesying by calling on the names of the female prophets who had gone before them. There was a line of succession giving them authority to speak – the daughters of Philip; Deborah, the wife of Lapidoth, a prophetess and the only female judge mentioned in the Old Testament; Mary, also known as Miriam, the sister of Aaron; Hulda, another Old Testament figure and the wife of Shallum who was the keeper of the royal wardrobe; and Anna, the temple-dweller and daughter of Phanuel (Origen, *Fragment on 1 Corinthians* 74).

> One of Origen's disciples, Firmilian, had heard of a Montanist prophetess (again in Asia Minor) who was causing havoc among the faithful. She was converting many lay people and clerics to her movement, baptising them and even celebrating the Eucharist (Cyprian, *Epistolae* 75:10).

As the name 'the New Prophecy' implied, the movement focused directly on visions, dreams and personal revelations. The followers believed that the 'three' prophets preached the Holy

Spirit's revelation for the present age. This 'New Prophecy,' at least as described by their enemy Eusebius of Caesarea, departed from established tradition and had the potential to destabilise the churches.

Eusebius Pamphili (historian, exegete and polemicist) began to write his *magnum opus*, *Historia Ecclesiastica*, in the latter part of the third century. In Book V, commencing at Chapter 14, he recorded the story of 'the false prophets of the Phrygians'. The devil, 'the enemy of God's church' and 'the hater of good and the lover of evil' had planted the seed of the strange heresies that were tormenting believers. Some followers of one of these heresies had believed that Montanus had been the Paraclete and that his two women companions had been prophetesses. They had behaved like 'venomous reptiles crawling on their bellies across Asia and Phygia'. As a historian, Eusebius was not what we have come to accept as a thoroughly impartial, disinterested storyteller. He was a partisan scholar and prone to colourful language.

These heresies had already been the target of a series of exposés – by Apollinarius of Hierapolis and others. According to Eusebius, one of these polemicists had visited Ancyra in central Asia Minor and had found the local church 'greatly agitated by his (i.e. Montanus's) novelty' and by his 'false prophecy'. He had spent 'many days' in disputation with false prophets and as a consequence, was well-placed to record what had transpired.

> There is said to be a certain village called Ardabau in that part of Mysia, which borders upon Phrygia. When Gratus was proconsul of Asia, as they say, a recent convert, Montanus by name, through his unquenchable desire for leadership, first gave the adversary opportunity against him. He became beside himself, and being suddenly in a sort of frenzy and ecstasy, he raved and began to babble and utter strange things, prophesying in a manner contrary to the constant custom of

the church handed down by tradition from the beginning (Eusebius, *Eccl. His.* V. 7).

This anonymous source reported that some of those who had heard Montanus's spurious utterances had concluded he was possessed by a deceitful spirit. They accused him of leading people astray. The devil had also stirred up two women who had been talking wildly, unreasonably and strangely, just like Montanus.

By way of a final knockout blow, the anonymous reporter pointed out that Montanus and his followers had not suffered for their beliefs as Jesus and his followers had done – persecuted, crucified and stoned. However, he reported that Montanus and his colleague Maximilla had exited this world by another route. The author had some doubts about the authenticity of the report, but even so, as a 'responsible' historian, he was prepared to repeat the rumours – and more than eighteen hundred years later I pass them on in their original form. These two false prophets had been incited by a spirit of frenzy to end their lives like the traitor Judas, at the end of a rope. They had hanged themselves, though not, as one would have expected, on the same branch.

> They say that these things happened in this manner. But as we did not see them, we do not pretend to know. Perhaps in such a manner, perhaps not, Montanus and Theodotus and the above-mentioned woman died.

Maybe this version of their flight was gossip spread by their enemies. In any event, by allowing on-going and uncontrolled 'revelations', the spirit raging through Asia clashed with officialdom. These people were the enemies of those who were trying to maintain order and orthodoxy. The bishops and their team wanted to preserve a direct line of continuity with the past.

On the death of Montanus, his female offsider took his place as leader of the movement. Of course the fact that the members of this prophetic movement were encouraging their women members to assume leadership roles within the community and within their liturgical gatherings, ordaining them as bishops, presbyters and deacons, disturbed the more traditional and conservative church leaders. This was not a direction in which the more orthodox leaders wanted to go.

Maximilla's opponents began to attack her. Rumours. Innuendoes. Slander and scandal. Allegations of immorality. Claims that in their mystery rites, the leaders used to slaughter children and mix baby blood in the Eucharistic chalices.

But we have to be careful not to read this polemical material too literally. Writers such as Irenaeus, Eusebius, Jerome and Epiphanius were on the attack, searching for points of weakness, ready to circulate rumours, gaining advantage over their enemies. They tended to base their material on prejudicial reports of the deeds of people they feared and despised – ancient versions of fake news and pre-election advertising spin.

Although the sayings and revelations of Montanus and his friends had been recorded in a substantial library, no documents have survived. What we know comes exclusively from the pen of their enemies, and for their own reasons, these authors were concentrating their attack especially on the women at the centre of the movement. Orthodox writers seemed unwilling to accept that women could make a meaningful contribution to the life of any faith community. They could not conceive of the possibility that women could enjoy some ministerial equality with men – with bishops and presbyters and with deacons and male prophets. These men couldn't entertain the thought that women could exercise the same ministry in liturgical gatherings as men, or could be involved in governance and in the daily life of the community.

Montanus and his female friends were challenging the authority of the episcopal leaders who sought to trace their legitimate line of authority to the college of apostles and to what they had taught. These parvenus had made an appearance in the centre of verdant Christian territory in Asia Minor, with a message that the Holy Spirit was continuing to reveal new truths through a prophet and his two female associates. They claimed to belong to a line of prophets and prophetesses, but they had been given no official commission to teach. They were not linked to any apostolic line of succession.

Like the Gnostic sects, these pretenders were attracting enthusiastic followers. Montanus was proving a danger to the institution, not least because he was accompanied by female prophets who were drunk on their power and who, under the influence of ecstatic religious juices, were babbling unwelcomed revelations. For an organisation seeking to be mainstream and socially acceptable, anxious to project a conservative image to the world, these women seemed dangerously reminiscent of the female seers of the pagan cultic centres. The institution could not afford to allow women like these to penetrate its structure and challenge the authority of its leaders.

The New Prophecy spread rapidly from Montanus's native province of Phrygia across the Christian world to Africa. There it was embraced by Tertullian (as some scholars have concluded), before reaching Gaul where it was repudiated by Irenaeus.

Although prophecy had been an important ministry in the primitive Christian communities, and female exponents of the art had been tolerated (if not positively encouraged), Irenaeus wanted his people to understand that this ministry was open to fraudsters and charlatans, and that those who were excessively pious could be hypnotised by practitioners of the art. The bishop of Lyon thought that women seemed particularly keen to participate in weird religious orgies where they would share their special favours, including untidy streams of subconscious nonsense from a world beyond.

According to this bishop, a devil who had taken possession of one of his Gnostic enemies was inspiring him and his followers to indulge their penchant for prophecy. Irenaeus reported that a Gnostic leader called Marcus was keen to encourage his female camp followers, especially the rich, elegant, aristocratic ones, to give voice to their personal revelations.

> He says to her, open your mouth, speak whatsoever occurs to you, and you shall prophesy. Vainly puffed up and elated by these words, and greatly excited in soul by the expectation that it is herself who is to prophesy, her heart beating violently, she reaches the requisite pitch of audacity, and idly as well as impudently utters some stupid nonsense as might be expected from one heated by a vacuous spirit (*Adversus Haereses*, I.13/3).

Irenaeus's pen was on fire. He used his special gift of invective to pursue his pastoral ministry. Marcus obviously had the gift of corralling and hypnotising women – rich women. He could fascinate his battery of devoted followers to such an extent that they were ready to hand over their considerable fortunes (or their husbands' accumulated wealth) and enthusiastically offer their bodies, 'desiring to be completely united to him, so that she may become altogether one with him'. Marcus obviously had a reputation as a ladies' man and the bishop was not impressed.

Some of the women who had left the more orthodox Christian community in and around Lyon, women who had tasted the forbidden fruits Marcus had had on offer, had eventually decided to abandon him and his followers and return to the church where Irenaeus was in charge. Of course, they didn't hesitate to describe what they had been involved in. If Irenaeus can be believed, during the festive gatherings the women used to draw lots to elect the one who could command the other girls to utter prophecies and to give forth as oracles from heaven whatever answered their base desires. The possibilities were endless.

According to Irenaeus, Marcus used to concoct love-potions and distribute hallucinogenic drugs to bewitch his female followers and 'fill them with a burning passion'. He would take unconscionable advantage of these silly, giddy women, or so Irenaeus would have his readers believe. At one stage, Marcus was said to have cuckolded one of the bishop's deacons, a man who had invited the prophet into his home. His wife was a woman of remarkable beauty. Like many of her sisters before her, she had fallen under the magician's spell, left her home and family, and for a long time travelled about with her hero, allowing him to do with her whatever took his fancy.

And it seems that Marcus had not been the only male member of the group who had had the chance to indulge himself. Irenaeus tells us that some of Marcus's lucky male followers could share in the spoils that were available to club members – to those who had attained a high degree of perfection by the infusion of some secret *gnosis*. These men enjoyed a level of special knowledge which was greater than Paul's or Peter's, or of any of the apostles.

> The followers of Marcus claim that they know more than all others, and that they alone have imbibed the greatness of the knowledge of that power which is unspeakable (*Adversus Haereses*, Book 1, Chapter 13:6).

Marcus and his gang of know-alls had made inroads 'into our district of the Rhone' and the damage had cut deep into the life of the community. They had deluded many of the women and seared their delicate consciences 'with a red-hot iron'. They had to be stopped.

We don't know exactly what was happening among these followers of Marcus. We only have an enemy's version, and his account undoubtedly contained elements of post-Truth religious spin. The bishop's account was highly coloured but in the absence of more trustworthy sources it became the standard version, a version that has supported an image of women as ill-disciplined, capricious sexual creatures who could undermine authority and cause untold damage to any movement. Still, it must be acknowledged that the bishop's mindset involving women was the stereotypical version shared by many of his brothers.

Whatever one might imagine was really going on inside his sect, by reputation Marcus was a handsome, charismatic religious leader. He could attract female followers and keep them engaged and happy. The ladies were fully occupied in the life of his company of followers – ordering others about, prophesying, presiding and praying publicly, as well as providing other services. Women were a fully functioning part of his community. The crudity and vehemence of the bishop's attack is significant, even if not historically accurate. No wonder the conservative branch of the movement Jesus had founded was opposed to female involvement.

One of the bishop's underlying messages was that female members were unreliable, untrustworthy and often hysterical. They were disruptive and disorderly. We can readily see that he was not keen to involve them actively in the life of his community.

Judging from his available writings, Irenaeus demonstrated little understanding of the cause of his pastoral problem, and unlike Jesus he had little sympathy for those who had gone astray. The phrases 'silly women' and 'buffooneries' would never have been found on Jesus' lips – and they don't seem appropriate in assisting in resolving the institution's problems, though Irenaeus was undoubtedly writing with his supporters in mind.

The bishop seemed keen to describe his own 'orthodox' community by contrasting it with the terrible Gnostics. He wanted to emphasise ecclesial order, discipline, a clear line of authority and conformity to traditional beliefs and practices. He seemed to think that the extreme defined the norm. Because women in the Gnostic sects were such a problem, his solution didn't involve negotiating a middle path and creating a culture in which women could participate fully and in accordance with the Gospel values. They had to be excluded altogether, contrary to the policy which characterised Jesus' public life.

But Irenaeus also accepted that prophecy had been an important part of the life of the church from the beginning. In the treatise which he wrote to confront various schools of Gnostic beliefs and practices he trained his episcopal sights on the New Prophecy and the followers of Montanus. By rejecting the Gospel of John and Jesus' promise to send the Paraclete, these heretics had destroyed the basis of the church's true prophetic ministry. They had effectively removed the ground from under their own religious system. 'Such stupid men! They want to be pseudo-prophets and at the same time suppress the gift of prophecy in the church.'

As Irenaeus saw it, the Montanists had been condemned by the rules of logic to repudiate what the Apostle Paul had to say:

> For in his Epistle to the Corinthians he speaks expressly of prophetical gifts and recognizes men and women prophesying in the church' (*Adv. Haer.* III. 11).

While the bishop was dealing with his particular situation in the south of France towards the end of the second century, he accepted that from the beginning, from apostolic times, some men and women had been recognised as exercising a special ministry. There had been space provided for them in the gatherings to communicate the spontaneous revelations which came to them from on high. These graced members of the community had been carrying out their prophetic ministry for the benefit of a particular congregation, in Caesarea or Corinth for example, or for various local churches in a particular region. These spiritual forces seem to have been particularly concentrated in the Asia Minor region, in places where the mystery cults were popular. Prophets and prophetesses were all the rage in the multicultural religious maelstrom round the rim of the Mediterranean in the first, second and third centuries, but Asia Minor was in the eye of the storm where most of the frenetic activity was concentrated.

In North Africa, Tertullian, ever the religious fanatic, had also been impressed by the personal power and the revelations of two high-profile prophetesses who followed the lead of Montanus (*De exhortatione castitatis* 10:5; *De resurrection carnis* 11:2; *Adversus Praxean* 1:5; *De ieiunio* 1:3). Despite being a classical misogynist, he was drawn into the world of female prophets.

In his treatise *De anima*, he had also painted a sympathetic portrait of a 'sister' who had been blessed with a range of special gifts – gifts of revelations and apparitions that she used to experience. These had come to her 'out-of-the-blue' in the course of the Sunday liturgy. Amidst the blinding shafts of mysterious visions and startling revelations touching the hearts of her fellow worshippers, she had conversed with angels, and sometimes even with the Lord.

At the conclusion of the liturgy (since liturgy was the exclusive domain of men), after the male celebrant had dismissed the faithful, this gifted female used to report to those in charge whatever had come to her in her vision. In order to ensure her probity, the community leaders would examine these communications with scrupulous care. According to Tertullian she had told them,

> Amongst other thing, there has been shown to me a soul in bodily shape, and a spirit has been in the habit of appearing to me; not, however, a void and empty illusion, but such as would offer itself to be grasped by the hand, soft and transparent and of an ethereal colour, and in form resembling that of a human being in every respect (9:4).

God was her witness. His apostle Paul had foretold that there were to be 'spiritual gifts' in the church, that God's servants *and his handmaids* would see visions, dream dreams and utter prophecies.

Tertullian was not deterred by his generally negative view of women. He had read what the situation had been in Corinth during Paul's time in the region. His support for the harsh practices of the Montanists and his faith in the divine inspiration of the scriptures forced him to accept that women had a place in the life of the church – but their participation did not extend to public worship. The sacred books had stated that women would receive divine visions, and he accepted the word of God.

> All these visions can be regarded as emanating from God, as being honest, holy, prophetic, inspired, instructive, inviting to virtue, the bountiful nature of which causes them to overflow even to the profane, since God, with grand impartiality, sends his showers and sunshine on the just and on the unjust (*De anima* 47:2).

But Tertullian was careful to maintain that these spontaneous interventions involving women were not part of any official liturgical event – not part of those occasions, such as Paul was supposed to have identified, when women were obliged to remain silent. They occurred only during the readings, for example, or while the psalms were being sung, during the homily or the prayers of the faithful.

Prophetesses dreamt dreams that came to them from on high and received stunning revelations from angels and other foreign figures. They were commissioned to pass these celestial messages on to the believers of their local churches. These gifted women, like their male counterparts, enjoyed an elevated status among the followers of Jesus. But the whole process was open to fakery and fraud. The practitioners of the art could cause turmoil in the ranks. Unsophisticated, gullible believers were ready, perhaps even anxious to put their faith in the most outlandish charlatan and swallow his/her crazy announcement of divine revelations. It was difficult, at times impossible, to distinguish between a truly graced prophetess and a crafty fake.

Even from this distance, it's easy to accept that there were tensions within the early communities. Tensions between those who claimed to possess the gift of prophecy from the Spirit of God and those who sought to impose their God-given authority on the gatherings to guarantee some form of continuity with the past, some semblance of order and orthodoxy. In the end, this tension involved a struggle between some female believers and the male members of the community – women who believed that they had an important role to play and the right to share in the spread of Jesus' message, and men who claimed the power and authority to regulate and govern.

Cliques of Angelic Virgins

At the end of the fourth century, the Christian emperor Theodorus disbanded the college of Vestal Virgins and extinguished the temple fire which, according to legend, these virgins had supervised for more than a thousand years. The vestals had been a community of virgin-priestesses consecrated to the goddess Vesta. They were vowed to a life of virginal chastity and charged with maintaining the perpetual sacred flame burning at her altar.

Vesta had been the Roman goddess of the heath – the *protectrice* of the home and family. While ideally the candidates for office had been selected by the emperor from the best Roman families, from among the rich and famous, since each candidate was expected to remain uncontaminated by sex and could be buried alive if she happened to falter and fornicate, some families were reluctant to put their daughter's name forward. Consequently, over the years, some candidates had come from the lower ranks of Roman society. Nonetheless they were consecrated and sacred young women.

Many of these Vestal Virgins had begun their thirty-year careers when they were children, somewhere between the ages of six and ten. They had been offered up to the state by their fathers who were acting as the head of the household. They had been removed from their family and friends to become members of an isolated team of girls and young women who lived together at the rear of Vesta's temple complex.

This team of six or eight virgins had watched over the temple flame and kept it burning bright. They had also looked after the wills and testaments of some important Roman citizens. As a body, they attended public ceremonies and were accommodated in special boxes or stalls on public occasions. They were dressed in white priestly garments and travelled around in a covered carriage. They never appeared in public on their own. Always in a group and until the end of the fourth century, these virgins had been an important public institution.

But by the end of the fourth century, when Theodorus disbanded the college, the importance of these women for Rome and the empire had diminished. Rome had undergone a conversion. She had become a Christian city. Paganism was on the wane, and the church in the ascendancy. Pagan beliefs and customs were being transformed and replaced with a new system of beliefs and customs, by a new institution, by Christian groups and organisations. The ancient institution of Vestal Virgins simply disappeared and rose again as a Christian movement of ascetics and virgins.

But the basis for any general acceptance of the importance of virginity and the celibate life at an early stage in the development of Christianity seems surprisingly thin. It is almost entirely to be found, as we have seen, in the writings of Paul and their later interpretation by commentators such as Jerome.

We can conclude from the Gospel literature that Peter was married, though while we read of his mother-in-law, we do not meet his wife. Some of Jesus' female disciples were married and it seems reasonable to assume that at least some (perhaps the majority) of his chosen twelve Apostles (presuming as a matter of historical fact that there were twelve in the initial team) were also blessed with wives.

In the Gospels we meet Jesus for the first time at the age of thirty as he launches his public career as a preacher. We have no idea what he had been doing up to that point – where he had lived, where he had travelled, who had been his friends, what level of education he had received or how he had earned a living – and perhaps whether he had been married or not, though for some strange reason tradition as it developed was certain beyond question that he had always been a virgin and a celibate. There is never the least hint that he had had a partner or a wife, though he certainly had a number of close female friends, and especially one who enjoyed a special relationship with him.

Apart from the living arrangements that emerge from reading the Gospel literature, there is also a hint that Jesus acknowledged and perhaps encouraged a sex-less celibate way of life for some of his followers. Certainly not for all, only for those who were minded to receive such a special message.

The general Jesus policy from the beginning was stated by the author of Mark's Gospel and harkens back to the story in Genesis.

> But from the beginning of creation, 'God made them male and female'. 'For this reason a man shall leave his father and mother and be joined to his wife, and the two shall become one. So they are no longer two but one. What therefore God has joined together, let not man put asunder' (10:6–8).

While virginity does not attract a great deal of press in any of the four canonical Gospels, Jesus adjusted his general policy in order to accommodate those of his followers who were minded to remain celibate 'for the sake of the kingdom of heaven'. If we can believe the Gospel accounts, virginity was not a matter on which Jesus had focused his attention. The author of the Gospel of Matthew reported, maybe with a burst of wry humour, that Jesus had encouraged some of his followers to live as 'eunuchs', as though they had been castrated 'for the sake of the kingdom of heaven'.

These words of Jesus are probably something he did say, because they give some expression to his dominant idea of the kingdom of heaven. We are not sure whether Jesus saw this option as a way of life or as a pragmatic decision for a brief period in order to journey about, preaching his message. His blunt dictum would be used to establish a spirituality founded on virginity which in turn led to monasticism and a number of very peculiar practices and customs. Of course these words of Jesus should not be taken literally, though over the years some religious fanatics have sacrificed their manhood on the say-so of Jesus.

One of Jesus' famous stories traces an imaginary moment in the lives of ten virgins. The author of Matthew (and only he) told the story of a group of young virgins' long wait for the arrival of a particular bridegroom. Jesus was drawing on a popular Jewish custom. Young maidens or virgins used to play an important role as torch-bearers in the torch-light procession of the bride to the groom's house – a procession which ended in a nocturnal torch-light celebration and dance outside his home. In the story, these girls were outside the bridegroom's home waiting for him to come out so they could accompany him to the bride's home then back to his house for the nuptial celebration. These young unmarried women or girls were an important part of the bridal party and would later become an important feature of a bishop's retinue.

In Jesus' story, a marriage was not pictured as an all-male event. Men and women were involved – a bride, the groom, the bridesmaids and guests – like the feast of Cana at which Jesus, his mother and his disciples had been guests. However, at weddings and on other occasions it may have happened that men and women celebrated at the same time but in different places.

The virginity motif in the canonical Gospels is rather flimsy. It consists of an announcement of a messianic virgin birth in the Gospels of Matthew and Luke; a typical Semitic raw observation about evangelical eunuchs in Matthew's Gospel, and a story about a bridal party of ten virgins. This theme of virginity shifted up a gear in some of Paul's letters which, as a matter of historical fact, predated the Gospels.

We have already considered at length what Paul had to say to the people in Corinth on the topic of 'not touching women', on the bedroom relationship of a husband and his wife, on marriage and Paul's own preference for a celibate life for Christians. Within a few generations, his advice and observations would be culled from its context, reinterpreted and exploited to promote a vigorous movement towards virginity and celibacy, especially in the Roman Catholic Church.

A number of the earlier Christian writers spoke of widows as though in the life of the church they were like sacred altars. This was probably because the gifts of the faithful that were distributed among these women used to be placed on the altar-table in their churches. The literary association may also have had something to do with the widows' special duty as pray-ers, and with the fact that they were encouraged to model themselves on the faith of the martyrs whose relics were buried in the altar. Later writers would use the altar image to persuade widows that they should remain in one place, at home, fixed and stable (like altars) and not be gadding about causing trouble.

And while widows were likened to *bronze* altars, Christian writers were depicting virgins as *golden* altars who were hidden like consecrated treasures in the Holy of Holies. Methodius spoke of virginity as a priceless treasure. A virgin was a girl untarnished by sex, a pure and stainless vessel, someone removed from the odours of ordinary human life.

> The golden altar within the Holy of Holies, standing in the presence of the testimony, an altar on which it is forbidden to offer sacrifice and libation, is a reminder of those in a state of virginity, to those who have their bodies preserved from carnal intercourse, pure like unalloyed gold ... Gold is suitably

a symbol of virginity which does not admit any stain or spot, but ever shines forth with the light of the Word. Therefore it stands nearer *to God* within the Holy of Holies, and before the veil, with undefiled hands (*Symposium*, V. 8).

In his collection of short biographies, the *de viris illustribus*, the scholarly Jerome described Methodius as 'a most eloquent martyr' who had written 'in a polished and attractive style'. One of his books was a lengthy treatise, written in the form of a dialogue, on the subject of virginity.

The bishop of Lycia in Asia Minor died in the first few years of the fourth century. His book *The Banquet*, or the *Symposium*, tells the story of a festive meal at which ten young virgins (modelled on the ten virgins of Jesus' parable whose lamps had been trimmed as they awaited the arrival of the bridegroom) were entertaining themselves by taking turns singing the praises of virginity.

According to the story, these girls were seated around a fountain 'flowing smooth in heavy oil', shaded under an *agnus castus* tree, a species of tree also known as the *chaste tree*, because it had a reputation for quelling the male libido. The chaste tree was considered to be sacred to the goddess Hestia who was herself a virgin. It has delicately textured foliage with lavender coloured aromatic flowers that are very attractive to butterflies and bees. These ten virgins were celebrating the beauty of their virginal lifestyle shaded by a tree which could quell their natural urges.

In the story, the first contributor, Marcella, opened her eulogy with a burst of ecstatic joyfulness, announcing that virginity is the soil which nourishes immortality:

> Virginity is something supernaturally great, wonderful, and glorious. This best and noblest manner of life alone is the root of immortality.

The Methodius paen is a parody of Plato's major work. In lieu of virgins, Plato had constructed his *Symposium* around a gathering of sexually active Athenian gentlemen. The bishop replaced Plato's principal participant, Socrates, with the leader of the ten virgins, a girl named Thecla, and in the course of his parody the author drifted far from the stories and adages of Jesus as they were recorded in the Gospels.

According to Methodius, Christ had restored the earth to its original virginal condition which God had created in the person of Adam. After a long and tangled history tracing the development of the human race, Christ had finally defeated the devil. As a result, humanity could become, in its flesh, what it was before the Fall – a beautiful, musical instrument of praise and thanksgiving in virginal flesh. This counterbalance between Adam and Christ was a theme that Paul had initiated in his letter to the Romans and that had been exploited by several of the early Christian authors, including Irenaeus of Lyon. Methodius inserted the same theme at the centre of Thaleia's contribution in Discourse III.

In order to return to the original perfection of pure virginity, mankind had passed through six stages. Methodius constructed human history in terms similar to Irenaeus – as the story of a slowly unfolding plan for the world which God has been forever in the process of creating. But the bishop had inserted his own particular slant on the subject. History was the story of the gradual taming of the raw sexual drive God had implanted in Adam and which was in the process of being sublimated. Once the earth had been fully populated, mankind could cease the 'shudder' of intercourse and concentrate on enhancing the harmony and peace experienced in the church of Christ. Sex had gradually, in stages, become redundant. As Theophila told her fellow virgins in Discourse II:

> When thirsting for children, a man falls into a kind of trance, softened and subdued by the pleasures of procreation as by sleep, so that once again something drawn from his flesh and

from his bones is fashioned into another man. To achieve a sense of harmony and peace in the bodies being disturbed in the embrace of love, as those tell us who have experience of the marriage state, all the marrow-like and generative part of the blood, like a kind of liquid bone, coming together from all the members, worked into a foam and curdled, is projected through the male genital organs into the living body of the female.

These young women's third-hand view of the way babies were made relied on the pre-scientific views of Aristotle and others. In the process of procreation, the male was the dominant, active force and the female was the oven which received the stuff the male produced. Nevertheless, despite their pre-scientific explanation, these virgins had a pretty fair idea as to how babies were made. The colourful description of what happens under the sheets leaves little to the imagination. These fictitious virgins knew more than their prayers.

Methodius listed the six ages of man:

1. The original, post-Fall inter-marrying between brother and sister – a period of brutal incest.
2. Choosing female partners from other families and marrying them – an age of polygamy.
3. The age of monogamous marriages.
4. The age of prohibitions against adultery or illicit relationships.
5. An age of continence within marriage.
6. The original pre-Fall and uncorrupted stability of the virginal state accompanied by a loathing of the flesh.

Methodius depicted his ten young women as members of an order, like a study group or a book club, and in his concluding discourse, their leader, Thecla, sung an antiphonal hymn of praise to virginity. The text is framed like a ceremony for the induction of eager young females into an order of virgins.

Theopatra (the narrator of the story) commanded her sisters who were standing under the *agnus castus* tree to send up to the Lord a suitable hymn of thanksgiving. She ordered Thecla to begin her song and to lead the others. Thecla is seen standing in the middle of the group, singing like a nightingale. The others are standing together in a circle, like a chorus, chanting the responses:

> *Thecla*: From above, O virgins, the sound of a noise that wakes the dead has come, bidding us all to meet the bridegroom in white robes, and with torches towards the east. Arise, before the king enters within the gates.
>
> *Chorus*: I keep myself pure for you, O bridegroom, and holding a lighted torch I go to meet you.
>
> *Thecla*: Fleeing from the sorrowful happiness of mortals, and having despised the luxuriant delights of life and its love, I desire to be protected under your life-giving arms, and to behold your beauty forever, O blessed one.
>
> *Chorus*: I keep myself pure for you, O bridegroom, and holding a lighted torch I go to meet you.
>
> *Thecla*: Leaving marriage and the beds of mortals and my golden home for you, O king, I have come in undefiled robes, in order that I might enter with you within your happy bridal chamber.
>
> *Chorus*: I keep myself pure for you, O bridegroom, and holding a lighted torch I go to meet you.

These are the first three verses of a song which continued for 24 stanzas. The sentiments are explicit – sensual, sexual and belonging to another, heavenly world.

Methodius was writing his imaginary dream-sequence well before the Emperor Constantine had convened the Council of Nicaea (325 AD). The virginal lifestyle had already been well established. Young girls had begun to live in communities away from their families and were dedicating themselves to an idyllic life together, living as consecrated virgins, reflecting in their lives the angelic realities of another world beyond the horizon. This distinct aspect of the life of the early church appeared for the first time around the time when the author of John's Gospel and the author of the Apocalypse were composing their works.

Methodius was one of many early Christian writers from the second to the fifth century who dealt at length with the glories and pitfalls of a life of virginity – from his imaginary dream world, as we will see, the anonymous author of the *Shepherd of Hermas* was singing the praises of virginity. He was followed by Tertullian of Carthage (c160–c225) who was also strong on the virtue of chastity, the rules around female modesty and the angelic values of virginity (*de cultu feminarum, de virginibus velandis, de exhortatione castitatis*).

Following Tertullian there was an explosion of treatises on virginity. These include fourth century works by:

- Cyprian who was also of Carthage (*de habitu virginum*);

- The author of the Pseudo-Clementines, a series of documents which included two Epistles to Virgins (*ad Virgines*);

- Athanasius of Alexandria (*On Virginity – Timely Advice*);

- Ambrose, Bishop of Milan (*de virginibus* and *de virginitate*);

- Evagrius of Pontus (*sententiae ad virginem*);

- Gregory of Nyssa (*On Virginity*);

- The Arian bishop, Basil of Ancyra (*de virginitate tuenda*, or *On the Preservation of Virginity*) produced a practical and blunt treatise on sex and how to avoid it.

There were also fifth century works including:

- Jerome of Rome and Palestine who wrote several long letters to his female friends on the subject - for example, his letter to Eustochium which he wrote in 384 AD was known by the title *De Custodia Virginitatis*;

- Augustine of North Africa (*On Holy Virginity*); and

- John Chrysostom of Constantinople (*On Virginity*).

A specialised literary genre dedicated to the practice of virginity was now appearing.

The physical integrity of a woman came to bear an exceptionally refined symbolic and religious meaning. It was a symbol of transcendent purity, of primeval physical integrity and of the state of innocence associated with God's sublime creature as she was before the Fall. Her sheltered, secluded, undisrupted and organised regular life of prayer and contemplation engendered a sense of mystery, holiness and power which permeated the whole community. In Methodius' time a virgin was viewed as completely Other – as belonging to another world. She was a bride of Christ – a playmate and companion of God in heaven.

Gradually, young girls who were living at home with their parents were choosing to renounce marriage, to dedicate themselves to a life of prayer and virginal purity and embrace the freedom of a celibate way of life. They were becoming a visible presence within the community. They sat together in the assemblies in a designated area, veiled and in silence. When they were not worshipping and praying together in the church they were expected to remain at home, off the streets and out of sight. They were the heavenly members of the community, the praying arm of the organisation. They were an important sign of witness, to be seen (but only at public ceremonials and liturgical gatherings), but not heard. They were trophies for the institution and living guarantees of what was in store for the true believer.

These women constituted a presence in the local churches of the third century, but a rather haunting presence: young girls removed from the sweaty odours of daily life, a constant reminder to all Christians of their calling to leave the world and escape the pull of the flesh, a message that intimate body contact stained a true believer. They were fragile angels – untouchable, passive, obedient, demure and disembodied.

From about the fourth century, this virginity movement would move up a gear and begin to transform itself into the wealthy nunneries and monasteries, thereby creating a whole new, parallel world inside the church.

In the middle of the fourth century there was a 'holy and heavenly profession' of young virgins which the heathens, at least in Egypt, saw and admired. Athanasius, the patriarch of Alexandria, claimed that such a distinguished profession existed nowhere else but among Christians. These virgins were a convincing argument that Christianity was 'a genuine and true religion', or so he told the emperor. These women were called the 'brides of Christ', 'most sacred persons' and 'lilies among thorns', and were the pride of the bishop himself. His cathedral seat of ecclesiastical power contained rows or benches on raised steps, thrones hidden behind curtains. Gatherings of believers witnessed extravagant processions of chanting virgins (Augustine of Hippo, *Contra Faustum*).

The bishop's retinue of virgins came to symbolise his status in society and within the community. These women reflected the purity of mankind's first parents before their tragic fall from grace. They reflected the holiness of the angels and saints in paradise.

These virgins were mostly young girls who had been volunteered by their family for service to the church and the bishop. They were hidden away from the outside world and imprisoned in a sacred language – sacred vessels dedicated to God (Eusebius of Emesa, *Homily* 6/18). When they appeared in public, they were dressed like brides in a white garment, fully veiled members of a group or sodality.

The members of the Christian community and their leaders idealised these young girls. They were like angels. They did not belong to the world. According to the Fathers of the church, they witnessed to an innate love of virginity, though at least Basil of Caesarea took a more pragmatic, even cynical view of the custom of consecrated virginity:

> Parents, and brothers and other relatives bring forward many girls before the proper age, not because the girls have an inner urge towards continence, but in order that their relatives may gain some material advantage from so doing (*Letter* 119/18).

Daughters could be moved around between families like pawns on a chessboard, in order to further the family's economic, political or social status. While the male believers who were inclined to heroic practices of asceticism tended to withdraw into isolated desert regions, their female counterparts followed the same way of life but hidden away within the household. Virgin daughters lived a life of domestic seclusion. They left the inner rooms of the family house and exposed themselves to the light of the sun only to attend ceremonies in the local church, and then only in a group, and in a specially designed space. These women were largely invisible. In one particularly egregious case, if the historian Palladius can be believed, a beautiful young girl in Alexandria spent her life sealed in a tomb and was fed occasionally on bread and water through a small opening (*Lausiac History* 5/2).

The pastoral policy of the period was that, as far as possible, every household should have its own resident virgin who would guarantee the salvation of all the members of the family.

> In every house of Christians, it is needful that there be a virgin, for the salvation of the whole house is that one virgin. And when wrath comes upon the whole city, it shall not come upon the house wherein a virgin is (*Canons of Athanasius* 98, cf. Eusebius of Emesa, *Homily* 7/24).

Gradually virgins began to live in small groups, renting rooms together, or one inviting a soul mate into her family home. Friendships developed between young women of similar aspirations. Rich widows or unmarried sisters of members of the clergy or of male ascetics encouraged local virgins to live with them in their house. Eventually they formed groups of fifty to a hundred (Palladius, *Lausiac History* 1/4; 5/3; 676/1; Theodoret, *Eccl. Hist.* 3/14).

> The women, gathered from every walk of life, quarrel continuously with each other (Palladius, 29/1).

Jesus' spoke of some of his followers becoming eunuchs for the kingdom. Paul's personal recommendation was that believers adopt the freedom of a celibate life. Together these words had given rise to what became a popular drive for many Christians towards an asexual life, or a life based on a form of 'angelism'. Some especially fervent members of the communities were inspired to try to avoid the contamination of sexual intimacy and to preserve their bodies in their original virginal condition, like Adam before the Fall, like Mary the mother of Jesus and Jesus himself.

Virginity came to be seen as a form of heavenly or angelic integrity which could be achieved here on earth. Virgins came to be seen as the spouses of Christ the bridegroom, and a sign that the kingdom of God, the heavenly Jerusalem, was present in our midst down here on earth. Although this was not the kingdom Jesus had preached, virginity was made the ideal for believers – the perfect way to live a Christian life. It was the highest possible state a person could achieve on earth – the original purity of Adam before his fatal fall into sin, before any sexual experience had addled his brain and contaminated his body.

Cohabiting with Virgins

The *Shepherd of Hermas*

The *Shepherd of Hermas* is an important Christian document from the end of the first century or perhaps from the first half of the second century. It predates the treatise of Irenaeus, the works of Tertullian and the writings of Clement of Alexandria. For some time it was considered by some to be part of the scriptures. Irenaeus accepted it as a canonical text, as did Clement of Alexandria, and also Tertullian, at least in his early years.

According to the story, Hermas was a Christian slave who had been sold to a lady named Rhoda, but who later became a successful and then bankrupt businessman. An angel graced him with a number of visions, a list of commandments and ten stories or parables, and these became the contents of the *Shepherd of Hermas* document. These had all come to him through an angel of repentance disguised as a shepherd – hence the title. The author was eventually enrolled, along with such figures as Clement of Rome, Ignatius and Polycarp, in the Honours List of Apostolic Fathers.

In Parable IX, the angel recounts a story about people, including twelve virgins, who were involved in the construction of a tower. The story is really a parable about the establishment of the church and was never intended to be read literally as historical fact. In the course of the narrative the reader meets the shepherd-angel, and Hermas, the storyteller. Hermas has spent a number of back-to-back shifts on the building site, watching what was going on and questioning the shepherd.

Hermas is fascinated by a gate which was cut out of a large rock and glittering in the sun. Twelve virtuous virgins, clothed in linen tunics and gracefully girded, are standing nearby, with their right shoulders exposed as if ready to make their contribution to the construction of the tower by carrying a heavy piece of timber, for example, or some scaffolding.

In the story, Hermas sees twelve other beautiful women on site, clad in black, shoulders bare and their hair cascading loosely down over their shoulders. Watching these twelve carting heavy stones, Hermas thinks that they look rather wild and fiery in appearance. (Full-flowing locks were a telling sign for the reader of women of easy virtue.)

At one stage, the twelve virgins (not the women in black) begin to sweep up the rubbish in the tower and sprinkle water around to make the building site fresh and clean.

The shepherd tells Hermes that if the Lord should come to inspect the tower, he will find nothing to blame them for, and announces that he intends to leave the site for a while.

Hermes catches hold of the shepherd's money-purse and says,

> I would like to know, sir, what is the meaning of the building of this tower? And what the rock and gate, and the mountains, and the virgins mean? And the stones which came out of the pit, stones which were not hewn but which came as they were to the building?

The shepherd replies, 'I'm busy for a little while. I'll explain everything to you later. Wait for me here till I come.'

Hermes wants to know what he is supposed to do there on his own, but the shepherd corrects him. He's not alone. The virgins would remain on site with him. Then he summons them and introduces Hermes to them. 'I commend this man to you till I come.'

Hermes continues the story:

> So I was alone with the virgins; and they were most cheerful and kindly disposed to me, especially the four that were the more glorious in appearance.

The virgins inform Hermas that the shepherd doesn't intend to return to the site that day and they invite him to stay with them. Hermes says that he will wait till evening and if the shepherd doesn't show, he will go home and come back the next day.

He is a man of prudence and surrounded by pretty girls. He has no need to expose himself to unnecessary temptation. But he has been entrusted to them and they insist that they will look after him in the shepherd's absence.

> Thou shalt pass the night with us, as a brother, not as a husband; for you are our brother, and from now on, we will dwell with you, for we love you dearly.

Here we have echoes of a custom involving virgins and 'wise' ascetics (or members of the clergy) living together – a custom we will come to in due course.

In the story, the virgin who appears to be the leader of the team begins to kiss Hermas and embrace him. The others join in and start to kiss him, to lead him round the tower and play with him. This must have been a most satisfying dream. A man's vision of what he can expect in heaven!

As the story unfolds, Hermas becomes young again and begins to enjoy the company of the young girls. Some of them start to dance, others to skip and sing.

When evening comes, Hermas still wants to return home but the virgins insist he stay with them there on site. He stays the night with them, sleeping by the side of the tower. The virgins spread their linen tunics on the ground and make him lie down among them. They pray together – and nothing else. They are happy when Hermas begins to pray with them – and he stays until the morning.

When the shepherd finally returns the next day, Hermas tells him how happy he had been to spend the night praying and sleeping with his workers.

But Hermas is curious to know who these workers are – the twelve women in black and the virgins who had entertained him:

> Declare to me, Sir, the names of the virgins, and of the women that are clothed in the black garments.

The names of the more powerful virgins, he was told, are Faith, Continence, Power and Long-suffering. And their companions are Simplicity, Guilelessness, Purity, Cheerfulness, Truth, Understanding, Concord and Love.

The names of the twelve women in black are Unbelief, Intemperance, Disobedience and Deceit (the more powerful ones) with their associates called Sadness, Wickedness, Wantonness, Irascibility, Falsehood, Folly, Slander and Hatred.

All beautiful women; some very tempting, all of them untouchable. All female characters in an elaborate allegory from the end of the first century or the beginning of the second – spiritual reading for the early believers. The Shepherd's fairy tale is the first indication of Christian virgins dancing and playing, praying and sleeping, with a male companion.

Dostoevsky

At the beginning of his novel *The Karamazov Brothers*, Fyodor Dostoevsky introduces his reader to the youngest of the Karamazov brothers, Alyosha, and to his spiritual director, the elderly monk Zossima. In doing so he traces the story of elders in the Russian orthodox monastic tradition – a story which, he tells us, goes back for a thousand years and more to Constantinople, and perhaps beyond.

In this Russian tradition an elder was a monk who had been touched by the divine and who took someone else's soul and will and incorporated it into his own soul and will. The novice or pupil was supposed to renounce his own will and yield himself completely, in total submission and self-abnegation, to his confessor, thereby enabling the grace of peace and personal freedom to flow. The two were bound together by an indissoluble bond. In this intense spiritual relationship, the elder exercised an unbounded and inexplicable authority over his companion.

While these elders were highly esteemed among the common people, some of their brother-monks in the monastery regarded them with envy, even hatred, and sought to undermine their authority. The ordinary people used to confess their doubts, their sins and sufferings to their chosen elder and to seek their advice and admonition.

Dostoevsky agreed that while this custom was meant to lead to a high degree of humility and self-abandonment, it could also end in 'the most Satanic pride' – and often did.

Alyosha the Karamazov brother-monk was infatuated with the quality of Zossima's soul. And the old monk, in turn, was fond of Alyosha and let him wait on him. He even lived in Zossima's cell in the monastery. This young man's imagination was deeply stirred by the power and reputation of his elder. Zossima was a very spiritual monk, deeply intuitive and much admired. Though he was relaxed and joyful, an aura of respect, even fear, surrounded him. He radiated in his person a sense of the transcendent and like other elders before him, he attracted a level of almost fanatical devotion.

A similar institution existed in the early church – in North Africa, in Asia Minor, in Rome and Constantinople. As we will see, such unconventional domestic arrangements were described in colourful detail by the archbishop of Constantinople.

Virginal house guests

The dangerous practice of sleeping with virgins was not just an episode in a fairy story narrated by an angel and recorded by a slave. Sometime after the author composed the *Shepherd of Hermas*, Irenaeus (admittedly a ferocious opponent of the many Gnostic schools of his era) reported that some of the heretical followers of Valentinus had given cause for scandal. They had been attending pagan festivals, enjoying the gladiatorial contests, yielding to the lusts of the flesh and justifying their sinful behaviour. They were also sleeping with their female pupils.

> Others of them, too, openly and without a blush, having become passionately attached to certain women, seduce them away from their husbands and contract marriages of their own with them. Others of them, again, who pretend at first to live in all modesty with them as with sisters, have in [the] course of time been revealed in their true colours, when the sister has been found with child by her pretended brother (*Adversus Haereses*, Book 1, Chapter 6:3).

According to Irenaeus, these innocent spiritual brother-sister relationships popular among the Gnostics had been found to produce miraculous, spiritual children.

Since not all virgins could rely on the protection and patronage of their family, a custom developed in the early church whereby unprotected women were adopted by members of the clergy or by some male ascetics or monks who (at least in theory) were ready to provide them with guidance, encouragement and protection. These young girls sought and welcomed this special relationship with holy men, and enjoyed the friendship of their patrons. In theory at least, deep spiritual friendships were free to develop, and sometimes friendships of another kind. This domestic arrangement was seen as a form of evangelical charity, like caring for the poor. There was merit in acting as a 'lover of virgins', or what was known as a *philoparthenos*. For obvious reasons, however, this custom led to spontaneous outbursts of unwelcomed practices.

Tertullian

While there has been some effort in recent years to rehabilitate him, by any standard Tertullian was something of a fervent fanatic who might now be listed as a reactionary, conservative misogynist, as we have already seen. Tertullian was troubled by men who had lost their wives and who thought they needed to contract a second, perhaps a third and fourth, marriage. Since they couldn't care for themselves, they had to have a wife to attend to their needs — to cook, to wash and clean for them. It was in this context that he casually mentioned the possibility of a widower cohabiting (chastely, sexlessly) with an elderly widow in a spiritual marriage, or even with a plurality of widow-wives.

Tertullian provides some evidence that the custom of male and female cohabitation of a Christian man and women, unmarried and living together, existed in North Africa in the second half of the second century. And he goes to straight to the heart of the problem:

> I'm aware of the excuses by which we colour our insatiable carnal appetite. Our pretexts are the necessities of props to lean on; a house to be managed; a family to be governed; chests and keys to be guarded; the wool-spinning to be dispensed; food to be attended to; cares to be generally lessened. Of course the houses of none but married men fare well! The families of celibates, the estates of eunuchs, the fortunes of military men, or of such as travel without wives, have gone to rack and ruin! For aren't we soldiers too? Soldiers, indeed, subject to all the stricter discipline, that we are subject to so

great a General? Aren't we, too, travellers in this world? Why moreover, Christian, are you so conditioned, that you can't (travel) without a wife?

In my present (widowed) state, too, a consort in domestic works is necessary. (Then) take some spiritual wife. Take to yourself from among the widows, one fair in faith, dowered with poverty, sealed with age. You will (thus) make a good marriage. A plurality of such wives is pleasing to God (*Exhortation to Chastity* 12/1–2).

In his treatise *On Monogamy*, Tertullian accepted the possibility of a widower not having to settle only for a second wife to keep him company when he could choose to welcome a plurality into his household.

What if he plead the loneliness of his home? As if one woman afforded company to a man ever on the eve of flight! He has, of course, a widow (at hand), whom it will be lawful for him to take. Not one such wife, but even a plurality, it is permitted to have (16/4).

Cyprian of Carthage

In the middle of the third century the bishop of Carthage penned a letter to bishop Pomponius on behalf of some of his colleagues, giving directions on a particularly delicate subject. Several Christian men, a deacon among them, were co-habiting with virgins vowed to chastity. Cyprian referred to a letter he had received,

> asking and desiring us to write again to you, and say what we thought of those virgins who, after having once determined to continue in their condition, and firmly to maintain their constancy, have afterwards been found to have remained in the same bed side by side with men; of whom you say that one is a deacon; and yet that the same virgins who have confessed that they have slept with men declare that they are chaste (*Letter* 61:1).

Cyprian was invited to provide his opinion about the virgins but not about the men involved. He let Pomponius know what he thought of this pious practice. He recommended discipline as a general principle to conquer the passions of lust, and he agreed that virgins could live in the same house as their patrons. But he drew the line at sleeping with their patrons in the same bed. Female virgins were naturally weak and young – they had to be bridled and governed like a horse in case the devil should entrap them. These young women had to be taken in hand – but we find no mention of the heroic men who were trying to sleep chastely by their side.

> We must interfere at once with such as these, that they may be separated while yet they can be separated in innocence; because by and by, after they have become joined together by a very guilty conscience, they will not be able to be separated by our interference. Moreover, what a number of serious misdeeds we see to have arisen in this way; and what a multitude of virgins we behold corrupted by unlawful and dangerous conjunctions of this kind, to our great grief of mind! (*Letter* 61:2).

'Dangerous conjunctions' seems such a delicate way to describe this pious practice that seems to have been rather popular and widespread.

> Assuredly the mere lying together, the mere embracing, the very talking together, and the act of kissing, and the disgraceful and foul slumber of two persons lying together, how much of dishonour and crime does it reveal! If a husband come upon his wife, and see her lying with another man, is he not angry and enraged, and by the passion of his rage does he not perhaps take his sword into his hand? And what shall Christ and our Lord and Judge think, when He sees His virgin, dedicated to Him, and destined for His holiness, lying with another? (*Letter* 61:3).

In Cyprian's day, there were young virgins who were dedicated to Christ, and some of these girls were involved, like the virgins in Hermas's story, in entertaining, comforting and servicing senior male members of the community.

The Pseudo-Clementines

The Pseudo-Clementines is a collection of early Christian writings from about the middle of the third century and includes two *Epistles to Virgins* which were (falsely) attributed to Clement I, the second or third bishop of Rome at the end of the first century. The anonymous author was pretending that the pope was writing to men who were supposed to be leading celibate lives. The collection probably comes from the region of Palestine. Some fragments of the original Greek text have survived in quotations recorded by a seventh century Palestinian monk from the monastery of St Saba and a complete version of the two epistles has survived in a Syriac translation.

Basing his advice on rumours and reports, the author takes us into the tangled world of 'holy', shameless, 'barefaced' men who, 'under the pretence of teaching' (1/11), were associating with maidens and virgins and pretending to be their spiritual guides. They were walking with them along pathways and in isolated spots. Others were eating and drinking with them, 'allowing themselves to indulge in loose behaviour and much uncleanness'. Others joined the company of these virgins for 'vain and trifling conversations and merriment'. They spoke evil of one another and shared rumours and scandals about each other. Some of these ascetics were wandering about, in and out of the houses of virgins, reading scripture to them and driving devils out of them.

> Is it not a matter of some surprise that, while the Lord did not allow Mary, the blessed woman, to touch his feet, you live with them, and are waited on by women and maidens, and sleep

where they sleep, and women wash your feet and anoint you! (2/1).

I would, moreover, have you know, my brethren, of what sort is our conduct in Christ, as well as that of all our brethren, in the various places in which we are. And if so be that you approve it, do you also conduct yourselves in like manner in the Lord. Now we, if God help us, conduct ourselves thus: with maidens we do not dwell, nor have we anything in common with them; with maidens we do not eat, nor drink; and, where a maiden sleeps, we do not sleep; neither do women wash our feet, nor anoint us; and on no account do we sleep where a maiden sleeps who is unmarried or has taken the vow: even though she be in some other place, *if she be* alone, we do not pass the night there (2/1).

We holy men do not eat or drink with women, nor are we waited on by women or by maidens, nor do women wash our feet for us, nor do women anoint us, nor do women prepare our bed for us, nor do we sleep where women sleep, so that we may be without reproach in everything, lest anyone should be offended or stumble at us (2/3).

The author was addressing his advice to celibate men, talking about women and young girls in the third person. He was admonishing the men, criticising them for their 'affrontery and folly', for their mindless lack of fear of God – but ignoring the women, talking about them as though they were mere objects. A modern reader might wonder what these young women were thinking and how they were reacting to the advances of dirty old men. Were they laughing at them behind their backs? Holding their breath and doing what they were told? Had they been 'groomed' into submission and exploited?

Bishop Paul of Samosata

Sometime later again, before 303 AD, in his *Historia Ecclesiastica*, Eusebius recorded the content of a letter addressed to Dionysius, bishop of Rome, and to Maximus of Alexandria – a letter sent to all the provinces, providing evidence of the same perilous practice involving Paul of Samosata, his presbyters and deacons. This notorious bishop had been excommunicated for spreading false doctrines, but his lifestyle had also come under scrutiny. He had accumulated fabulous wealth by plundering the possessions of those who in all simplicity were ready to give generously to their bishop so that they might obtain reconciliation and entry to heaven.

According to Eusebius, Paul of Samosata had behaved like 'an arrogant cock', full of himself, with his rooster feathers puffed out as he paraded with his retinue. He had assumed worldly titles and places of honour, 'preferring the title *ducenarius*, 'leader' rather than his ecclesial title 'bishop'. He strutted about in the marketplaces, reading letters and reciting them as he walked around attended by his bodyguards with his admirers milling around him.

And then there were the women, the *subintroductæ*, (as the people of Antioch called them) who belonged to him, to his presbyters and his deacons.

> For how can he reprove or advise anyone not to be too familiar with women – lest he fall, as it is written – when he has himself sent one away already, and now has two with him, blooming and beautiful, and takes them with him wherever he goes, and at the same time lives in luxury and surfeiting? (*Hist. Eccl.* VIII. 30:14).

From very early on, from at least the middle of the second century and perhaps earlier, in an attempt to prove their worth by performing feats of extraordinary heroism, there seems to have been a practice in some Christian and Christian-Gnostic communities of 'saintly' men sharing their lives, and even sleeping (modestly) with one or several virgins – but abstaining from any untoward activity. Both parties (the holy men and the virgins) would take vows of chastity. They engaged, courageously, in a type of spiritual marriage, agreeing to live together (even sleep together) in perfect purity, as brother and sister. Whether such an arrangement was possible for ordinary mortals seems highly unlikely. These ascetics were playing with fire. But the reward, if successful, would be eternal bliss. The saintly men were making their rocky way to heaven – and the women were the instruments of their success – or failure. Women were the tormenters, temptresses. The men were trying to prove their heroism by placing themselves in imminent danger and emerging without a wound or blemish.

In some circles these companionable females were known as *virgines subintroductae* (virgins introduced into the house through the back door, under cover of darkness), or *syneisaktoi* or *agapetae* (lovebirds). They were chaste objects of desire which an ascetic could patronise and on which he could test his resolve. To objectify women in such a crass way seems profoundly alien to the message of the Gospel, but typical of the attitudes of some of the Fathers of the Church – Tertullian, Clement, Origen, and further down the track, Jerome, Ambrose, Augustine, the Gregorys from Cappadocia, John Chrysostom and on into the Middle Ages. Women were objects of resistible desire rather than partners in ministry.

But these men were not all successful ascetics, or saints, or capable of feats of heroism. Young beautiful women, virgins, were being used and abused. Those among the male believers who were truly virtuous and were able to attain the heights of heroism, on the standards of today, were treating their female counterparts as objects on whom they could harden themselves and prove their virtue. One can only imagine the confusion in the lives and minds of these young women who were sharing the beds of the 'saints'. Frightened little girls *en fleur* called by God to test the mettle of a bishop, a monk or a deacon, and required to do so by the head of her household. A sacrificial offering who was trying to sleep peacefully in the same bed as a tormented man of God. It takes little imagination to see that the custom was exceedingly dangerous for the spiritual guide and patron, but particularly for his impressionable *confidante* and *femme de chambre*. Naturally it became the subject of close scrutiny from councils and religious leaders like John Chrysostom and Jerome.

Councils

In the fourth century, the practice of virgins and widows cohabiting with church officials and leaders had become widespread across the globe – from Spain in the West to modern Turkey. A number of local councils sought to close the practice down and to regularise the sexual and social lives of those in their charge.

In 309, for example, those present at the Council of Elvira in Granada decided that bishops and other members of the clergy could live with a sister or a daughter who were virgins, but with no other woman. Immediate female relatives were permitted, but no-one else.

At about the same time, early in the fourth century, the local council held at Ancyra in Asia Minor prohibited the practice of virgins cohabiting with men 'as sisters'. No reason was given but the prohibition appeared in the same canon (Canon 19) which dealt with women who had promised to maintain their virginity but who failed to honour their promise.

But the problems associated with cohabitation were not confined to a few local areas. The practice was across the board in the church. The general council summoned by the Emperor Constantine in the town of Nicaea in the northern region of Asia Minor also addressed the issue.

> The great synod has stringently forbidden any bishop, presbyter, deacon, or any one of the clergy whatever, to have

a *subintroducta* dwelling with him, except only a mother, or sister, or aunt, or such persons only as are beyond all suspicion (canon 3).

The Council of Trent attempted to control the sexual urges of the clergy, nevertheless the practice of spiritual marriages continued. Couples shared the same house, often the same room, sometimes the same bed, living as brother and sister – or so they would have the world believe. Virgins continued to be abused under cover of spiritual discipleship and Christian companionship.

Jerome of Rome and Gregory of Nyssa

Jerome was not known for his diplomacy or for his soft, charming words. He was a blunt man who lived on the edge, making enemies with his poisonous pen. He was friendly, however, with a wealthy Roman widow by the name of Paula and her four daughters. Eustochium was his favourite. She had taken a vow of perpetual virginity and as her adviser and confidant, Jerome had written a long letter to her on the subject – now known as letter 22, *De custodia virginitatis*.

In the course of his letter, he told his correspondent that he was deeply shocked to learn of a Roman plague of lovebirds (*agapetarum pestis*) who were living in their midst. He described these women as 'unwedded wives', as a new kind of concubine (*novum concubinarum genus*) and as 'one-man prostitutes' (*meretrices univirae*). They often slept with a stranger in the same bed, pretending to be together as brother and sister (*saepe uno tenentur et lectulo*). They wanted people to believe that they were seeking spiritual consolation, but Jerome had a good idea what they were about.

> There is another scandal of which I blush to speak; yet, though sad, it is true. They call us suspicious if we think that anything is wrong. A brother leaves his virgin sister; a virgin, scorning her unmarried brother, seeks a stranger to take his place. Both

alike pretend to have but one object: they are seeking spiritual consolation among strangers: but their real aim is to indulge at home in carnal intercourse (ch. 14).

Jerome invited Eustochium (and his other readers) to expel these wanton women from the community.

Gregory, the bishop of Nyssa was a contemporary of Jerome, and a brother to Basil of Caesarea. In about 370 he wrote a treatise entitled *On Virginity* in which he exposed the myth of monks enjoying a relationship of brotherly affection with women living in their houses. He was having none of that nonsense.

> Who could enumerate all the pitfalls into which any one might slip, from refusing to have recourse to men of godly celebrity? Why, we have known ascetics of this class who have persisted in their fasting even unto death, as if 'with such sacrifices God were well pleased'; and, again, others who rush off into the extreme diametrically opposite, practising celibacy in name only and leading a life in no way different from the secular; for they not only indulge in the pleasures of the table, but are openly known to have a woman in their houses; and they call such a friendship a brotherly affection, as if, forsooth, they could veil their own thought, which is inclined to evil, under a sacred term. It is owing to them that this pure and holy profession of virginity is 'blasphemed amongst the Gentiles' (ch. 23).

John Chrysostom of Constantinople

John Chrysostom, however, unlike Jerome or Gregory, passed no moral judgment on the behaviour of the monks and ascetics who were involved in spiritual marriages. He refused to condemn them and, in an effort to persuade them to change their living conditions, he accepted that they were all as virtuous as they claimed. He wanted to convince them only that they were giving scandal to others, that others believed that they were living in sin, engaging in carnal intercourse and that anyway, it was far easier for men to live with men, women with women, and that when the sexes cohabit there is always friction and unhappiness.

John Chrysostom was one of the great archbishops of the fourth to fifth centuries. He was born in Antioch on the Orontes around 349AD and became the archbishop of Constantinople in 397. Though he died before the age of sixty, he was to become immensely popular and influential – a Saint Augustine of the eastern churches.

In two lengthy essays Chrysostom addressed the popular practice of mixed cohabitation, of intimate friendships across the gender barrier, of what was known as 'spiritual marriages'.

There is some dispute about when he composed these treatises. Some believe he wrote them when he was working as a deacon in Antioch – in the 380s or early 390s. His early biographer Palladius, however, was convinced that he was already archbishop of Constantinople when he addressed the burning issue of the scandalous, intimate relationships between spiritual gurus and their battery of doting virgins (*Dialogus* 5).

The archbishop was troubled when he heard reports of monks and other religious leaders fraternising in their homes with females. They were enjoying the company of women, fostering a spiritual and emotional intimacy with consecrated virgins and thereby damaging the church's reputation. This practice provided salacious scandal for the pagans and ignored the sensibilities of their weaker brothers and sisters. He argued his case with wit and sarcasm, without alleging, as Jerome had not hesitated to do, that the participants were secretly copulating.

In the first of his two essays, Chrysostom addressed argument to those males who were involved in the practice of spiritual marriages, and his second essay addressed the participating women. There is no doubt that Chrysostom would have taken a very dim view of the domestic arrangements involved in these intimate spiritual friendships. In his treatise on the priesthood, for example, he spoke of the dangers of contact with women and how prone they are to lead men astray.

> There are in the world a great many situations that weaken the conscientiousness of the soul. First and foremost of these are dealings with women. In his concern for the male sex, the superior may not forget the females, who need greater care precisely because of their ready inclination to sin. In this situation the evil enemy can find many ways to creep in secretly. For the eye of woman touches and disturbs our soul – and not only the eye of the unbridled woman, but that of the decent one as well (*De Sacerdotio*, Bk. 6, Ch. 8).

The archbishop had form. He wrote disrespectfully of women, sharing with some of his brother bishops and other theologians a seriously distorted opinion of them and their frightening sexual attractiveness.

> The whole of her bodily beauty is nothing less than phlegm, blood, bile, rheum, and the fluid of digested food. If you consider what is stored up behind those lovely eyes, the angle of the nose, the mouth and cheeks, you will agree that the well-proportioned body is merely a whitened sepulcher (*Ad Theodoram lapsum*, para. 14).

The author commenced his first essay by observing that there were two reasons, according to his ancestors, for men and women to live together – marriage was the reason from the beginning, and prostitution followed. More recently, however (and we don't know when the practice commenced, or where), a third way of life had been 'dreamt up':

> There are certain men who apart from marriage and sexual intercourse, take inexperienced, unmarried girls,

set them up as permanent residents in their homes and keep them sequestered there until [a] ripe old age – not in order to bear children with them (for they deny that they have sexual relations with these women), and not out of licentiousness (for they claim that they preserve them inviolate) (164–5).

While the author was not prepared to commit his suspicions to writing, he clearly entertained his own hypotheses and argued that there would not be 'so many scandals if a violent and tyrannical pleasure were not found in their cohabitation' (165).

What that pleasure might have consisted in we can only guess. Violent, rough sex? Sadomasochistic activities? The joys of gender domination? The author suggested instead that the 'violent and tyrannical pleasure' was living with a gaggle of virgins without a man being able to satisfy his powerful desire for sexual coupling. In any true marriage, a man's basic drives were properly satiated while at the same time a woman grew less attractive as the years passed. She gave birth to children, reared them and suffered prolonged sicknesses. The bloom of her youth faded and the male's 'sting of pleasure' gradually diminished. But virgins were different. No labour pains. No child-rearing 'to dry up her flesh'. No drudgery.

> Since they remain untouched, these virgins stay in their prime for a long time ... (They) retain their beauty until they are forty and rival the virgins who are being escorted to the nuptial chamber (166).

Consequently, according to Bishop John, the hapless old monks who chose to live with consecrated virgins were 'stirred by a double desire' – the terrible torment of no sex and therefore no satisfaction, while their house guests remained pristine and attractive for years.

When John Chrysostom turned his attention, in his second essay, to the virgins involved in spiritual marriages, he accused them of degrading the sanctity of their virginal state. Virginity was, according to him, a way of life more honourable than marriage, similar to the Holy of Holies in the Temple in Jerusalem where God's mysterious presence was focused. Virginity was a state of being which was 'august and full of terror', a condition here on earth which mirrored the way we will all be living in heaven, male and female together, without the embarrassment of sexual attraction and activity.

The archbishop had a poor opinion of these pretend virgins. He seems to have known them well. They used to stroll around the marketplace like birds spreading their wings of pleasure. They were loud and undisciplined, flighty and debauched. They would giggle and laugh at the wrong time. They played the coquette and broke men's hearts. These nominal virgins were hypocrites – worse even than common prostitutes.

> She grinds the same poisons, mixes the same cups, prepares the same hemlock (as a prostitute) (210).

But they also paid a high price for engaging in their domestic arrangements. Their reputation suffered. The author observed that midwives were making regular (daily) visits to these irregular households as though some of their occupants were expecting and ready to deliver a baby. While this had occurred 'on some occasions', the midwives were more often summoned in order to discern who had lost her virginity, or who were in fact 'untouched', unspoiled.

These consecrated women were subjected to the same treatment as common female slaves before a purchaser would part with his money. In order to prove their angelic condition, some virgins agreed to undergo a close inspection of their private parts, but others would refuse and would suffer the disgrace of losing their reputation, even those who had not been deflowered.

But even if the midwife could establish by a 'minute examination' that some of the virgins were physically intact, it still remained true that 'the healthy section of the virginal choir' living in a shared house was tainted.

> But how is that necessarily so, the virgin asks, 'when we can show that our body has not been deflowered or prostituted?' It is precisely this proof (of virginity) which is not manifest at the present but will be clear on that future day of judgment. For the wisdom and skill of the midwife can see only such things as whether the body has experienced intercourse with a man. But whether it has also fled the rude touch, the adultery of kisses and embraces and their defilement, that day (of judgment) will reveal (218).

While 'virginity in the company of men' was receiving more slanderous press than prostitution, and while the noble life of a virgin had lost its 'own proper place' and rolled down into the abyss of harlotry, those women who wanted to have men live with them should never have chosen virginity as their way of life. They should simply have agreed to marry. It was obvious to Chrysostom. It was better by far in the eyes of God to live as a married woman than pretend to be a virgin while cohabiting with a man.

As much as he tried, the archbishop couldn't convince himself that the domestic arrangements created by the religious cohabitants in the city and suburbs of Constantinople were kosher. He mocked the offending monks by congratulating them for their Herculean super-strength. He referred to them as 'fine gentlemen', living a life of self-sacrifice, of piety rather than lust. 'O wondrous man!' who was living as though among stones rather than among weak flesh-and-blood humans like himself. The author was incredulous.

> I do wish our accusers could also persuade us that a young man bursting with vigor can cohabit with a girl, sit side by side with her, eat with her, talk with her all day long (not to mention

all the rest – untimely laughter, merriment, sweet talk, and so forth, which is perhaps not nice to speak about here), have the house, the table, the salt in common, share everything openly, and yet not be seized by any human sentiment, but remain pure of evil desire and pleasure (171).

According to the archbishop, these virginal women used to 'intoxicate' their pathetic spiritual friends. They made the men they captured an easy prey for the devil. They enticed and dominated them. They turned these men into effeminate fops – softer, more hotheaded, shameful, mindless, irascible, insolent, ignoble, crude, servile, niggardly, reckless and irrational. The archbishop wasn't mincing his words.

These women take all their corrupting female customs and stamp them into the souls of these men (197).

In his essays, John Chrysostom spent a little time exploring these corrupting female customs. He considered that as a general rule, any member of the female sex would be, as he said, 'totally despicable' unless she had been given the special 'power' exclusive to her gender – the power of sexual attraction, and that no man would ever choose to live with a woman if he did not feel the pull of sexual desire. They may have other incidental uses (such as childbearing and housekeeping), but they were annoying and difficult, demanding and unreasonable. Sex was the only driving force keeping a man and a woman together.

Cohabitation is not based on law but on love and lust (178–9).

How did Constantinople's spiritual cohabitants justify what they were doing? According to the archbishop, while he personally thought they had no 'simple, decent, plausible excuse' which they could offer, they would argue their case.

These monks needed someone, for example, to keep an eye on their possessions and to keep house for them – to oversee their chests of drawers, their cloaks, to set the table, boil the kettle, make the beds, light the fire, wash their feet and provide all the other little comforts of life (191). When a stranger entered the house of a monk or religious guru who was sharing his abode with virgins, the visitor would see women's shoes hanging up, girdles, headbands, baskets, a spindle for spinning wool and weaving equipment (192). The archbishop was obviously familiar with the scene. Perhaps, in the course of his pastoral work, he had visited these communes and seen how the household functioned.

Furthermore, in Chrysostom's city and suburbs, some virgins had no male relative to protect them from the world. No husband or in-laws, and often no family relatives. A woman needed a male protector to defend her from harm, to establish her in a secure haven, to support and comfort her. By nature, men had been provided with a wealth of resources while women were considered weaker, more vulnerable and in need of more protection (179 & 184). They could not appear in public or in the marketplace if they were unaccompanied (222). Cohabiting virgins themselves agreed that they needed men to look after them and protect them, and according to the author men made the same claim. They needed women to reside with them and provide for their daily needs – and the local, consecrated virgins eagerly offered their services. It was a perfect arrangement.

The archbishop was convinced, however, that the men involved were motivated 'by a bleak and wretched pleasure'. Despite their vow of celibacy and their commitment to a spiritual way of life, they loved living with women, and particularly with young, pretty, nubile virgins. Women, on the other hand, were inspired by a desire for esteem rather than a desire for sensual, if not sexual pleasure. They loved the status associated with sharing a house with someone of importance. They enjoyed living with a housemate who enjoyed considerable power in the church – someone from a brilliant family or a man of great eloquence or a 'friend' with a reputation for holiness, or wisdom, or learning. They took pleasure in the notoriety, in the admiration of shoppers and stallholders in the marketplace – the whispering, the stares, the nudges, the envy of the crowd, the vanity. They were celebrities in their little world. John Chrysostom thought he knew what it was all about – and pretty women always had the upper hand.

> The whole human race is vain, but especially the female sex (229).

According to the archbishop, the natural, established relationship between a man and woman was often thrown out of balance in these unofficial households. Instead of being respectful and obedient as women should be, these virgins became aggressive and domineering. The women took control and began to treat the man of the house with disrespect. He became enslaved to his female companions. His domestic life was lived under a cloud of shame and disgrace.

From the beginning, God had ordered the world in such a way that the man would rule over his consort. There was a hierarchy of power and status within any domestic setting. The man was the head of the house and by nature he was in charge. Chrysostom quoted the Book of Genesis (3:16) and Paul's first epistle to the Corinthians (11:3) in support of his argument. However, when a religious leader shared his house with unmarried women, with a number of consecrated virgins, God's natural order was often thrown into chaos. The domestic world became topsy-turvy.

> It's a huge disgrace when the upper assumes the position of the lower so that the head is below, and the body above (231).

We can have no idea how widespread the custom of cohabiting monks and virgins was in the city and suburbs of Constantinople, but it was considered important enough for the archbishop to produce two substantial essays on the topic. He was determined to stamp the practice out. Monks and ascetics living with admiring, virginal devotees were inciting serious scandal among the faithful. And they had become the cause of satire and mockery in society at large.

The bishops and their delegates who assembled at the General Council summoned by the emperor at Nicaea in 325 considered the practice so serious that they had to take steps to delegitimise it. As we have seen, there is evidence of cohabiting men and unmarried women, of monks and clerics living with widows and virgins from North Africa and from Gaul at the end of the second century. And with widows and virgins from Rome, central Asia Minor and Constantinople from the end of the fourth century. It had become a patriarchal practice which was not easy to control, and it exploited women. While John Chrysostom was not the only one to take serious steps to eradicate this obviously pernicious practice which had taken root in various parts of the Christian world, he is the only author who dealt with it expansively in his writings. He tells us more about the custom than any other writer (all males), though we have to be careful to take into account that he, like all the others, was an opponent of the practice. None of the writers spoke favourably of those involved or wrote sympathetically of their goals and motivation. Hostile material, written from such a distance, has to be interpreted with caution. And we have no idea, from this distance, how successful Chrysostom and the others were in counteracting such an attractive, engaging practice.

A Struggle for a Place at the Table

The Gospel of Matthew

In treating the Gospel of Matthew as a classical historical record of events, a straight reading of the text would show that during his lifetime, Jesus had established a structure for a church which would continue his messianic work after his death. He had commissioned a spokesman, a leader who would be the rock-foundation of his institution. He had also appointed a group of male followers to act as a board of directors and an advisory committee, with a kitchen cabinet of three – Peter, James and John. Peter was chosen to be the CEO of the organisation and chairman of the board.

Jesus gave these men the authority to preach and to baptise, the power to drive out devils and to heal. While he was with them, he sent his followers out two-by-two to spread the message and later to extend his influence to all nations, and he provided a program for dispute resolution among the believers (Chapter 18). Before his death, Jesus celebrated a last meal and his guest-list had been restricted to his twelve male followers. He authorised these followers with the words 'Do this in memory of me' to preside at future liturgical celebrations held in his memory.

According to the author of the Gospel of Matthew, Jesus had designed the future architecture of his organisation by appointing and commissioning a male leadership and twelve male apostles, thereby establishing the Roman papacy as well as a body of apostolic successors – the bishops and archbishops. A loose band of followers, men and women, but a tight inner circle of men who were to be in charge and these had been appointed by Jesus himself. The only other substantial component of the institution – the one which Jesus had neglected to initiate and the one that would eventually be responsible for electing his vicar on earth – was the exclusive College of Cardinals.

No place in the boardroom for women. No place for women around the Last Supper table or on the altars scattered around the globe.

This Gospel of Matthew which appeared under the name of the tax-collecting apostle was almost certainly not written by him. It had been put together (artfully) by a representative of a second or third generation of followers. The composer was possibly a converted rabbi who was working as a teacher and church leader in the latter half of the first century, and he had put together a Gospel for his community somewhere between 80 and 90 AD.

Over the years, scholars have been in dispute about the author's purpose in composing his Gospel. Was it to produce a liturgical lectionary perhaps; or to confirm the Jewish members of his community in their belief that Jesus had been the fulfillment of the Old Testament messianic prophecies and that the church was in fact the New Israel? Or perhaps the Gospel of Matthew was to be a strong polemical work to refute the beliefs and practices of Judaism as it was practised at the time of Jesus? Then again, was Matthew created to be a handbook for church leaders to assist them in their teaching and preaching, and in defence of the message? The author's goal could have been any one or all of the above.

The Gospel of Matthew begins with the fabulous account of Jesus' birth in Bethlehem and contains many of his wonderful parables, his famous Sermon on the Mount, stories of his miracles and his kingdom message. However, one of the principal considerations explored by the composer in this Gospel was to find a way to promote the argument that Jesus had concentrated his power and authority in the hands of Peter and the apostles in order to legitimise the position of the successors of Peter and the other apostles.

The legitimacy of the current leaders' power base seems to have been an important consideration for the Gospel composer. He was focused on excluding any rivals, on undermining any possible alternative claim. These passages in the Gospel are fundamental to the hierarchical structure of the church. They establish the origin of the Pope's and bishops' central position in the organisation. According to the members of the hierarchy, these passages in Matthew (and a few in the Gospel of John) support the claim that their power and authority derive directly from Jesus himself – from Jesus to Peter, to the Twelve, to bishops throughout the world, to popes down the centuries.

But these passages which record sayings attributed to Jesus have created a storm of exegetical and theological controversy, at least among scholars. The ordinary worshippers, male or female, and probably the greater portion of the clergy, have not participated actively in this cerebral controversy. Obscure, academic considerations don't affect their day-to-day lives. They simply go about their business and accept without difficulty what those at the wheel tell them. The political and theological agendas of those on top of the structure normally pass by under the radar.

Nevertheless, we have to ask the question whether these utterances attributed to Jesus are sayings which the founder himself actually uttered (as they are presented in the Gospel) or if they were a product of the early church. Do they truly reflect the mind of Jesus and his intention to establish a clear line of authority, an organisational structure for his religious movement? Did he really establish a church, and one with a hierarchical structure? Or do the Matthew passages speak of an early Christian ecclesiology penned by the author and based on the structure of the faith community at the time? So how should we read and understand the Gospel of Mathew?

These are complex questions for scholars, and their answers could prove critical for the future direction of Christian churches and for true believers. Does the Gospel literature record what we understand to be historical facts, accounts of incidents which really occurred, or are the Gospels to be understood in some other way?

A straight reading of the original Gospels which were composed so long ago could prove to be a misreading of this specialised literature. The Gospels are not historical records as a modern reader has come to understand the science of history. They are heavily flavoured with mythology and metaphor, and mixed with strong theological undercurrents. They have been artificially styled to answer a particular need and to reflect the religious mood of the times. To come close to a true reading, we have to examine each passage, each event, each saying, one by one, carefully, because none of the four canonical Gospels is made up of a continuous seamless stream of undifferentiated literature. To begin with there is the Petrine primacy passage in Matthew 16:18 ('Thou art Peter and on this rock I will build my church') which bears all the hallmarks of a post-resurrection invention from the early church, and which is presented as occurring at Caesarea during Jesus' public ministry.

The authors of the various Gospels sometimes wrote their accounts of particular incidents in a backward direction – projecting the present reality into the past. Writing some decades after Jesus had left them, the Gospel composers wrote back into his life-story what had developed in the community only after his death. Post-resurrection events were made to appear as if they had occurred during the founder's lifetime. For example, in positioning this encounter between Jesus and Peter in Caesarea, as in many other passages throughout the Gospels, the author of Matthew was writing his history backwards. This author was justifying the present situation in the church in and around Jerusalem in the period 80-90 AD by reference to an imaginary event and to a critical saying attributed to the founder.

Without becoming bogged in the complexities of academic exegesis, we need to touch on some of the reasons why this difficult primacy passage might not reflect the historical sayings of Jesus. We also need to consider how it can be better understood as an attempt by leaders within the early church, several generations after Jesus' disappearance, to trace the structure of their community back to the founder. This they did by attributing words to him which would reflect what they believed was (or should have been) in the mind of Jesus, words he would have uttered if he had addressed what would later become the critical issue of leadership and authority.

First, once anyone has read the four canonical Gospels and listened to the words and phrases, it is difficult to hear the Jesus revealed in this literature uttering the sayings recorded in Matthew 16. Besides, this particular incident in Matthew – 'Thou art Peter and on this rock I will build my church' – is not replicated in any of the other three Gospels.

Chapter 18 of Matthew's Gospel (where the Greek word for 'church' appears twice) deals with a disciplinary procedure which had undoubtedly developed in the early church – how to restore order in the community and resolve disputes, and who were the proper arbiters of disputes among Christians. The procedure reflected the situation of dispute resolution in a particular community, the early church in Jerusalem, at the time the passage was composed. But to clothe it with some authority, the author was putting his words into Jesus' mouth.

Besides, the word 'church' does not rest easy on the lips of the founder. The word 'church' appears only three times in the Greek version of this Gospel (once in Chapter 16, and twice in Chapter 18), and 114 times in the rest of the New Testament. According to the Gospels, and especially the Gospel of Matthew, he talked incessantly about a kingdom – not about a church. That type of language came later, from the pen of the Apostle Paul and even later still from the author of Acts.

When Jesus came to commissioning his disciples to preach and teach, the number recorded of those he sent out on a mission, namely seventy (or 72), was probably chosen by the author of the Gospel to reflect the number of the members of the Jewish Sanhedrin. And while Jesus almost certainly had a special team of followers at his side during his public ministry, the number of these apostles in the New Israel was probably chosen (whether by Jesus, or probably later) to reflect the twelve Patriarchs of the Old Israel.

Furthermore, the direction to baptise 'all nations', which comes at the conclusion of the Gospel of Matthew, reads like another imaginary historical event from the pen of the author. Apart from the fact that as far as we know Jesus never baptised a single follower, the word 'baptise' does not sit comfortably in any statement Jesus made during his lifetime. It appears unexpectedly at the end of the Gospel. The author took the practice of baptising believers into the community, a practice which had developed in the early stages of the church, and wrote this back into the immediate post-resurrection life of Jesus, creating an incident in the course of which he commissioned his eleven apostles to preach and baptise.

The author of the Gospel was determined to bolster the position of those who had assumed the role of leadership within the early church. He wanted to defend them from potential rival claims, to call on the authority of Jesus to confirm the developing status quo and to respond to any counterclaims. The undercurrent of these passages points to some tension, some anxiety within the early church about the legitimacy of certain roles and positions taken up by Peter and his associates after the founder had finally disappeared.

The New Testament tells of the tension which emerged between Peter and Paul of Tarsus, and the leadership rivalry in Paul's church at Corinth. There is also evidence of a struggle developing between the authority of a few members of the apostolic college on the one hand, and another, totally different, style of leadership. This latter style is based on gifts of the Spirit – a leadership associated with personal faith, based on visions and dreams and messages revealed to individuals (including women) who belonged to an ancient lineage of prophets.

Jesus had commissioned Mary Magdalene to deliver a message to his apostles, but when she had told them that Jesus had risen, Peter had dismissed her as an unreliable witness. The apostles had greeted the news as 'just idle talk'.

In some of the Gospels, Mary Magdalene and some of the other women had been first to the empty tomb, and first to see Jesus in his newly risen state. In other Gospels, the narrator recorded that Jesus had appeared first to some of his apostle-disciples – not to women.

And again, in his letter to Corinth, as we have seen, Paul identified a number of post-Resurrection appearances, but none to any woman – not to Mary Magdalene, or to any other female. For some mysterious reason, while some of the Gospel authors included them, Paul omitted to mention women as witnesses to Jesus' resurrected existence.

From the New Testament literature we can see the authors insisting that on Jesus' disappearance, Peter and some of the other apostles had immediately begun to assert their authority – an authority which was to be handed down to others within the community, from male leader to male leader – to James, the brother of Jesus, in Jerusalem, to a committee of male presbyters or elders, and to male deacons. Gradually, from a council of presbyters modelled on the Jewish authoritative structure, the Christian communities began to settle on a three-tiered structure. This structure comprised a male overseer or manager, a council of male presbyters under him, and a group or order of male deacons also under the *episcopos*.

Early on, the leaders had begun to look with suspicion on any claim based on a member's (male or female) gift of prophecy and personal faith. 'Idle gossip' was a typical way of dismissing the power of a female witness. Nevertheless, he competition for supremacy between Peter and Mary Magdalene grew in intensity in the churches of the second and third centuries. This battle was a 'battle to the death' between the powers-that-be and a Gnostic form of Christianity based on some special hidden knowledge which could restore harmony and introduce a believer into an intimate, spiritual relationship with the world and its Creator. In this battle the institutional church sought to suppress the power of prophecy, the influence of women, women teachers and preachers, and the ministry of women.

The tension we have seen in the New Testament literature, where women were at work and involved in ministry, but where their contribution had to be at least controlled and regulated – this tension was on show for all to see in the Gnostic-Christian Gospels of the second and third centuries. Believers were telling themselves stories about Mary Magdalene, about her special status, her influence with Jesus, about her authoritative voice and her gift of prophetic revelations. She was seen as a woman who had been given a position of authority, a female with a contribution to make to the life of the faith community, a woman the male apostles disliked and were suspicious of.

The Gospel of Mary

Towards the end of the nineteenth century, a fifth century papyrus codex was resurrected in Egypt and found to contain four ancient works written in a Coptic dialect – the *Apocryphon of John*, the *Sophia of Jesus Christ*, a summary of the *Acts of Peter* and a document which became known as the *Gospel of Mary*. The scorched sands of Egypt had proved to be a providential place to preserve precious ancient documents which are now conserved as Berlin Codex 8502 (also known as the Akhmim Codex) in the Berliner Museum. There are also some fragments of the *Gospel of Mary* which were among half a million or so fragments of papyri found by two English papyrologists on a rubbish dump in Egypt. These can be found in the Sackler Library at Oxford (*Papyrus Oxyrhynchus* 3525); and in the in the John Rylands Library in Manchester (*Papyrus Rylands* 463).

The original *Gospel of Mary* had been composed in Greek, probably during the second century – maybe sometime between 120 AD and 188 AD – before or about the same time as Tertullian and Irenaeus were composing their treatises. The Mary to whom this gospel is attributed, or at least after whom it was called, is almost certainly Mary Magdalene – the controversial female friend of Jesus also referred to in the *Gospel of Thomas* as well as in the *Pistis Sophia* and the *Gospel of Philip*. She was apparently the focus of some division and ill will among the members of the early Christian communities. She was the person who had stood up to Peter and Andrew and challenged their authority.

Unfortunately, in its present reconstructed form, the *Gospel of Mary* is incomplete. The first six manuscript pages are missing. The text opens in the middle of a conversation, probably a post-Resurrection conversation, between 'the Saviour' himself and Peter. Peter had enquired about 'the sin of the world' and Jesus was telling him that there was no such thing as sin in the abstract, that people themselves made sin when they acted in 'an adulterous way'. In the course of this controversy Jesus gave some strangely enlightened advice to Peter – advice typical of the Jesus we meet in the four canonical Gospels:

> Do not lay down any rule beyond what I have determined for you, and do not promulgate laws like a lawgiver lest you be constrained by it. When he said this he departed.

This was a revolutionary position taken up by Jesus and one which was in harmony with Jesus' kingdom preaching, though the audience to whom 'the Saviour' was talking didn't take it upon themselves to preach the Gospel message of the kingdom or Jesus' message of freedom from the law. When it came to the law and to regulations, Jesus had been a minimalist. No canon law. No regulations. No authority above our own conscience. 'Don't lay down any rule beyond what I have determined for you.' No wonder this *Gospel of Mary* was lost for so long. The institutional church would not have found Jesus' advice very attractive.

Once 'the Saviour' had uttered his advice, he had disappeared. As the story went, his followers were naturally distressed and frightened. But Mary had stood up and assumed command. According to the author, she was acting both as a prophet with a personal message for the early church, and as the moral conscience of the disciples. Her ensuing address and her interaction with Peter and Andrew occupy the bulk of the surviving document, though the record of this important meeting is again interrupted and the participants reduced to silence because four more pages are missing from the manuscript.

For any Christian, liberal or evangelical, the *Gospel of Mary* is a curious document. Not a classical orthodox Christian work (or at least not reflecting the orthodoxy of the past fifteen centuries), and yet not a classical Gnostic document. There are good reasons to classify it as a product of the Gnostic world, not least because it was found in an old codex with several other Gnostic writings. Furthermore, it was written in a form similar to other Gnostic works – in a dialogue-form containing revelatory discourses framed within a narrative. There are equally good grounds, however, to hesitate, because the author hadn't adopted a typical Gnostic dualistic view of creation or the world. The text reflects a classical Christian monistic view – one God who was the creator of all things, spiritual and physical, heavenly and earthly.

Despite any confusion as to its origins, however, this gospel has much to teach us about life in the early church. At the time,

Christianity was a turbulent, often chaotic movement struggling to embrace or exclude competing influences. The primitive community was finding its way – exploring the meaning of Jesus and his life, establishing structures, discussing and resolving practical questions, determining who was in charge, how to regulate the life of Christians living together, what teacher/preacher to listen to, where God's Spirit dwelt, and who had the power. Confusion was energised by a constant ebb and flow. Open clashes of pressure groups. Arguments. Lobbying and competing loyalties. People leaving one community and joining another, and then coming back. Leaders attracting members from rival groups. Christians converted to a secret Gnostic sect, or simply attending meetings out of some kind of religious curiosity. Gnostics returning to their former Christian community. There were cross-currents swirling around, producing an intoxicating mixture of ideas. Theology, discipline, liturgical celebrations – were all developing in a churning theological whirlpool. This *Gospel of Mary* was the product of a world now past.

The author of the apocryphal *Gospel of Mary* (some think it was Mary herself) addressed questions which were vital to every Christian – questions about truth, insight and leadership. As Christians, where were they to look to find answers? Who was going to replace Jesus once he had disappeared? Who held the keys of the kingdom? Whose visions could be trusted? Who had the strongest link to Jesus? Can a woman be a leader among the disciples? How was anyone to discover true freedom? This gospel was about Christian controversies, the reliability of a disciple's witness, the validity of teachings that were communicated by personal revelations and visions, and about the role of women in the community.

After the Saviour disappeared, Mary spoke to the assembled brothers and sisters, telling them to be strong and resolute, that Jesus had made them 'true human beings'.

Like the author of the *Gospel of Thomas*, the author of this text had not adopted the interpretation of Jesus' life which would become the orthodox message, at least until recently, namely that Jesus' suffering and death constituted a redemptive sacrifice by which mankind would achieve eternal life. The author presented a more radical interpretation of the person of Jesus and his teachings – Jesus was the Truth, and the Way (as he was reported as claiming in the Gospel of John), and his teachings were showing mankind a path to an inner spiritual knowledge by which each believer could achieve the peace and freedom he or she sought.

In their community setting, according to the author the members began to discuss the Saviour's message. Peter invited Mary to share her special knowledge. She had been privileged in Jesus' life. He had shared secrets with her.

> Sister, we know that the Saviour loved you more than all other women. Tell us the words of the Saviour that you remember, the things which you know, that we don't know because we didn't hear them.

Mary replied by recalling a conversation about visions which she had experienced when she was with Jesus:

> I saw the Lord in a vision and I said to him, 'Lord, I saw you today in a vision.'

> He answered me, 'How wonderful you are for not wavering at seeing me. For where the mind is, there is the treasure.'

> I said to him, 'So now, Lord, does a person who sees a vision see it with the soul or with the spirit?'

> And the Saviour answered, 'A person does not see with the soul or with the spirit. Rather the mind, which exists between these two, sees the vision and that is what …'

According to this ancient author, the Saviour had said that the inner self was composed of soul, spirit and a third element, mind, which hovered somewhere between the other two and which saw visions. But this is not the same Jesus whom we meet in the canonical Gospels, nor was this a conversation that Jesus would have had with his beloved Mary Magdalene. 'Soul', 'mind' or a human 'spirit' were not concepts he would have encountered in his Semitic world in Palestine. Not part of his mindset. This was a dialogue which the author had constructed – again, writing history backwards.

When the narrative takes up again after the absence of four more manuscript pages, Mary is in the middle of recalling the revelation she had received in her vision. As a prophetess, she was making her contribution to the stock of revelations which had come from Jesus. On its ascent to its final destination, the soul had engaged in a Gnostic dialogue with those powers that had been trying to hinder its progress.

But Mary's vision and her revelation did not please some of the brothers, Andrew and Peter particularly. Addressing his brothers and sisters, Andrew remarked:

> Say what you like about the things she has said, but I do not believe that the Saviour said them. These teachings are strange ideas.

Knowing what we know of Jesus from the canonical Gospels, I would tend to agree with Andrew. In any event, he was simply giving expression to the problem which the institution was experiencing with their prophets and prophetesses. The leaders were finding it increasingly difficult to recognise any contribution prophets were able to make to the life of the church.

Peter joined in to express his concerns.

> Did he, then, speak with a woman in private without our

knowledge about it? Are we to turn around and listen to that? Did he prefer her over us?

Mary was upset. Because she was a woman, the male apostles were casting a shadow of doubt over her authenticity and over her right to speak. The Gospel of Mark records that when she told the apostles about the resurrection, Mary Magdalene had met with the same reaction – rejection.

> She (Mary Magdalene) went and told those who had been with him, as they mourned and wept. But when they heard that he was alive and had been seen by her, they would not believe it (Mark 16:10–11).

However, the more ancient manuscripts of the Mark Gospel conclude the whole Gospel at verse 8. The longer ending does not appear in the best and earliest manuscripts, or in the manuscripts dating from patristic times. The longer version is probably a summary of material from the Gospel of Luke (Chapter 24) and perhaps from the Gospel of John (Chapter 21), though the narrative of Jesus' appearance to Mary Magdalene and of her reporting to the apostles is different. In the Gospel of Luke, Mary Magdalene was in the company of other women (Joanna, Mary the mother of James 'and others'); they had not seen Jesus, but had encountered two men 'in dazzling apparel' who announced that Jesus had risen.

> Returning from the tomb they told all this to the eleven and to all the rest. Now it was Mary Magdalene and Joanna and Mary the mother of James and the other women with them that told this to the apostles; but their words seemed to them an idle tale, and they did not believe them (Luke 24:9–11).

According to the *Gospel of Mary*, when challenged by Peter, Mary Magdalene burst into tears and said,

> My brother Peter, what are you imagining? You think that I

have thought up these things by myself in my heart or that I am telling lies about the Saviour?

Then the apostle Matthew intervened with a startling put-down. Contemporary Christians are familiar with what is now accepted to have been Peter's established position within the little apostolic group, with how the authors of the canonical Gospels attempted to prop up his authority and primacy, with what we presume was his status, in the primitive community. We know of how his successors have prized their link to him, expanding their institutional control over the universal church. This is why Matthew's contribution to this unpleasant confrontation is surprising, maybe even scandalous. He was putting Peter and the other apostles back in their place.

> Peter, you have always been a wrathful person. Now I see you contending against the woman like the evil spirits. For if the Saviour made her worthy, who are you to reject her. Assuredly, the Saviour's knowledge of her is completely reliable. That is why he loved her more than us. We should be ashamed. We should clothe ourselves with the perfect Human, acquire it for ourselves as he commanded us, announce the good news, not laying down any other rule or law that differs from what the Saviour said (page 18 of the Coptic manuscript).

Cardinals and other contemporary leaders might hesitate to clothe themselves 'with the perfect Human' – with Jesus – and announce the good news of the kingdom rather than the reactionary news of the institution.

On any view of the author's description of this scene, Mary Magdalene was depicted in the document as a central character in the early Christian community. She was seen as an especially cherished companion of Jesus, the repository of exclusive visions and divine revelations, with a ranking and an authority which implied a leadership role, as someone truly worthy – made worthy by the Saviour. If the Saviour had made her worthy, the apostles were obliged to listen to her. They were prohibited from making decisions which differed from what Jesus had said.

If the author's information be true, this apocryphal gospel clouds any romantic notion contemporary Christians might entertain about the level of harmony and communion in the early church. It challenges us to reconsider the basis of power and authority within that institution. The author provides an insight into the life of the primitive church, describing the discussions and controversies among them about the source of revelation, the random gift of the Spirit, the reliability of the disciples' witness, about ministry, leadership, authority, control, and about the role of women such as in the guise of Mary.

The Pistis Sophia

The tension between Peter and Mary Magdalene also featured in another Christian-Gnostic document which was discovered in 1773 and which had probably appeared on the scene in the third century (or the fourth century at the latest). This text is available in only one Coptic manuscript, known as the *Askew Codex* which the British Museum purchased in 1785. The codex originally contained 178 leaves of parchment but the contents have since been reduced to 174.

The author of *Pistis Sophia* purported to record the secret Gnostic teachings of the transfigured Jesus. As the story unfolded, Jesus had remained on earth for eleven years after his resurrection and had engaged in dialogue with his disciples, his mother, Mary Magdalene and Martha. In this apocryphal document, the disciples are heard asking questions which Jesus is answering – and Mary Magdalene is presented as a privileged interlocutor.

> Excellent, Mary. You are blessed beyond all women upon the earth ... Speak openly and don't be afraid. I will reveal all things that you are looking for.

The work contains lengthy and often strange revelations dealing with the complex structures of hierarchies in heaven, introducing the reader to many female figures in Gnostic cosmology – figures such as Sophia the Universal Mother, the Power on High, the Wife of Male, the Revealer of Mysteries, Heavenly Mother, Consort of the Man, the Virgin, the Moon. The *Pistis Sophia* author describes in exhausting detail the descent and ascent of the soul, and he lists thirty-two carnal desires, all of which had to be overcome before a follower could achieve salvation. This is material which appears to be nonsense to a modern reader, and totally foreign to what we read of Jesus and his disciples in the original canonical Gospels.

Mary Magdalene and John the Virgin appear in the document as the principal disciples of Jesus, and because of their ranking they possess the greatest measure of *gnosis*. Mary Magdalene asks one question after another, and sometimes excessively long ones. The author paints her as a garrulous, overbearing woman. When Peter complains, Jesus admonishes her. Because of her deep spiritual understanding, she monopolises the discussion (asking thirty-nine of the forty-six recorded questions). Peter is irritated by her overbearing presence and interrupts twice to register his annoyance.

> My Lord, we can't suffer this woman who's dominating the conversation, robbing us of our opportunity. She doesn't allow anyone to speak. She's doing all the talking.

Jesus agrees and directs Mary to give others an opportunity to ask questions. Peter thinks she is supplanting his authority, and the authority of his brothers. However, when he urges Jesus to silence her, Jesus rebukes him (Bk. 1, ch. 36). In Book 2 Chapter 72, Mary Magdalene confides to Jesus that she is reluctant to speak to him freely:

Peter makes me hesitant. I am afraid of him because he hates the female race.

Perhaps he did. Maybe Peter was a misogynist. Apparently Mary thought so. In any event, there was obviously some tension in the early church, some antipathy towards pushy women, at least as the author of the *Pistis Sophia* imagined the situation to be in the third or fourth century. Women dominant. A contest for control. Men not happy. It was reminiscent of Paul's community in Corinth as it was portrayed by the faceless author who introduced verses 34-36 of Chapter 14 into Paul's first epistle. If the canonical Gospel accounts can be believed, Jesus had never made his female companions 'hesitant' as Mary of Magdala complained Peter had done. Jesus never embarrassed the women he was encountering in the street.

The Gospel of Thomas

At the conclusion of the *Gospel of Thomas*, in passage 114, as we have seen, the author provides an example of the tension which existed in the early church between one of Jesus' male apostles and Mary Magdalene. This Gnostic gospel purports to record the hidden sayings that 'the living Jesus' had spoken, and which Judas Thomas the Twin had recorded. It was composed during the second century, maybe even during the latter stages of the first century, at about the same time as the later canonical Gospels were being composed. We read how Peter was portrayed at an early stage in the life of the Church as sexist, seeking to reduce Mary Magdalene's influence with Jesus and to put her back in her place.

> Simon Peter said to them, 'Mary should leave us, for females are not worthy of life'. Jesus said, 'Look, I shall guide her to make her male, so that she too may become a living spirit resembling you males. For every female who makes herself male will enter heaven's kingdom.'

The Gospel of Philip

In *The Dialogue of the Saviour* (another Nag Hammadi Library document), Mary Magdalene had been identified as one of the three disciples (together with Thomas and Matthew) whom Jesus had chosen to hear his special teachings. It was a strange trinity of disciples Jesus had selected to share his secrets. The canonical Gospels had suggested Peter, James and John had been the 'kitchen cabinet' that Jesus had appointed. The author of *The Dialogue* praised Mary above the other two, describing her as someone who 'spoke as a woman who knew the All' (139:12 – 13).

According to the author of the *Gospel of Philip*, and following a theme explored in the Gnostic gospel narratives, some of the male disciples of Jesus were jealous of Mary Magdalene and her access to the Master.

We should not presume, however, that the *Gospel of Philip*, or for that matter any of the ancient Christian-Gnostic texts from the second, third or fourth centuries, should be accepted as reflecting the real situation between Jesus, his disciples and Mary Magdalene. It's obvious that the further we move away from the critical events of Jesus' life, the less likely it is that any document which purported to describe these events and his relationship with others accurately reflected the historical facts they describe. These were imaginary narratives created by their individual authors, reflecting their view of the world, their problems and their perception of the dynamics and interactions within the group, and their prejudices and struggles. In telling us about Jesus and his life, they were telling us something about their own times, their local community and about themselves. They were writing history backwards, beginning with themselves, superimposing their own problems and solutions on the text about Jesus. Consequently, these writings give us some insight as to what it was like inside the Christian-Gnostic communities at the time they were being written.

The *Gospel of Philip*, for example, is a Christian-Gnostic work originally written in the Coptic language sometime in the second half of the third century. Like other documents we have seen, it had been lost until rediscovered as part of the Nag Hammadi library in Egypt in 1945. The work was bound into the same codex as the *Gospel of Thomas* and is a collection of Gnostic teachings and reflections – a mishmash of parables, aphorisms, polemical statements, dogmatic propositions and biblical exegesis. It especially focused on the book of Genesis and the Adam-and-Eve story, presenting peculiarly Gnostic teachings on the origin of the human race.

The Gnostic school of knowledge at the base of the *Gospel of Philip* (maybe a school associated with the Valentinian Gnostic tradition) viewed marriage as an archetype of the spiritual union which everyone must seek in order to reach the state of perfection. The intimate embrace uniting a man and a woman in the nuptial bed was a sacred sign, a metaphor, a mystery, a sacrament mediating a deeper, spiritual union. Consequently, the close relationship between Jesus and Mary Magdalene was afforded a privileged treatment in this work.

The author described Jesus as Mary Magdalene's 'companion', and the word had the potential to imply that the bond between them was an intimate, even sexual one. In *logion* 32 the author observed,

> There are three who always walked with the Lord: Mary, his mother, and his sister, and Magdalene, the one who was called his companion. His sister and his mother and his companion were each called Mary.

In contrast to this (Isenbery's) translation, the concluding statement is translated with a different and puzzling meaning by Jean-Yves Leloup: '... and Myriam of Magdala who was known as his companion as Myriam is for him a sister, a mother and a wife [*koinonos*]'. To confuse matters further, the second Mary is identified in some translations as the sister of Jesus' mother, and in others as the sister of Jesus.

In several places in this gospel, Mary Magdalene is referred to as Jesus' companion, his partner or consort. The Greek word used had a range of possible meanings, but at root it denoted a person engaged in some kind of fellowship, or a sharing with someone or in some common project.

What exactly a *koinonos* (a companion) could share with his or her partner could take many forms, ranging from a common enterprise or experience to a shared business. In the Bible, *koinonos* was sometimes used to refer to a spouse (Mal 2:14; 3 Macc 4:6), but the word could also mean a 'companion' in faith (Phlm 17), a co-worker in proclaiming the Gospel (2 Cor 8:23) or a business associate (Luke 5:10).

The Greek word *koinonos* in its Coptic form, as well as some of its various Coptic equivalents, is used with a number of meanings in the *Gospel of Philip*. It appears, for example, in its literal sense to refer to a pairing of men and women in marriage and to sexual intercourse. But it is also used in a metaphorical sense, referring to union of a spiritual nature, or to the mysterious communion with and immersion of a gifted believer into the divine realm. And importantly, there are occasions in the *Gospel of Philip* where the regular Coptic word for wife was used directly in reference to people who were married, thereby suggesting that the term *koinonos* was reserved for a more specific usage by the author.

According to the author, relying on oral tradition, or maybe drawing on his own imagination, Mary Magdalene's influential relationship with Jesus was the cause of jealousy and tension. His male disciples were unhappy.

> The companion of the (Saviour is) Mary Magdalene. (But Christ loved) her more than (all) the disciples and used to kiss her (often) on her (mouth). The rest of (the disciples were

offended by it) ... They said to him, 'Why do you love her more than all of us?' The Saviour answered and said to them, 'Why do I not love you as (I love) her?' (*Nag Hammadi*, II, 3:63/32–64/5).

This passage referring to Jesus kissing Mary Magdalene is tantalisingly incomplete, though the sexual language and imagery can't be mistaken. The original manuscript is damaged. Several critical words are missing. What appears in brackets is the translator's attempt to feel for the meaning. Unfortunately, there is a hole in the manuscript after the phrase 'and used to kiss her often on her ...' The passage describes Jesus kissing Mary Magdalene, but the nature of that kiss is uncertain. One translator suggests he kissed her on the mouth, another, on the hand. It is just as plausible that Jesus kissed her on the cheek, or the forehead. Whatever word is missing in the text, the passage clearly suggests that the gesture was an expression of a special, intimate relationship of love between the two, and that this intimacy caused some friction in the larger group. In some circles, religious people would have been scandalised by Jesus even talking to Mary Magdalene. She was not one of his blood relatives. Touching was thought to be more serious. Kissing was strictly forbidden.

The kiss that was shared by those who had attained perfect *gnosis* had been explained earlier in the text:

> For it is by a kiss that the perfect conceive and give birth. For this reason we also kiss one another. We receive conception for the grace which is in one another.

According to the author, those who had reached the higher stage of perfection by acquiring the true *gnosis* could exchange kisses that were grace-filled. Life, true life, was generated when couples kissed, physically and spiritually.

When Jesus kissed Mary Magdalene, he filled her with grace. They were able to share because Mary had proved herself worthy of 'the kiss'. The disciples were jealous of her because they were not worthy of the same intimacy. Mary and Jesus had been united in a mystical marriage of man and woman forever – Logos and Spirit; Adam and Eve again; male and female. The circle was complete.

> If the female had not separated from the male, the female and the male would not have died. The separation of male and female was the beginning of death. Christ came to heal the separation that was from the beginning and reunite the two, in order to give life to those who died through separation and unite them. A woman is united with her husband in the bridal chamber, and those united in the bridal chamber will not be separated again (*Nag Hammdi* II.3:70).

By the second and third centuries when the Gnostic-Christian gospels were being composed, the 'orthodox' Christian communities had resolved the tensions and mixed messages created by the likes of Mary Magdalene, or by officious widows, prophetesses or enthusiastic women seeking to assert themselves as leaders in the Group. These women challenged the authority of Peter, and of the other apostles and their male successors. The 'orthodox' communities had drifted away from the values and attitudes which had guided Jesus' personal ministry. His kingdom message and his policy of prioritising the poor and marginalised, of welcoming women into his inner circle and involving them in ministry, had proved too radical for the members of the early church – too unpopular for those joining the movement, too difficult to sell – and the church was slowly moving up in society, making converts from among the middle class, the rich and powerful. Christians were becoming a force in society – recognised and established in country areas and cities where women were still regarded as inferior to men and unable to take part in public affairs. Society was hostile to the idea that women could enjoy a leadership role outside the home. The 'orthodox' Christian churches sought to be part of the world, accepted in the wider community, melding in as part of the landscape – and the world was not ready to accept Jesus' kingdom preaching or his way of involving women in his ministry.

Gnostic groups, including Christian-Gnostic groups, were different. They were more secret than the orthodox communities were – more exclusive, more unconventional, more charismatic, more fascinated by visions and mystery revelations with outpourings of ecstatic energy. As we have seen, by reputation some Gnostic groups were engaging in unconventional sexual practices. They provided a forum where the Christian message and liturgical practices could interact with the mystery religions of the East, where women could preach and prophesy and where they could be leaders, adopt a public role and celebrate the mysteries. Since the more 'orthodox' communities didn't want to follow them down that track, the tension which had existed for a time in the early churches was lost forever. From then on, Christianity would be a top-down institution governed by dogma, by theologians and bishops, by a canon of books, by rules and tradition, and by men.

Female Participation in the Mysteries

In his *De virginibus velandis*, Tertullian took up Paul's supposed embargo on women talking publicly in the assembly, expanded it, and later explained his extension of Paul's prohibition in his treatise *De baptismo*. As far as he could see, it was obvious from the laws of nature (as well as from the precepts of ecclesiastical discipline concerning women), that the apostle's prohibitions applied to all women, including virgins. Women were not permitted to speak in the assembly. They were not free to teach, or to baptise, or to offer the Eucharist, or to claim a part in any manly function, and especially in any sacerdotal office (*De virginibus velandis* 9:1–3).

> How could we believe that Paul should give a female power to teach and to baptise, when he did not allow a woman even to learn by her own right? Let them keep silent, he says, and ask their husbands at home (*De baptismo* 17:5).

There must have been something going on in North Africa that Tertullian didn't like. From the tone and details of his explicit prohibitions, we can assume that there was trouble in Paradise. Women must have been acting up behind the scenes, asserting their Jesus-given rights, claiming to be able to do 'irregular' things, getting above themselves. From time to time, and reading between the lines of course, we can sense that the church was not functioning as smoothly as the bishop and his deacons would have liked. Women were pushing themselves forward and threatening the good order of the community, just like they had done in Corinth when Paul was on the scene there. Those in authority had to keep pulling the females into line.

This tension within the community – between the female believers injecting themselves into the liturgical celebrations, popping up where they weren't welcome, becoming more active in worship than was considered proper, on the one hand, and those in authority making laws and regulations to control their female members, on the other – this tension had been a smouldering feature of life since apostolic times.

In the late fourth century (a little outside our period of reference), at the Synod of Laodicea, a team of local bishops would decide that women had to be kept well away from the altar (canon 22). Subsequent teams of episcopal celibates repeated the same ruling, at the Synod of Nimes at the end of the fourth century, and again at the Synod of Nantes in the seventh century, and again in the eighth century at the Synod of Aachen. Here the assembled bishops would decide that admitting women even to the lower ranks of the hierarchy was not allowed because it was 'indecent' and contrary to apostolic church order. Why were they considering the issue? What was happening in these churches?

At the end of the fifth century, an angry Pope Gelasius, in a fit of ecclesiastical temper, would write to a team of bishops in the south of Italy, saying,

> As we have learnt to our anger, such contempt for the divine truths has set in that even women, it has been reported, serve at the holy altars. And everything that is exclusively entrusted to the service of men has been carried out by the sex that has no right to do it (Decree 26, PL. 59/55, Mansi VIII. 44).

The minutes of the Reform Synod of Paris from the early ninth century would go on to record,

> In some provinces it happens that women press around the altar, touch the holy vessels, hand the clerics the priestly

vestments, and even dispense the body and blood of the Lord to the people. This is shameful and must cease ... No doubt such customs have arisen because of the carelessness and negligence of the bishops.

From the beginning, women – assertive women – proved a problem for the men who were in charge of the show.

Tertullian's nuanced view was that while men and women were equal before God their creator, they were unequal by the laws of nature and the laws of the church. Men and women had the same souls and could look forward to the same celestial reward (but only after the female believers had become men), but in all other respects a woman was inferior. Tertullian's misogynistic mindset has not lost its ecclesiastical impetus. While secular society has undergone a revolution of gender roles, the relationship between men and women within many of the Christian churches was set in concrete almost from the beginning. It is the same today as it was in the second century – a policy bound tight by what has been twisted into a form of dogmatised tradition. Women's participation in the mysteries has been governed by clerical minds befogged by pre-scientific prejudices.

While the more 'orthodox' Christian churches were holding the line, albeit against some opposition, and excluding women from an active participation in the mysteries, there were other churches (Gnostic-Christian communities) which weren't falling into line. They were encouraging their female members to step forward and take their place. Members of various Gnostic sects were also infiltrating the more 'orthodox' communities of believers and corrupting the message, twisting beliefs, challenging day-to-day practices and causing dissension.

It is difficult from this distance to assert with any confidence the principal factors which persuaded the church leaders to exclude women from active ministry. This exclusion was from liturgical involvement, teaching, participating in governance, and from being part of the institution's hierarchal structure. However, the following factors were an undoubtedly important element in the mix.

There was the sexual freedom which existed in some of the Gnostic communities, the energetic involvement of women in some of the Gnostic sects, their dominance and exuberant participation in the ceremonies and administration. As well as all this there was also the radical dualism which permeated most of the Gnostic theological mindset (good and evil, spirit and flesh, heaven and earth, spiritual and material, male and female). If these factors didn't cause the authorities to take a hard line on female participation in the mysteries, they almost certainly provided a good rationale for their conservative, reactionary policy.

It would have horrified the male leaders of the more conservative Christian communities to learn that some Gnostic communities were basing their theology on traditions handed down by women – by Mary Magdalene in particular, but also by women such as Salome and Martha, and the two Montanist prophetesses, Priscilla and Maximillia. Some Gnostics simply didn't accept that the authentic message was being passed on along a line of exclusively male executives, from the apostles to their successors. The Spirit was far more dynamic. Its force was overflowing institutional boundaries and energising men and women.

Although Gnostic beliefs and practices varied from group to group, and although the intermingling of Gnostic and Christian beliefs and practices were forever in flux and varied from region to region, there are common features which suggest that some Christian-Gnostic communities used to involve women in their ceremonial activities. It is important to follow this line of development for a little distance because for some centuries and for some Christians, Gnosticism was a serious threat to the purity of Jesus' message. Although for other Christians, the

Gnostic view of the world and their spirituality enriched their lives.

Unlike the 'heretical' or 'unorthodox' sects in and around Carthage where women were teaching, exorcising, healing and probably baptising, Tertullian was convinced that women were meant by nature and by divine ordinance to remain passive in the assemblies.

> I must not omit an account of the conduct of the heretics – how frivolous it is, how worldly, how merely human, without seriousness, without authority, without discipline, as suits their creed. How wanton are the women of these heretics! For they are bold enough to teach, to dispute, to enact exorcisms, to undertake cures – it may be even to baptise. Their ordinations are carelessly administered, capricious and fickle (*De prescriptione haereticorum* 41).

We have to be careful. Tertullian wrote with a poisonous pen when he was attacking his enemies. He was prone to exaggeration and was hostile to what some women were doing.

The Alexandrine theologian, Didymus the Blind, writing his commentary on 1 Timothy 2:14 in the fourth century, would agree with Tertullian that the involvement of women in the assemblies had to be tightly controlled. While scripture had recognised the existence of prophetesses (the four daughters of Philip, for example, and Deborah, Mary, the sister of Aaron, and the mother of God), Didymus observed that you could search the scriptures without finding one book written by a woman. Taking up once more the myth of Adam and Eve, Didymus was certain that women were not permitted to teach – and the reason was obvious, at least to him. A woman's teaching had caused considerable havoc to the whole human race. As Paul had told his readers, it was not a man who had engaged in deception, but a woman (*On the Trinity*, III. 41:3). The evil Eve again!

In the second century, Irenaeus was struggling in Gaul with the same problem Tertullian was confronting in North Africa, namely the pernicious influence of Gnosticism in his region, including the challenge of countering women's active interference in the mysteries. He had been appointed as the second bishop of an area in southern France and after a pastoral service of approximately 25 years he had died in office in about 202 AD. In his major work, *Adversus Haereses*, he set out on a mission to expose and crush the teachings of various Gnostic schools which had been contorting the minds of his flock into ugly patterns of belief.

In the course of a diatribe, the bishop penned his salacious description of the intimate relationship between a Gnostic leader by the name of Marcus and his female followers. He detailed the outrageous behaviour of the female members of his sect. In reading this material, we must keep at the back of our minds how much the bishop loathed these people who were infiltrating his flock, how mischievous his description of their practices probably was, how aggressively polemical his writings were, and how tainted the source of his knowledge of the Gnostic beliefs and practices could have been.

So was it all just gossip and rumour from disillusioned adherents? Was there any personal, first-hand experience of any of the enemy's activities? Were there inter-faith meetings or ecumenical encounters? What he wrote may record shadows of historical truth, but we must be careful to flavour his slanderous material with a healthy dose of scepticism. The author was running a line. His aim was to expose, belittle, defame and destroy a movement which was running secret fifth-column activities and undermining his work.

While his treatise purports to describe a dominant role for females in the religious life of the followers of Marcus, Irenaeus was certainly not trying to produce a balanced, objective history of his opponent's religious practices. According to him, Marcus was a fraud. He was presenting himself as someone who possessed secret knowledge, who knew more than anyone else, even the apostles – He was a man blessed with the gift we all hanker for, perfection. Marcus believed he had personally received the highest power 'from the invisible and ineffable regions above'. Perfect? Irenaeus thought that he was perfect as an imposter, as a magician. He had the ability to fascinate and mesmerise many men and more than a few women. His 'senseless and cracked-brain followers' saw him as a miracle-worker, but the bishop regarded Marcus as the 'precursor of the Anti-Christ'.

Not a great character reference. Casting aside his sense of political correctness and the Gospel dictate about turning the other cheek, Irenaeus felt free to tell his readers exactly what he thought of Marcus and his buffoons. He went on to describe a liturgical ceremony akin to the Eucharist, one in which Marcus's crazy female followers assumed a presidential role.

As the story unfolded, Marcus used to pretend to consecrate cups of wine and, while he was reciting lengthy prayer formulas, by a sleight of hand, by some trick, he gave the liquid a purple and reddish tint. Consequently, it appeared that as a result of his prayers, a divine female spirit (whom he called 'Charis') had dropped her own precious blood into the cup. He invited those present to sip from the cup so that by the power of 'this magician', Charis would 'flow into' the communicants. His was a ham-fisted version of the real presence in the Eucharist.

The bishop told how Marcus would hand the cups of wine to 'the women' and direct them to consecrate them in his presence. Then he used to take a much larger cup and pour the wine from the cups which the 'deluded women' had consecrated, into his own, at the same time pronouncing a prayer:

> May Charis who is before all things and who transcends all knowledge and speech, fill your inner man and multiply within you her own knowledge.

Repeating certain other similar words, and thus goading on the wretched women to madness, he appears as a worker of wonders when the large cup is seen to have been filled from the small one, so as to overflow by what has been emptied from it (*Adversus Haereses*, Book 1, Chapter 13:2).

Magic and superstition. A female deity and silly women at the centre of their liturgical worship. It is clear that Irenaeus didn't like what he was hearing on the rumour mill. He was not going to let his community generate similar public scandals.

But this active participation in the mysteries by Gnostic and 'heretical' women was not confined to Gaul. The same scandalous practice was going on elsewhere. As we have seen, according to Cyprian, Firmilian the bishop of Caesarea in Cappadocia knew of a Montanist prophetess in Asia Minor who, around 235 AD, was converting lay people and clerics to her movement and who was even celebrating the Eucharist (Cyprian, *Epistolae* 75:10).

The story of Marcus and his followers provided the impetus to persuade more conservative male leaders (bishops, for example) to prohibit active female involvement in the life and work of their faith communities. Women were erotic beasts. Dangerous and forever causing trouble, they were being ordained and celebrating a Eucharistic-type meal in some of the heretical sects. They had to be discouraged. A clear line had to be drawn. Admitting women to the inner sanctum could only lead to disaster so the situation called for continuing vigilance.

Some Factors behind the Female Hate Speech at the Heart of Christianity

While Jesus had set a truly unique example of how to respect and honour women, in the second, third and fourth centuries his followers exhibited a level of misogyny which is troubling for people of faith. These followers whose works have been preserved and quoted with approval down the centuries were men with mothers and sisters (presumably) who had loved and nurtured them. They had put their faith in Jesus as the person who could show them the way to a happy, fulfilling life, and yet they had wandered off the track their leader had marked out for them and stumbled about in swamps.

The authentic letters of Paul (and others who came after him) contain material which was once considered by its authors and their readers as completely acceptable, 'orthodox' and reasonable. But a modern reader can only view some of this material as crazy theology, as expressions of blind prejudice. The level of misogyny which existed within the Christian churches of the period is shocking. The fact that it was there in the churches, without any apparent opposition, is far more important than any academic reflections as to its origins. These alien attitudes tainted the fabric of church structures and poisoned the message Jesus had preached.

But nearing the end of this essay, some attempt should be made to identify at least the principal factors which contributed to the long tradition of misogyny within the history of Christianity.

How did such perverse attitudes and prejudices arise? How to explain them?

A *philosophical*, pseudoscientific basis for the popularity of hate speech in the Western world can be traced directly to the influence of men such as Plato and his pupil Aristotle, to Aristotle's friend Theophrastus and their disciples, as well as to the re-emergence in the second and third centuries of the present era of the ethical principles of the Stoics as a way of facing the trials of human existence.

The schizophrenic mindset at the heart of Christianity in the second, third and fourth centuries (traces of which can be seen in the writings of Paul) grew out of Plato's philosophical worldview, and more particularly from the later version modified by Plotinus and the Neo-Platonists. In addition to the early Christian writers who had been exposed to the ideas of Greek philosophers (writers such as Origen and Clement), the prevailing Greek mindset also influenced many of the Gnostic schools of thought which in turn contaminated the faith of many 'orthodox' believers. These schools promoted the concepts of a distant, ineffable deity and a demiurge who created all physical reality; an endless series of divine and demonic emanations; the body-spirit divide; good and evil; heaven and earth; male and female; Adam and Eve; good and bad angels. These binary categories facilitated a tidy explanation of the world and of the experience of evil. Women and female beings were inevitably placed on the dark side of the cosmic divide, with male deities and emanations, and men on the side of light and reason.

In contrast to Plato's dream-world, Aristotle based his view of the world on a process of observation and experimentation. As far as he could see, there was no essential physical difference between men and women – both were basically constructed with the same parts. Women were merely an inferior version of the male species. They were males who had gone off the boil in the womb and had turned out a little distorted, or at least 'undercooked'.

These ancient philosophical and 'scientific' considerations on the subject of women were powerfully reinforced by the scurrilous attitudes and values reflected in the writings of the Greek and Latin poets and playwrights. And in turn, the works of these pagan authors were on the school reading lists for many of the Christian writers when they were boys and easily influenced.

Then the ancient philosophical principles of the Stoics made a reappearance in the writings of men like Seneca and Epictetus, and in the reflections of Emperor Marcus Aurelius who had employed Galen as his personal surgeon. Their jaundiced view of the human condition produced a philosophical enzyme which leavened the theology of the Christian authors of the early centuries and beyond.

At its origins, Stoicism had been an integrated system of metaphysics, logic and ethics, but as it developed and became popular it had turned into a way of living for many of the citizens of the Roman Republic of the first century.

The basic ethical principles of Stoicism became accepted as a way of dealing with misfortune – with death, loss and defeat. It sought to cultivate a mentality of indifference to the external world and to the vagaries of life. The path a Stoic had to tread was arduous, but by exercise and discipline, he was able to develop the ability to separate those dimensions of his life which were ruled by his ability to reason, from his rebellious desires and powerful urges. By a program of rigorous training and self-control, he could achieve a sense of acceptance and a degree of indifference to pain and pleasure. Imbued with these principles, a man was able to face the trials of life with dignity and with a certain aloofness. While women and children were emotional, weak creatures, a true man was strong and constant.

Gaius Mucius Scaevola had proved his manliness to the Etruscans by thrusting his fist deep into a brazier, without flinching, and Christians were made of the same mettle. They could demonstrate their fervour and faith by an enthusiastic espousal of harsh ascetical practices, by vowing themselves to a life of celibacy and ultimately by their acceptance of death under torture.

While Stoic principles were infiltrating the ranks of believers in the early centuries, traces of which can be seen even in Paul's letters and especially in the later Pastoral Epistles, some pagans also shared the hair-shirted seriousness and stoical contempt for the world practised by the Christians. They too pursued what they regarded as the manly virtues – courage, fortitude, nobility and honour, and the ability to live a life where the mind remained separate from, and in control of the body, where temptations could be resisted. Fornication was the dreaded nightmare of every male, young and old. Sex was associated with sin and the serpent. The female was someone to be feared and avoided. She was dangerous and her ability to lead men astray was diabolical.

As the Christian movement was expanding into the Greco-Roman world, it was shedding some of the elements of Jesus' original vision and taking on some of the beliefs and values, the attitudes and prejudices of the world it was encountering on a daily basis. Some of those prejudices of course involved women.

Some of the early Christians authors, men such as Origen and Clement of Alexandria, Tertullian of Carthage, and later Jerome and Augustine, had as youths been schooled in the works of pagan philosophers and the literature of the pagan classics. They were familiar with the ideas of Plato and Aristotle, for example, and with the poetry of Homer and Hesiod, of Semonides and Juvenal. They had been exposed as young men to the classical stereotypical descriptions of women – fickle, silly, giddy, gossips, empty vessels, greedy, crafty, cunning and dangerous. These stereotypes were passed on from one generation to the next by male teachers, male preachers, male supervisors and leaders.

A *theological* basis for the Christian tradition of women-haters and women-fearers can be found in the exploitation of the powerful, religious myth of Adam and Eve and in other fabulous stories about creation and the Fall. The early Christian writers, as well as Jewish thinkers such as Philo, had been hard at work expanding these primeval stories and embellishing the details surrounding them. Caught in the web of these myths, female figures – Eve, Lilith and women in general – were condemned to carry the load of guilt for sex and sin.

Paul and those who followed him argued that Adam had been created as the stereotypical male figure, fashioned in the image and likeness of God, and therefore the leader, the head, the captain, the patriarch. Eve was the stereotypical woman – second in line, created as the companion, after Adam, and fashioned from his flesh, inferior and submissive.

A further theological basis for disparaging the female sex can also be traced to the teachings of Paul and his followers. He promoted a worldview for Christians which invited them to see themselves as new creatures, living a life on earth which mimicked the angels' life in heaven, an asexual life such as the angels and God himself (all males) lead.

The *sociological* basis of the developing anti-feminist tendency within the church is somewhat more difficult to trace. The story involves what was going on inside the communities themselves, and what was happening at the interface between 'orthodox' Christians and society at large. The leaders of the churches were keen to present an institution which could function comfortably in society, which could attract members from various strata of society, which looked normal and trustworthy. And, of course, it has to be remembered that the members of the various local communities who came from the pagan world were joining the movement in ever-increasing numbers and that they didn't arrive with their heads completely empty and ready to absorb all the details of the developing religious message. While they were making a radical change to their religious and social lives, they all arrived with baggage. They came with all their individual flaws, their acquired attitudes and prejudices, and with many of their previous customs and practices. Preaching the message and establishing a community of believers was not a simple task for those in charge.

Women were dominant in some of these other communities, and on occasions their behaviour was ill-disciplined, sometimes immoral. The more 'orthodox' Christians wanted to be differentiated from those groups which were encouraging women to take up leadership roles and failing to conform to the norms of society.

Furthermore, there is some evidence of tension within the Christian communities themselves. Women were seeking to establish a basis for a more flexible type of authority. They were claiming secret revelations coming directly from the Master himself. They were calling for a power structure founded on the Founder's exclusive love. Some Gnostics were infiltrating the community and leading believers astray. Mary Magdalene had become somewhat of a symbol of resistance to the way in which the authority structures had begun to crystallize exclusively in the hands of men. Some of the practices of mystery cults were gaining a toehold within the churches. The male-dominant hierarchy had to be vigilant and ready to take defensive action. Control of the institution was paramount. Men had to assert their authority and preserve their exclusive position in the hierarchy.

Over time, the efforts being made to appear part of the mainstream and to blend seamlessly into society were not proving successful. Christians were suffering persecution. Believers were being challenged to choose between denying their faith by sacrificing to idols, and becoming sacrificial victims themselves. Vicious rumours were spreading. Christians were seen throughout society at large as aliens and traitors, and they began to see themselves as unwelcome, as outcasts, strangers in the world and surrounded by pagan decadence. A cult of the martyrs was developing. Some believers began to emulate the sacrifices of their heroes. Fasting, mortification, vigils, consecrated virginity and other extreme ascetical practices replicated in miniature the challenges of martyrdom. The more pious members of the faithful began to withdraw from the world, living alone or with others in the desert lands, praying in caves and on mountain tops. Believers were struggling to convert themselves into heavenly beings, leading their lives outside the world, in an antechamber to heaven. They were disembodied beings trying to return to man's primitive existence when Adam had been God's perfect creature, living alone in Paradise before the appearance of Eve, before base sexual drives had kicked in, before any sexual contamination and inevitable sinning.

The soul fought against the body for dominion. Our angelic selves were in a constant struggle against our diabolical urges and desires. The world was evil. The male member of the species had to safeguard his superior status. Self-denial, ascetical practices, virginity, control, prudence, and the forces of reason were all on the side of the angels, whereas women, sexual indulgence, coupling with females, the flesh and the world were on the side of the powerful forces of evil. A schizophrenia had infected the religious mind of Christians so that all flesh and particularly the flesh of women (and their devious minds) had taken up residence on the dark side of creation.

As membership grew, the wealth of the institution had also been increasing. Even before Constantine, the church was acquiring land, building churches, attracting people who occupied positions of power – moneyed people, members of the elite. The Jesus vision of a kingdom for the poor and marginalised was fading. His original Gospel message was being mangled, or at least seriously refashioned. For some of the serious-minded Christians, a life of poverty was becoming more and more attractive. They wanted to remove themselves from the world, even from the institution of the church itself, to become like angels – touched by poverty, indifferent to possessions and untainted by sex.

The works of writers which were copied and preserved in libraries and collections had been produced exclusively by men –

trustworthy men, conforming men. They were written principally for male readers – leaders, monks, bishops and other clerics. These works reflected the values and beliefs which had become mainstream, and which were passed on from one generation to the next. Other works (of Gnostic-Christians, for example) which supported different opinions and other theological views, were overlooked or destroyed.

An Epilogue

Jesus' kingdom vision had encompassed the world of the Creator in all its beauty and all its messiness. God's gifted prophet had been embedded deep in the world, among people, and had ministered to these people in their homes and on the streets. He had been a man of the world.

In the second half of the first century, the anonymous authors of the four Gospels that eventually would make their way into the canon of the New Testament were recording the community's prized memories of Jesus. They were recounting stories which depicted him as a radical revolutionary, a thorn in the side of the religious establishment. They saw him as a 'wonder worker', a rabbi, a country wisdom-lover or a street philosopher and charismatic storyteller. A decade or two before them, another high-profile author had been busy writing pastoral and theological letters to various communities of believers that were already spread around the Mediterranean in places such as Corinth, Galatia, Thessaloniki and Rome, for example. This preacher was more conservative than Jesus had been. More educated, more establishment oriented and a Roman citizen. He didn't want to disturb the peace or challenge the status quo. He wanted to encourage the followers of Jesus to fit comfortably into wider society – not to be too visible, too different or too counter-cultural.

The image of Jesus presented to the early Christian communities by the Gospel writers was of an extraordinary man who often spoke about a mysterious kingdom, of a world of love and compassion in which people of faith would turn the other cheek and forgive the insults of their neighbours – seventy times seven times. It was a kingdom which was to come to fulfillment at a time unknown and unknowable, but a kingdom that their leader had launched in present time.

By contrast and though he sometimes wrote about and listed some of the kingdom values (love, compassion, humility, forgiveness, joy etc.), rather than concentrating on the kingdom and on God as Jesus had done, Paul had focused his missionary mind on the person of Jesus Risen and on his significance for all humanity.

Before the Gospels were composed, Paul had been busy transforming the person of Jesus into some kind of ethereal figure who inhabited the world above and beyond. His perception of Jesus was as a saviour of the universe, a mystical, ungraspable presence – a figure that he had refined down to its essence and removed from the visible, material world.

In such a short time the Jesus movement had moved away from the streets and alleyways of Galilee and Jerusalem into a world of personal spirituality. And then on into a world of hierarchy and clericalism. Baptism launched a believer on an individual, interior journey of ascetical practices, into a struggle for perfection. This journey would take believers away from services to the poor. It would take them away from a kingdom seeded in this world, a kingdom which included everyone and which had been based on the belief that God's will was that his followers (including women) should be serving the real, daily needs of his little people. The leaders were taking believers away from Jesus' dream for the world and guiding them toward liturgical practices, hierarchies and power structures. This movement had become a well-constructed institution with buildings and bureaucracies, thriving in parallel with all the other institutions, and searching (often unsuccessfully) for accommodation in the world.

A group of simple fishermen from Galilee, a tax collector named Matthew, and other faceless followers had accepted a Greek-speaking Roman citizen into their 'A' team. The early church had somehow enticed an educated Pharisee into its ranks. Paul brought with him a new style of playing, new moves, new organisational and administrative skills. He had arrived with his briefcase full of new ideas – new visions, a new set of arguments, a different style and a colourful creative mind. New problems to confront and new subjects to discuss, including sex and sin, the relationship between the Jewish law and Jesus' message, a vision of freedom, ideas on marriage, the tensions between the world and the Spirit.

With a gifted creative mind and different ways of looking at religion and life, Paul was speaking a different language and displaying an openness to a foreign world. He had been a great find and after some initial hesitation, the team had made him welcome and let him show his talents. The historical Jesus was replaced by a series of abstract, cerebral, distant figures – the Messiah, the Saviour, the Second Adam, another Moses, the true son of Abraham. The image of a Christ with mystical, cosmic features then followed in the deutero-Pauline letters.

The movement had migrated from the isolated Semitic world of Palestine into the wide world of Greco-Roman cultures with all their diversities and cross-cultural influences. The sudden upheaval within the Christian message as understood and interpreted by Paul the Pharisee when coming into contact with the world outside Palestine, was life-changing. With mystery cults from the East and Gnostic sects to grapple with, Paul had to convince the followers of Jesus and the citizens of cities and villages that his congregations were not just followers of another mystery religion or Gnostic sect.

Through Paul and his missionary colleagues, Christianity came into contact with a world beyond Palestine – the cosmopolitan centres of Asia Minor and Greece and their rural regions. Paul spoke their language and felt at home in their culture. He was a man of their world. He dedicated his life to persuading these Gentile people from various social and religious backgrounds to join his crowd. In doing this he was careful to ensure that his conduct and the conduct of other believers didn't alienate the audience, and that his people didn't appear as a bunch of undisciplined 'crazies'. In the congregations he had established there would be no outlandish behaviour. Women would be properly dressed, modest and demure, subservient to their husbands as one would expect. They would be silent in public and provide no cause for scandal. They would make no sudden, loud outbursts in the assembly. Everyone would be on their best behaviour so as to give a good impression to outsiders. Though he had been freed by the power of the Gospel message and was answerable to no-one except the Lord, Paul had made himself a slave to all, to Jewish people first, then to those outside the law (the Gentiles), in fact to everyone so that 'I might by all means save some' and win more converts to the cause (1 Cor 9:19 ff).

Despite his best efforts, however, Paul's churches were coming under scrutiny. Their members were subjected to criticism and occasional persecution. The community leaders and their preachers were trying to increase membership and avoid unnecessary conflict. In order to appear as part of the mainstream, they needed to differentiate the Christian groups from the mystery cults and the increasingly popular Gnostic sects.

> Give no offence to Jews or to Greeks or to the church of God, just as I try to please all men in everything I do, not seeking my own advantage, but that of many, that they may be saved (1 Cor 10:32–33).

Within the first few centuries the institution travelled into foreign lands, into troubling territories, and on this journey it lost contact with Jesus' message. It was finding ways of living and relating to the world beyond, ways which were foreign to Jesus' way of life, to his way of behaving and thinking. He had nourished his spiritual life and his contact with his Father in heaven, while remaining in the world and of the world. But after he left the scene, the movement soon began to identify itself as a heavenly reality in opposition to the world.

Women were involved in some limited way in the life of the early churches. As the decades rolled by and became centuries, their role within the local communities became more structured. Their involvement fell far below the level it had reached in the life and ministry of Jesus when they had been with him in Jerusalem, on Calvary and when they were the first witnesses to his resurrected condition.

Women were offered ministries at the bottom of the scale, and had no involvement in governance. They were given minor work to perform and some of it was kingdom work *à la* Jesus' preaching, such as ministering to the bed-ridden, to the sick and elderly, the house-bound, and spending time in prayer. Some of the Christian writers soon began to speak of women in the same way as Hesiod, Seminides and Juvenal had done – disrespectfully, patronisingly, disparagingly.

Men became involved in the administration of the institution (in key areas such as finance), and as visible actors in the celebration of the liturgy – in the baptismal ceremonies and the Eucharistic gatherings. The women's role was mostly restricted to the works of mercy, to the advancement of the kingdom, and their ministries were limited to women only.

Despite their struggle for a place in the sun, to achieve recognition of their ability to make a meaningful contribution to the life of the Christian churches, women didn't stand a chance in a male-dominated world. The overall impression emerging from the available literature of the post-apostolic period is that women were dealt cards from the bottom of the deck. The leadership team were wary of them, perhaps even frightened. There was no way they were going to be invited into the game as key players. Management was not going to surrender to them any meaningful responsibility. The policy was that they were to be kept at arm's length and their behaviour strictly regulated. The old stereotypes prevailed – females were considered irresponsible, weak and frivolous, cunning, materialistic and sensual. They posed an obstacle to salvation. The young male members would be warned how to avoid the snares that women set to entrap them.

While the followers of some Gnostic schools and some lukewarm Gnostic-Christians were ready to exploit the talents of their female members and involve them in their ceremonies, the standard 'orthodox' leaders of the Christian communities were determined to keep the female members in their place – silent, submissive, inferior and where possible, virginal.

The apostolic and post-apostolic churches were in turmoil on a number of fronts. The converts from Judaism were keen to present the memory of Jesus in the context of their Old Testament cultural setting. They wanted to preach his movement as a smooth continuation of the Jewish law and traditions. Jesus was the second Moses – the true son of Abraham. While the Jewish converts were anxious to preserve their precious Jewish laws and customs, the converts from the Greco-Roman world could see no point in maintaining contact with a past which was foreign to them. If they were ever going to gain a foothold in the world outside Palestine, they would need to project a more inclusive message – one geared to gather all comers. Gradually the ever-increasing number of pagan converts was smothering the influence of the followers of Jewish origin.

Furthermore, for some time the structure of the various churches was fractured. The members couldn't decide whether to prefer the stabilising authority based on a line of succession traced back to the apostles, or to go with the excitement and energy generated by a line of charismatic prophets. One promised a secure contact with the past; the other, a future of dreams and visions involving mysterious revelations associated with the Spirit Jesus had promised.

The tension between Jesus' vision of a kingdom of heaven on earth which served the poor and dispossessed, and the movement within the primitive communities to establish a structured institution, was being resolved in favour of the organisation. Instead of a movement whose members were gazing hopefully over the horizon into the future, the leaders voted for establishing an institution which looked backwards, into the past – an institution founded on memory and tradition, one which pretended to follow an authentic re-interpretation of Jesus' message and which was structured on an authority based on apostolic succession.

There is also some convincing evidence that for a time there had been a struggle for power and status between the male members of the movement and their female counterparts – a struggle in which the men were the victors. Women had entered this struggle under a huge disadvantage. The cultural norms and attitudes had been against them. Jesus had acted as their friend and coach, but after he left, his male followers began to assume the positions of leadership and to play by the old rules. Those authors who came to represent the Christianity of the period wrote disrespectfully and spoke disparagingly of their sisters and mothers. Unfortunately, we don't hear even one female voice in the crowd.

Writers of the second and third centuries put us in contact with some strange beliefs which reduced women, and especially virgins, to the status of chattels and robbed them of their God-given dignity. Those in authority never gave them the respect which Jesus had shown them.

Putting to one side what was written about Mary the virgin-mother of Jesus, what is surprising about the post-apostolic era is the almost complete silence in those documents which have made it through the tunnels of history about matters of central importance. There is very little said about the kingdom Jesus preached; about the inclusion of women in his team; about the dignity of all women. Nothing about the central role of Mother

Eve in the history of the human race and in the plan of the Creator; about the female role in God's plan for his creation and in Jesus' life. The misogynistic sentiments sprinkled over the early Christian literature is an occasion of shame and embarrassment to any serious believer. These sentiments make a mockery of what we know of Jesus and his teachings. They are repugnant to those of us who live in the modern world. The tragedy is that there is no parallel, alternative narrative from the period – no bishop, theologian, lawyer or layman writing in support of the women in their communities; no words dignifying their membership in the churches; no passages replicating Jesus' refreshing, revolutionary approach to women and their place in his world; nothing to counter-balance the negativity of the author of the Pastoral Epistles and of heavy hitters such as Tertullian and Clement.

If the available documents from the period are a reflection of the attitudes and prejudices of the early Christians, then the church officials and teachers were living theological and spiritual lives with their minds throbbing with a toxic view of women. The men in charge did not take up the lead Jesus had given to his followers. They did not embrace their sisters in faith and include them at all levels of their lives.

From this distance, we might have expected the early Christians to have listened to Jesus' message. His was a message of a kingdom including the poor, the dispossessed, the marginalised – and the women. But the male followers of Jesus did not promote this Jesus message. Instead they prioritised male membership, shared power among themselves, excluded the female members and spoke poisonous rubbish about them.

Even the apostles never really got the message of the kingdom. As Jesus was leaving them to disappear into the clouds, they were still asking when the kingdom which had been foretold would appear. They wanted to be installed as patriarchs in the new dispensation. Despite the clear warnings Jesus had delivered, at least as recorded in the four canonical Gospels, the apostles hadn't understood the mysterious character of his kingdom. Instead of becoming figures of power and influence, dressed in fine clothes, wearing ruby rings, gold chains and patent-leather sandals, in Jesus' kingdom they were destined to be slaves like their master, to be the last among men and women, to be sitting down the back with the servants and sinners. This was the kingdom they were called to preach – and though he had explained it to them in words of one syllable, they hadn't understood.

Yet despite the cowardice of the Twelve and the absence of the other male disciples in their leader's time of need, the male members continued to maintain their position in the community. Women had been intimately engaged in Jesus' life and mission as friends and companions, witnesses, exemplars of faith, messengers and disciples, but men remained at the helm while the women were gradually moved below decks.

Would Jesus have been in favour of elevating women to priesthood? It's undoubtedly true that such a question would have had no meaning for him. Priesthood associated with his message would have been the last thing to enter his mind. The priests of his generation were in his line of fire as pompous hypocrites. Perhaps a more relevant question would be, 'Did Jesus discourage an active, public female participation in the preaching and serving ministry which had characterised his life?' Based on what we know, the answer has to be 'certainly not'.

According to the Gospel records, the early Christian believers hadn't heard Jesus refer to himself as a priest. He was a layman, and the thought of being a member of a priestly caste would have horrified him, or amused him. He would have been insulted to hear anyone, even one of his enemies, describing him in such a pejorative manner. The priesthood characters he encountered were the butt of his invective.

Jesus was described in the New Testament literature as an anointed, consecrated Messiah; as a gifted preacher who belonged to a kingdom 'not of this world'; as a prophet, a revealer of divine truths; as the long-suffering servant of Isaiah; as a lawgiver like Moses, and as a second Adam. There is only one *sui generis* piece of literature, of comparatively late origin, which describes Jesus as a priest. The priesthood metaphor was a late theological development. It stemmed from the faceless author of the Epistle to the Hebrews drawing heavily on details of the Jewish institution of priesthood.

The early Christian community used to come together regularly for prayer and to sing hymns, to listen to readings and break bread together, and to encourage one another and give thanks (1 Cor 11:23 ff). They would have had no idea of what was to come in the centuries ahead, of the subterranean tunnels through which their initial religious experience would travel.

And nowhere in the Gospels do we read of Jesus referring to any of his disciples as 'priests'. As the story was told, at a farewell meal he invited his Twelve (and probably others, even women) to continue to break bread and to share a cup, giving thanks in his memory. Nowhere in any of the books of the New Testament, even the later ones, was any individual in the community described as a 'priest'. Elders, teachers, prophets, deacons, disciples, apostles, overseers, preachers – but not 'priests'. Someone must have presided at the prayer meetings to keep order. Someone would have led the prayers, invited others to reflect on the readings, determined simple matters like when to begin and when to close the proceedings – but the idea of a priesthood as we have come to know it was a development which arrived centuries later. It has come to us heavily overlaid with theological insights and doctrinal nuances, especially from the Middle Ages and Scholastic scholars.

The idea that women could be priests would never have entered Jesus' head, any more than the idea that men could be ordained to 'say' Mass daily and pray the Breviary. These sacramental procedures were not on the horizon in Jesus' time. Such concerns would have left the members of the early church asking, 'What is this strange person talking about?' 'What planet has he come from?'

But can an acceptable theological answer be provided to the question of female ordination? Is there a case for supporting a female presence at the table, in the boardroom, with a role to play in the organisation's system of governance, with authority to make decisions, in a leadership role and able to preside at the assembly?

Jesus preached radical change and freedom from the law. He showed a disregard for and maybe even a disdain for the establishment. In opposition to the law and the prevailing cultural norms, he encouraged women to be active members of his fellowship. He saw them as witnesses, disciples, companions in arms. He valued and embraced them. In his ministry, he sought to give preference to the marginalised, to the poor – and to women. Status and gender were of no consequence in the kingdom, or on the road. A person's plumbing system was not a relevant consideration any more than was his or her status. Even the hated tax-collectors could be apostles and participants in the kingdom, and a woman from the other side of the tracks, from whom seven demons had been expelled, could be a disciple.

Jesus hadn't regarded himself or his disciples as bound by external rituals or religious traditions. The Jesus we meet in the Gospels challenged his followers to free themselves from the shackles of petty regulations and the restrictions of ritual purity. They had to be ready to change, to be part of a new, Spirit-filled world. They were to be ready to be citizens of the Kingdom of Heaven – living in the real world, but free of the trappings of institutional religion and trivial restrictions, and the fetters of twisted power structures.

The basic question for all Christians is, what is normative within the Christian tradition? What indispensable principles must govern our behaviour within the institution? How much notice should any of us take of what Paul said or of what was written in his name?

With this in mind, there are two possible answers to the question of whether the church can or should involve women fully in her sacramental ministry.

First, those who happen to be in charge for a moment of history are duty-bound to find a place in the ministry for all – including women – as Jesus had done. Leaders within the faith-world of Christians are committed to discern Jesus' way of thinking and to ensure his Kingdom-principles find a reflection, however blurred it is, in the life and ministry of the church. Otherwise, those in charge would be engaged in a frolic of their own.

Second, the Gospels tell us that at 'the Last Supper', a gathering of early believers had broken bread together and shared a cup of wine with Jesus. Paul the Apostle and the author of Acts recorded that after Jesus' disappearance, his followers used to gather, pray together and break bread in his memory. It was in these gatherings that the believers had learnt to recognise the presence of the risen Jesus. Bread and wine, when shared by those of faith, created a mystery, a sacrament which allowed Jesus' face to be glimpsed again, if only in shadows.

According to the stories, as we have seen, women were the first to recognise this face after his resurrection and the men were reluctant to believe. The women were responsible for spreading the news and introducing the apostles to the mysterious experience of faith. They acted as messengers of the risen Lord. Their search and their faith empowered them to become witnesses of the resurrection and agents of the message. But then, after an unequal struggle in the early church, women lost the important ministry which Jesus had entrusted to them.

If the Eucharist is truly a common meal at which believers can encounter the presence of the risen Lord, in view of the stories told by three of the evangelists (Matthew, Luke and John), women of faith are the natural religious leaders to call the community together and to preside at the celebration of the mysteries. If anyone has a legitimate claim to a sacramental ministerial role, our sisters can find theirs embedded in the Gospel stories.

The simple communal experiences of Jesus' presence among his followers were not the highly ritualised Masses we have come to accept as the standard. No vestments or incense in the Gospel stories, no golden chalices, no immaculate, dry discs of heavenly bread, no missal, no rigid structures or any hint of transubstantiation, or any eternally fixed formula of words, no processions or tinkling bells. A simple event celebrated among friends and believers has changed radically over the centuries. Layer upon layer of cloudy ceremonial has been superimposed on a simple meal. Now the Eucharist is wrapped in a protective armour and repels all attempts to examine its dimensions, including the gender of the one who presides.

Following the example of Jesus, and conscious of the rough territory through which Christianity has travelled over the centuries, the institution should feel free to change and adapt, radically, to create workable structures which reflect the mores and attitudes of each culture. Paul of Tarsus felt free to manufacture a personal theological worldview, to devise an administration, to frame a suitable language and to plant a modified message in foreign soil. At least according to the Gospel accounts, Jesus chose to commission a small group of men who were called apostles. In the early church, a few extra apostles were added to Jesus' team, but without consulting him. Then the team was expanded to include 'elders', and ministries emerged – social workers later became deacons and deaconesses. An order of widows was created and sodalities of virgins, prophets, teachers, interpreters and others. Later still, individual supervisors were ordained to oversee local communities. Much later, when these 'bishops' needed assistance to minister in their rural centres, they ordained agents to represent them. These men came to be called 'priests', but only after a few centuries.

In the early church, the various communities were looking to the future, fine-tuning a message for the Greco-Roman world and establishing an institutional structure. The early Greek and Latin Fathers of the church continued down the same road – interpreting, adapting, expanding, condemning, rejecting, and changing. Gradually, while continuing to change radically, the official church began to pretend that it was not deviating from the norm; that it could not move because its duty was to preserve faithfully what Jesus himself had set in place, even though he hadn't. It wasn't a bad line as long as it lasted. It wasn't true, but for a long time nobody knew. Believers had no way of checking what they were being told. For centuries there was no basic education for all, no community libraries, no internet, no books or magazines, and ignorance was conserving the status quo.

However, when the Western world and its scholars devised the historical method of research and began to reconstruct critical editions of ancient texts and develop methods of interpretation, when ancient texts began to be uncovered in the deserts of Egypt or on rubbish heaps, the dogmatic protective facade collapsed. The church and its complex history of traditions and dogmas was not as monolithic and inflexible as everyone had been required to believe. Christianity was never meant to be what it became – an old, established institution looking back into the supposed glories of the past. Jesus had preached a vision for those looking to the future. That vision saw vast spaces out there for change, and opportunities to dream dreams without leg-irons and follow the path Jesus had mapped out.

The four canonical Gospels were composed by their authors with such bright colours. The interplay between Jesus and women of all sizes and shapes, the female presence which pervades the pages of the Church's foundational documents reads in stark contrast to the shocking misogyny of Tertullian or Clement, Jerome and Augustine, to the tasteless statements of John Chrysostom, the gross sexist outbursts of Innocent III and the deep-rooted prejudices of many theologians, canonists, bishops, monks and religious poets down the centuries. All these people (typically men) claimed to be faithful followers of Jesus, listening attentively to his message. The early writers and leaders, untroubled by the Gospels, proceeded to poison the minds of those who came after them. The air they breathed, the water they drank, the books they read, the prayers they recited, the earlier leaders they listened to, conveyed the message that Eve and her giddy sisters were the temptresses, that though one of their ranks had been immaculate, women in general were inferior and dangerous, untouchable, somehow unworthy to minister, and alien to the hierarchical structures of the institution. Messages passed down along the streams of tradition, often unspoken, in the bland monastic food, in the poisonous clerical wine, under the text, from power to powerless – a message of exclusion, of submission, of inferiority and sinfulness.

Even though Jesus had spoken, gradually the female followers were being relegated to the back of the line. The status they had enjoyed in Jesus' company was undergoing a makeover. They were being returned to the socially acceptable position they had enjoyed before they had been caught up in Jesus' life and mission – submissive and inferior – and gradually reduced to passive participants in the movement. Although there is little evidence to support a conclusion that Paul was a dyed-in-the-wool misogynist, there is evidence that while he did involve women in his ministry, he propagated a policy of male superiority. There is no denying women were there from time to time, and sometimes in important, visible positions, but the dominance of men within the movement, men like Peter and Paul, James the brother of Jesus and Barnabas, was never questioned.

Reading his authentic letters, one gains the impression that Paul was beginning, almost from scratch, to design and establish an institution with a set of beliefs which he was articulating from his own theological insights, but without the benefit of any record of a shared memory of Jesus' lived experience. As a result, the female members of the emerging institution had suffered.

Whatever Paul might have written or thought, it is no longer appropriate to describe a woman who is someone's wife as a receptacle of his seed or sperm, or as a vessel or sheath to receive his sexual organ. And marriage is no longer to be seen as the solution to the problem of a man's natural drive to fornicate.

No-one I know believes that before a woman can present herself at the gates of paradise, she has to hand in her extra rib and return to her original masculine condition, or that she has to cover her head in public as a sign of her husband's authority over her.

Whatever aura surrounds Aristotle as a universal genius and as the mind of the millennia, no-one now considers a woman as a misbegotten male, as the product of a copulating couple that was meant to be a male but that was not properly cooked in the womb and ended up a female.

Adam and Eve were never meant to be seen as real people – only mythological figures – and the story about them which was composed in a patriarchal culture does not tell anyone how God wanted us to live our lives, how men and women should relate to one another.

None of my friends think that men are superior, more pre-eminent, and more intelligent, logical and reasonable than their mothers, or their wives. None of them think that women as a job-lot are silly and giddy, more frivolous, more emotional, less trustworthy and deviant; that they were created to be inferior and submissive to men; that they are more prone to evil, easier for the devil to tempt, more lustful and craving of erotic experiences. None of my friends or acquaintances consider that men are far better company than women; or that the celibate life is better, more virtuous, happier, more fulfilling for a man than living and working in a loving union with a woman of his choice and the mother of his children.

If anyone in the world ever believed these things (and we know they did – or said they did), we now know their minds were filled with nonsense. The world has moved on – and for the better. Female prime ministers, governors, judges, lawyers, surgeons, cricketers, soldiers, commentators, journalists and jockeys – but not archbishops or bishops or even common priests (at least not in the Roman Catholic Church).

If he was living today (as Christians believe he is, in some mysterious form, in the believing community and in the world), Jesus would undoubtedly favour sharing once again his work and ministry with his female followers. The purple bishops and the fiery red Cardinals of the modern era have taken the place of the 'whitened sepulchres' of old that had plotted to destroy Jesus and his work. They are desperate to conserve the status quo and maintain a system which guarantees 'jobs for the boys'.

When will they ever learn?

A Bibliography

The literature surrounding the issues addressed in this book is considerable – hundreds of books, thousands of published articles, acres of pages and a lifetime of material on the internet.

I have attempted in this bibliography to provide a list of books that I have relied on and some titles that might prove interesting to you. But you will also find that the internet is a vast reservoir of information on the bearded characters who make an appearance in the pages of this book, on their tattered manuscripts and treatises, on the worlds they inhabited and the movements that surrounded them. Click on any name or title and a world of new horizons will open up before you.

I have provided references in the text itself for you to find the passages I have quoted from the original authors, but as a general rule I have not directed you to any particular printed edition or translation of the source material. Once you have a reference, most of the quoted passages can be found on the web, in state libraries and often in local, municipal libraries. Even the recently discovered Gnostic Christian material is available on the internet.

General Histories of the Period: 1–4 Centuries AD

Brown P, *The Body and Society: Men, Women, and Sexual Renunciation in Early Christianity*, Columbia University Press, 2008.

Ehrman B D, *Lost Christianities: The Battles for Scriptures and the Faiths We Never Knew*, Oxford Uni. Press, 2005.

Geoltrain P, *Aux origins du christianisme*, Folio histoire, Gallimard, 2000.

Kösterberger A J, *The Heresy of Orthodoxy: How Contemporary Culture's Fascination with Diversity Has Reshaped our Understanding of Early Christianity*, Crossways Books, 2010.

Fox R L, *Pagans and Christians in the Mediterranean World from the Second Century AD to the Conversion of Constantine*, Penguin, 1986.

Lee A D, *Pagans and Christians in Late Antiquity*, Routledge, 2000.

MacCulloch D, *A History of Christianity: The First Three Thousand Years*, Penguin Books, 2010.

McKechnie P, *The First Christian Centuries: Perspectives on the Early Church*, InterVarsity Press, 2002.

Vermes G, *Christian Beginnings – From Nazareth to Nicaea*, Yale University Press, 2013.

New Testament Studies

Deming W, *Paul on Marriage and Celibacy: The Hellenistic Background of 1 Corinthians 7*, second edition, Wm B. Eerdmans Publishing, 2004.

Saunders R, *Outrageous Women Outrageous God: Women in the First Two Generations of Christianity*, E J Dwyer, 1996.

Tabor J D, *Paul and Jesus: How the Apostle Transformed Christianity*, Simon and Schuster, 2013.

Witherington III B, *Women and the Genesis of Christianity*, Cambridge University Press, 1990.

The Adam-and-Eve Myth and Other Stories

Godawa B, *When Giants Were Upon the Earth: the Watchers, the Nephilim, and the Cosmic War of the Seed*, Embedded Pictures Publishing, 2014.

Henning W B, *The Book of Giants: The Fallen Angels and their Giant Sons*, Forgotten Books, 2007.

de Jonge M & Tromp J, *The Life of Adam and Eve and Related Literature*, Sheffield Academic Press, 1997.

Kvam K E, Schearing L S and Ziegler V H, ed., *Eve & Adam: Jewish, Christian, and Muslim Readings on Genesis and Gender*, Indiana University Press, 1999.

Lumpkin J B, *The Books of Enoch: The Angels, the Watchers, and the Nephilim (with Extensive Commentary on the Three Books of Enoch, the Fallen Angels, The Calendar of Enoch, and Daniel's Prophecy)*, Fifth Estate, 2nd. ed., 2011.

—, *The Book of Giants: the Watchers, Nephilim, and the Book of Enoch*. Fifth Estate, 2014.

—, *Lost Books of the Bible: the Great Rejected Texts*. Fifth Estate, 2011.

Lumpkin J, ed., *The First and Second Books of Adam and Eve: The Conflict with Satan*, Fifth Estate, 2009.

Pagels E, *The Gnostic Gospels: Adam, Eve, and the Serpent*, Random House, 1988.

—, *The Origins of Satan*, Quality Paperback Book Club, 2005.

Stone M E, *A History of the Literature of Adam and Eve*, Scholars Press, 1992.

Christian-Gnostic Literature

Barnstone W and Meyer M, *Essential Gnostic Scriptures*, Shambhala, 2010.

Doresse J, *Les livres secrets des gnostiques d'Egypte*, 2 vols. Plon, 1958–1963.

Ehrman B D, *Lost Christianities*, Oxford University Press. 2002.

—, *Lost Scriptures: Books that Did Not Make It into the New Testament*, Oxford University Press, 2003.

Filoramo G, *A History of Gnosticism*, Basil Blackwell, 1990.

Grant R M, *Gnosticism and early Christianity*, Harper Torchbooks, 1966.

Grant R M, ed., *Gnosticism: an Anthology*, Collins, 1961.

Hedrick C W and Hodgson R, ed., *Nag Hammadi Gnosticism and Early Christianity*, Hendrickson Publishers, 1986.

Hoeller S A, *Gnosticism: New Light on the Ancient Tradition of Inner Knowing*, Quest Books, Theosophical Publishing House, 2002.

Hutin S, *Les gnostiques, collection Que sais-je?*, 4th edition, PUF, 1979.

Jacobs A, *The Gnostic Gospels: Including the Gospel of Thomas, the Gospel of Mary Magdalene (Sacred Texts)*, Watkins Publishing, 2016.

King K L, *The Secret Revelation of John, Images of the Feminine in Gnosticism (Studies in Antiquity and Christianity)*, Bloomsbury T&T Clark, 1st edition, 2000.

—, *What is Gnosticism?* Harvard Univ. Press, 2003.

—, *The Gospel of Mary of Magdala: Jesus and the First Woman Apostle*, Polebridge Press, 2003.

King K L, ed., *Images of the Feminine in Gnosticism*, Fortress Press, 1988.

Koester H, *Ancient Christian Gospels: Their History and Development*, Trinity Press International, 1992.

Kraemer R S, Mary Rose D'Angelo, eds., *Women and Christian Origins*, Oxford University Press, 1999.

Lacarrière J, *Les Gnostiques*, Albin Michel, 1994.

—, *The Gnostics*, City Lights Publishers, 2001.

Leloup J, *L'Evangile de Thomas*, Albin Michel, 1986.

—, *L'Evangile de Maria-Myariam de Magdala*, Albin Michel, 1997.

—, *The Gospel of Mary Magdalene*, trans. Joseph Rowe, Inner Traditions International, 2002.

—, *L'Evangile de Philippe*, Albin Michel, 2003.

—, *The Gospel Of Philip: Jesus, Mary Magdalene, And The Gnosis Of Sacred Union*, Inner Traditions International, 2004.

—, *L'Evangile de Jean*, Albin Michel, 1989.

Meyer M, *The Gnostic Discoveries*, Harper Collins Publishers, 2006.

—, *The Gospel of Thomas: The Hidden Sayings of Jesus*, Harper Collins Publishers, 1992.

Meyer M, ed., *The Nag Hammadi Scriptures: The Revised and Updated Translation of Sacred Gnostic Texts*, Harper Collins, 2007.

O'Grady J, *Heresy: Heretical Truth or Orthodox Error?* Element Books, 1985.

Pagels E, *Beyond Belief: The Secret Gospel of Thomas*, Random House, 2003.

—, *The Johannine Gospel in Gnostic Exegesis: Heracleon's Commentary on John*, New Edition, SBLMS, 1989.

—, *The Gnostic Paul: Gnostic Exegesis of the Pauline Letters*, Trinity Press International, 1975.

Pagels E and King K L, *Reading Judas: The Gospel of Judas and the Shaping of Christianity*, Viking, 2007.

Porter J R, *La Bible Oubliée – Apocryphes de l'ancien et du nouveau testament*, Albin Michel, 2004.

—, *The Lost Bible: Forgotten Scriptures Revealed*, University of Chicago Press, 2001.

Puech H, *En quête de la gnose, tome II Sur l"Evangile selon Thomas*, Gallimard, 1978.

Robinson J M, ed., *The Nag Hammadi Library in English*, E J Brill, 1996.

Also from this author

How did Jesus treat women? Chris Geraghty delves into the scriptures and history showing how Jesus practised a radically inclusive approach to women that challenged the inequitable beliefs and practices of his own culture and community.

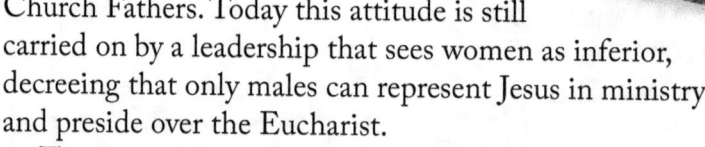

Yet the Church has historically failed to follow its own founder's example, instead taking its direction from the early tradition of male only apostles developed by misogynist Church Fathers. Today this attitude is still carried on by a leadership that sees women as inferior, decreeing that only males can represent Jesus in ministry and preside over the Eucharist.

This learned, humorous, irreverent book reminds us that Jesus was a feminist and argues that the Church must repent and honour this in order to restore women's place as fully equal to men, in the Church and in the world.

Geraghty has brought his forensic skills as a former judge of the District Court and (his) impressive research of the primary sources to produce a myth-busting wake-up call for the Church.
– Paul Bongiorno,
veteran political journalist and commentator

www.ingramcontent.com/pod-product-compliance
Lightning Source LLC
Chambersburg PA
CBHW070748230426
43665CB00017B/2295